Choosing the Right Educational Path for Your Child

What Are the Options?

Edited by
Paula J. Carreiro
and Eileen Shields-West

ROWMAN & LITTLEFIELD EDUCATION
Lanham • New York • Toronto • Plymouth, UK

Published in the United States of America
by Rowman & Littlefield Education
A Division of Rowman & Littlefield Publishers, Inc.
A wholly owned subsidary of The Rowman & Littlefield Publishing Group, Inc.
4501 Forbes Boulevard, Suite 200, Lanham, Maryland 20706
www.rowmaneducation.com

Estover Road
Plymouth PL6 7PY
United Kingdom

British Library Cataloguing in Publication Information Available

Library of Congress Cataloging-in-Publication Data

Choosing the right educational path for your child : what are the options? / edited by
Paula J. Carreiro and Eileen Shields-West.
     p. cm.
  ISBN-13: 978-1-57886-826-1 (cloth : alk. paper)
  ISBN-10: 1-57886-826-2 (cloth : alk. paper)
  1. School choice—United States. 2. Education—Parent participation—United States.
I. Carreiro, Paula J., 1947– II. Shields-West, Eileen.
  LB1027.9.C535 2008
  379.1'11—dc22   2008010146

Contents

Preface

Paula J. Carreiro and Eileen Shields-West

For both of us, American education has been an interest and a passion. This book of essays is an outgrowth of those feelings and our mutual experience. In September 1996, we formed a partnership for leadership of an independent elementary school in Washington, D.C. In our respective roles as head of school and governing board chair, we spent hours working on behalf of the school, its students, staff, and families. Our hopes of creating a caring community with a genuine focus on the needs of young children and a genuine joy in learning were realized in ways that extended far beyond our planning or imaginations. While the energy and optimism of children almost inevitably create a positive atmosphere, the beliefs and values of the adult community also weigh intensely on each educational environment. Parents may differ in beliefs and even values, but there is almost always some overlap in a cohesive school community of the hopes and dreams that the adults have for their children.

Over the years, as our own children grew and enrolled in various educational institutions, our observations and involvement in many kinds of schools grew as well. After serving on numerous boards and becoming involved in volunteer efforts in the educational arena, we became interested in the issue of "school fit." We observed that even the most wonderful of schools might not be equipped to meet the essential educational needs of all children or, for that matter, of all their families. As a result, we were drawn to an Oxford Round Table that focused on many different models of schooling. In summer 2003, participants from all over the United States traveled to Oxford University, bringing with them a thorough knowledge about the schools with which they were associated and a desire to learn about other models of education. The result was a dynamic dialogue on the merits, challenges, and possibilities of the many educational programs we discussed.

The essays in this book were written by well-known professionals in the field of education, some of them by participants in the Oxford discussions. In spite of different perspectives expressed in the book regarding the design of good schools for the twenty-first century, the reader will find common themes: the respect for the knowledge that students bring to a learning environment, a belief in the need to continue the growth and development of educators as the research on teaching and learning expands, and a passion for the education model described by each individual writer. The uniqueness of American education is the opportunity for and challenge of educational diversity. None of these authors argue for the supremacy of their model for all children. All of them, however, assert the value of their model for specific students and specific families. The challenge in the offering of these many educational choices is the societal desire that all students possess common values of citizenship. But even the public schools have not been exempt from the tensions of the debate over what those values should be. In some ways, the availability of a diverse educational system has provided the United States with a safety valve that relieves the pressures of significant conflicts of belief.

It is our hope that this book will provide a useful perspective on America's rich educational choices. Parents can use it as a starting point to understand the various missions and philosophies of schooling models that they are considering for their children. Policy makers may gain understanding of the point of view of advocates of specific public and private schools with whom they find themselves in dialogue. Educators who sometimes find themselves in conflict with advocates of another approach may be able to reflect on the similarities, as well as the differences, between them. For all its faults, America has shown how a society, how a country of many cultures, religions, races, and national origins can work and live together: E. Pluribus Unum. American education has demonstrated how the many, becoming one nation, do not have to go to the same schools, follow the same curriculum, have the same texts, or have the same teacher requirements in order to contribute positively to the democratic whole.

So long as that option of educational choice continues to be available to families, the unknown intellectual challenges of the twenty-first century will find America ready with a response. If America is the Great Experiment, American education, for all its faults and frustrations, is the Great School Experiment.

Acknowledgments

"The beginning is the most important part of the work."

—Plato

*T*his book is fashioned by many minds and many hands. We are especially grateful to all of our fellow contributors, many of whom first heard from us about the idea for this book five years ago. They stayed the course as we refined the idea and added essays along the way to keep pace with developments on the educational landscape, such as, Virtual Schools, Islamic Schools, and School Calendar Reform. We feel the collection is far better for its breadth.

As mentioned in the Preface, the idea for this book came to us at an Oxford Round Table, held at St. Antony's College, Oxford, England, July 2003. We personally want to thank Dr. Kern Alexander, professor of Educational Administration at the University of Illinois, for inviting us there to discuss "Choice in Education" as a timely and riveting topic. We also applaud Ann Grogg, our book's copyeditor, for her careful reading of each essay for flow and style.

Finally, we want to acknowledge and thank all of those in the field of education who are working day after day to make their schools, whatever model, better and more imaginative places for our children to learn and to discover joy in that learning. As Henry Adams once said, "A teacher affects eternity." This is true yesterday, today, and tomorrow.

School Choice: A Personal History

Michael Thompson

*W*hen I grew up in New York in the 1950s, there was no such thing as school choice, at least not for me. Like all children, I went to the school to which my parents sent me. I imagine that if I had struggled there or been unhappy there, they would have concluded sadly that I wasn't much of a student. I doubt that they would have thought they had chosen the wrong school; after all, I was sent to one of the "best" schools in the city.

One interesting question for me is how much of a choice my parents felt that they had. They are no longer living, so I cannot ask them, but this I know: the Upper East Side of Manhattan was full of many different kinds of schools. For reasons of economics, tradition, and psychology my family may not have felt that they had much of a choice at all. Because my grandmother had left money in her will for her grandchildren's education, and since both my parents had attended single-gender private schools when they were young, they settled on a boys' school for my brother and me and a private girls' school for my younger sister. The only upset over school choice that I ever heard about was that my younger sister was not admitted to my mother's old school (my mother never forgave her alma mater, although my sister thrived in her new school). I never heard my parents mention public schools or any other school as a possibility for me, not once in my entire childhood.

Of course I was aware that there were other schools out there. When I walked south on Madison Avenue I regularly passed a public elementary school that the grown-ups said was very good and very competitive, maybe almost as good as a private school. (Was it an exam school to which children had to apply or just in a favorable district? I can't recall.) I can remember looking in its windows and staring at the student artwork taped there. The pictures didn't look that much different from the ones we drew, so although I

1

tried, it was impossible for me to figure out the possible differences between public school students and me. I was also vaguely aware that there was a Catholic boys' school only two blocks from my home, but I knew that because we were Presbyterian I would never go to a Catholic school of any kind. People spoke in reverent tones about the extraordinary magnet public schools in New York such as Stuyvesant and Bronx High School of Science. They had nothing to do with me or my future. It was only much later, perhaps when I was in middle school, that I became aware that there was an academically powerful, secular, coed private school just five blocks from my house. It could have been a neighborhood school for me—I could have walked to school all those years instead of taking two buses to the West Side!—but of course my parents wouldn't have let me go there because the majority of the students were Jewish. In New York in the 1950s, social background and religion were the dominant factor in private school choice. I received an excellent , traditional education surrounded by upper-middle-class white boys from high-achieving New York families—boys like me.

I often run into adults who have lived the mirror image of my early education. They say to me, "I didn't even know private schools existed when I grew up. I just went to the public school in my town." They then add, "It was a really good school," or "It was great for me," or "We could never have afforded private schools." Quite commonly they report, "We thought the weird kids and the snobs went to private schools." Sometimes, a person from an affluent family might refer to choice by saying, "My parents would never have sent me to private school. They believed in public education."

What is odd is that I, too, believed in public education, with great ideological fervor. Though I was a product of private schools from nursery school through high school I was philosophically committed to the idea of strong public schools. I believed that such schools were the foundation of our democracy, the crucible in which good citizens were created. Although kids of privilege like me might be sent to private schools, and might, as a result, get extra preparation for "leadership" (that's what we were told) we were, in fact, the aberration. The vast majority of kids in the country were going to go to public schools, and all of us—indeed, the future of the country—required great public schools.

After college I went to work as a seventh-grade teacher in a public school in a poverty-stricken town in rural New Hampshire. There were thirty-five students in a classroom designed for twenty-five; space, paper, books, and support services were in short supply; some of my seventh-graders were functionally illiterate; one of my seventh-grade girls became pregnant that year. The local John Birch Society monitored our classrooms closely to make sure that the teachers were sufficiently anticommunist, and they were rightly suspicious of my liberal political views as well as those of the sixth-grade teacher, who had served in the Peace Corps in Brazil. It was a tough environment in which to start a career, and I left after a year, discouraged about myself as a teacher and uncertain whether I should stay in the profession. Philosophically, however, I was even more committed to the idea of a strong public school system as the foundation of American democracy. What I understood that to mean was a traditional, excellent public school in every neighborhood and town. I knew that a small percentage of religious families would always choose parochial, Christian, and Jewish day schools (the idea of a Muslim school never occurred to me) and that a small number of families of privilege would inevitably choose private schools, but they were the exceptions to the rule of no choice. That's the way American educational system was. I accepted the status quo, believed that it was fundamentally sound, and thought that we should all work to make it function better. The idea of universal school choice for all families was, simply, a thought that never crossed my mind. That is, of course, until my own children were of school age.

By the time I became a father at what seemed to me the advanced age of 38, the public schools in the United States had been allowed to deteriorate to a frightening degree. Proposition 13 had swept the state of California, and Prop 2½ had been adopted by the voters of Massachusetts. Soon the fine public school systems in those states were being starved of funds, along with the public schools in most other states. Americans, in general, were no longer willing to support public education as they once had. The majority wanted lower taxes and less government, and they perceived schools as a part of burdensome, bloated governmental bureaucracy. Report after report on the American high school documented that, on average, our schools were not performing at the same level as public schools in Finland, France, Japan, Taiwan, and many other countries. Wave after wave of reformist efforts were directed at struggling public schools. Most failed because of a lack of political will to fund them, the incompetence of administrators, meddling by politicians, the intransigence of teacher unions, and, most important, because of enduring racism and poverty in this country that educators could not fix.

Over a period of three decades, from the mid-1950s to the mid-1980s, people who could do so moved to the suburbs in search of better public schools and found themselves more or less pleased. Like so many others, when we were still childless, my wife and I bought a house in a town outside Boston which had a highly rated school system. We were told that we were moving into the "best" district, with the "best" elementary school in the town. Our future child-education problems, it seemed, were solved. (Except that they weren't. Neither of our children attended that excellent school. More about that in a minute.)

When we moved into our small cul-de-sac neighborhood, we learned that all the parents on the street were involved in a sometimes frantic effort to find just the right school for their children. All around us were homes with children attending public, parochial, and a large variety of independent schools. One of my neighbors had served with distinction on the school committee in town for years while her son was in the local elementary school. When he reached eighth grade she decided to send him to an independent secondary school and resigned her position on the school board. Another neighbor bought an empty condo in a nearby town and became a property tax payer there so that his son could go to a better public high school less than three miles away. Yet another, a graduate of parochial schools herself, sent her children to the public schools and expressed annoyance about families who chose independent schools. The choice of schools was not without its political tensions in our neighborhood; the message, however, was unmistakable. When people had the means, the information, and the access to a variety of schools, they should spend an enormous amount of effort to find the "right" school for their child. And it was not just my suburban neighbors who were talking about choice.

My friends who had stayed in the city and my friends who were committed to public education were entering their children's names in lotteries for specific public schools and were waiting anxiously to find out whether their children had "gotten in." Soon I was hearing the words "charter school" for the first time. Everyone we knew who cared about education wanted a choice. Indeed, every parent I know socially and every parent I met in the course of my work as a psychological consultant to schools wanted to find the "best fit" for his or her child. Of course, that's what my wife and I wanted for our children.

I will spare the reader the complete history of my children's school transitions. Suffice it to say that we have at various times delivered our children to the front doors of: a public school (in my town but out of our district, because it was the better "fit"), a high-powered preschool (not a "fit"), a lovely preschool in a church basement (a great "fit"), a Montessori school in a nearby town, a new "alternative" independent school in yet another town, a traditional boarding school that has been in existence for more than a century, two different independent schools that admit only learning disabled children (both schools a long commute from our house). Between the ages of 3 and 18, each of my children attended four different schools.

Neither of my children has ever gone to a neighborhood school to which they could walk. My wife has borne the burden of car-pooling for nineteen years, and the number one expense on our family budget during those years has been independent school tuition. Earning the money to pay for the "right" schools for my children has shaped almost every career decision I have made.

Perhaps the reader thinks I am nothing but an impossibly picky psychologist. All I can say in my defense is that I feel both sane and lucky. We may not have always made the right choices for our children, but we have had the economic freedom to look for the "right" schools, and we have tried our earnest best to find schools that matched our children's temperaments, learning needs, and, at different periods in their lives, particular developmental requirements.

For a long time my ideological belief in an excellent universal public school system coexisted alongside the pursuit of the right school for my children and my work as a psychologist in independent schools. As a political matter I mistrusted the school voucher movement as a right-wing conspiracy, an underfunded attempt to undermine public schools. I continued to think that an excellent neighborhood public school was the correct educational solution, even though the top-flight public school in my neighborhood wasn't right for my children. How could the school that was wrong for my kids be right for everyone else's children? How could the wonderful all-boys' school for which I worked as a psychologist be so wrong for a number of boys? How could some boys who hated the school where I work find so much happiness at a local parochial school? It was the right place for them. How could some boys who were floundering and unproductive in a local high school turn around so completely when they came to my school? Answer: it was the right fit for them.

My children and my work led me to two conclusions: First, that school "fit" is the thing that every child needs, and, second, that the parental impulse to find the best possible school situation for a child is absolutely universal and must be honored by society. I have never met a parent who did not want his or her child to thrive in school, and, indeed, many parents have made much larger sacrifices than we have to ensure their child's best education. Immigrants leave their families and countries behind to find good schools for their children. I have known families who have sold their houses and moved to new towns to avoid a bullying problem in their child's school. We all want choice for our kids, and, ideally, every family should have access to a choice of schools for their children. How that is to be accomplished is the work of educators and politicians in the next decade. What I know is that families cannot wait; they will pursue choice in any way that they can.

The fact remains that it isn't always easy for parents to know what is out there. How many people can educate themselves quickly about the huge variety of educational opportunities in their world? Personally, I have had the tremendous advantage of working in schools for more than twenty years. I have personally visited more than five hundred schools in the United States and around the world. I have seen differentiated learning in action; I know what Montessori and Reggio Emilia schools look like. My travels have exposed me to a vast array of creative, passionate, thoughtful educators in public, independent, and international schools from whom I have learned a great deal. I wish every parent could visit the number of schools I have. It would help them to make an informed choice of school for their children.

Because not all parents can visit a lot of schools, they need to learn what choices are available to them through reading, and that is the reason to read a book like *Choosing the Right Educational Path for Your Child: What Are the Options?* Here is the vast array of school choices laid out before the reader, presented by passionate, committed educators. Here are the big issues, public and private, involved in school choice. I learned so much by reading this book, and I expect that you will, too.

I

GENERAL PRINCIPLES

Model and Mission

What a School Wants, What a School Needs

Keith Weller Frome

$\mathscr{T}$he mission of a school expresses its goals, its values, and its most cherished dreams. To paraphrase a pop song by Christina Aguilera that was once adored by the eighth-grade girls at my school, the mission is what a school wants, what a school needs. A school's model, on the other hand, is the set of tools and structures it has created to achieve its mission. The model should be the servant of the mission; the mission should never bend for the model.

For example, the school calendar is part of a school's model, not its mission. Yet you would not know that from the controversy and rhetoric ringing in my part of the world about the length and timing of spring break. Should it be two weeks around Easter? Should it be one week in February and one week in April? The question is hotly contested at school board and parent council meetings. The arguments spin around and around and are left unresolved because the calendar debate is not mission driven. We never talk about how the school's calendar serves the school's mission. Essentially, the spring break crisis in western New York State is about families who like to go to Florida for two weeks and need to make reservations a year ahead of time. This is hardly the heady stuff that should be at the core of our conversations about schools and children. Yet our leaders get wrapped up for weeks in disputes about the timing of spring break because, at heart, the mission/model distinction is not fully appreciated or understood by their constituents. To press the example further, if the mission of the Maple Syrup School is to teach children reverence for the sap of the maple tree so that they can learn the science and craft of tapping maple syrup, then one would hope that the issue of when spring break ought to occur would be quite easily decided by the school's mission. Whenever the sap flows, one would expect the Maple Syrup School to be in session.

Every institution in the nonprofit and for-profit sectors should be able
to recognize the distinction between its mission and its model. Yet while this
is an easy intellectual distinction, many school board members, school
trustees, and school employees have a most difficult time putting it into practice. The managers of for-profits have an easier task than schools because no
matter the poetry of their purposes and objectives statement, their mission is
simply to make a profit. Healthy companies always change or refine their
models to serve the bottom line. The mission of GE is not light bulbs and re-
frigerators; it is enriching its shareholders. Hence, Jack Welch, its CEO, had
no intellectual problem starting a financial services division. In essence, he
created a new model to serve his company's mission.

The nonprofit sector has a more difficult time distinguishing the mission
from the model. To explore this concept in more detail, I will discuss the cases
of three nonprofit organizations that illustrate, in turn, an example of equat-
ing the mission with the model, of emphasizing the model over the mission,
and of holding the mission sacrosanct and the model ultimately flexible. The
first two cases represent two organizations I worked with in the past that
grappled with the mission/model distinction without even knowing it. Since
neither could recognize and differentiate its model from its mission, each had
difficulties navigating necessary change.

The more stable of these institutions, which I will call Preparation Academy, tutors and supports economically disadvantaged students so that they
can attend the finest secondary schools in their region and then matriculate
at elite universities. The trustees, through a long strategic planning session,
discovered that the students, as an aggregate, were beginning to decline on
three measures: standardized test scores, high school performance, and the
quality of college acceptances. These data stopped the trustees in their tracks,
as did the sudden resignation of the program's director, who had been on the
job for less than a year, because of the persistent incivility and insubordina-
tion of the staff. Clearly there was something wrong at Preparation Academy
that went beyond the need for more classroom space and computers. There
was a crisis in the management of the mission of the organization and in its
practice.

This crisis led to an intense examination of the exact nature of the mission of the program. We discovered that there was not total consensus among
the trustees about their understanding of Preparation Academy's goals and objectives. Some thought that the program should help students of average to
above-average abilities; most, though, agreed that the program should serve
only academically elite students and should expect them to achieve certain
minimum standardized test scores and enjoy the choice of an array of the most
competitive colleges when they graduated from high school. After reaching

consensus, the trustees felt that they had achieved an important objective, namely they had simply and clearly articulated Preparation Academy's mission and developed benchmarks for measuring its success.

They had done just that, but then they stopped their work. When one of the trustees suggested that now that they had agreed on their mission they go about redesigning the program and the curriculum to better strategically achieve its goals, the rest of the trustees balked. They gave two familiar arguments: the argument of time and the argument of credibility. The time argument should be familiar to anyone who serves on a nonprofit board. It goes like this: We've spent x years developing these ways of delivering our mission; now that we know what we want to achieve, let's not be drastic; let's see if our existing programs work now that we have a clearer understanding of our vision, and then we can always reassess. The corollary to the time argument is that the staff, who have put their hearts and souls into existing programs, will resist changing them, and the trustees need the loyalty and goodwill of the staff. Let's not rock the boat. Given a clearer set of goals, inevitably a happy staff will achieve them. Hey, we can always reevaluate.

The credibility argument follows from the time argument. It goes like this: Our loyal donors have invested a lot of money in our existing programs; if we go to our supporters now and say that what we've done in the past needs to change, we will in effect be telling them that their money has been wasted, that we've failed, and, consequently, they may not give anymore.

Persuaded by these two lines of thought and with a vague commitment to keep an eye on the situation, the trustees of Preparation Academy completed their strategic planning session with a more focused mission and the same models that had been serving what they had discovered to be the previously ill-defined and vague mission statement. In addition, the time and credibility arguments were so forceful and universally accepted that they became potent obstacles to substantive progress to the achievement of Preparation Academy's mission. I find this case fascinating because it was, in the end, the mission that had to be worked over while the programs, which were determined to be faulty, stayed the same. One could argue that the mission did not change; the trustees just came to a better understanding of it. Granted. Still, the mission and the model were treated as equals, and the model was never refined or changed. It was as if a baseball team said that it needed better pitching to win the World Series and then did not recruit new pitchers, hoping that its existing pitchers would play better now that it has been made clear just how important pitching was to winning. The point of this example is that it is not enough to diagnose a situation; boards need also to implement remedies, which always entail change.

My next case, the Striving School, treated the model as superior to the mission, and the consequences were tumultuous. The Striving School is a tuition-free private school located in one of the poorest sections of the United States serving an oppressed population of children who suffer from health risks, a high crime rate, poverty, and unsafe public schools. The mission of the school seeks to provide a classic liberal arts education so that each child will be able to recognize his or her potential and be able to imagine a wider scope of possibility for his or her life. Once educationally liberated, Striving School students are then given the means to make a meaningful high school choice including the possibility of attending boarding school. The curriculum is rich in music and art and literature. The children of the Striving School learn to read at an early age, and their nutritional and health needs are monitored. Medical, educational, and vocational interventions, through a rich network of friends of the faculty and trustees, are offered to the families when needed. In essence, the cultural capital of the educated upper middle class is donated to the school's families. Through this same network, the teachers take full advantage of the city's rich cultural institutions for their curricular needs.

Given the nature of the mission, there was nothing wrong with the educational model of the school. When the children were deemed ready, they enrolled in prestigious private schools whose headmasters were more than happy to play a part in the grand vision of the school and its founder. The trouble was financing such a venture. Fiercely independent, the school would not seek any kind of government assistance; private donations from individuals and foundations generated its only revenue stream. The founding head insisted that he could both run the school and raise the money through his individual contacts. To his way of thinking, the trustees' primary responsibility involved making up any cash shortfalls for the fiscal year through personal giving. The directors, who were all friends of the founding head, asked, in return, for greater financial accountability in terms of a yearly budget and a strategic development plan. The school's staff simply could not deliver either, partly because they were unskilled in these areas and partly because the founding head saw no reason to waste time on these administrative tools and tasks. He was saving lives; the board should simply fund the effort.

When the board looked into the future of the school, they saw a fiscal disaster looming that would put it out of business. When they asked the business manager and the founding head where the money for the next academic year was going to come from, they were told that the money just always came in. Faced with a development program based more on faith than strategic planning, the trustees voted to take over the development functions of the school. In their first act, they told the founding head, who was a dynamic but temperamental fellow, to spend two days a week doing nothing but fund-raising.

The board would initiate the contacts and produce the materials. They then asked one of the teachers to run the school on the two days the founding head was busy raising money.

In essence, the board held the mission sacred and sought to change the administrative model in order to preserve the work of the school. Hasty in its zeal, the board neglected to consider the psychology of change. The founding head rebelled against having his job description revised. He rallied his teachers to support him; held unofficial board meetings with trustees with whom he had long-standing relationships; and finally wrote a letter saying that he would close the school down if forced to hand over its operations to anyone else. Offended by the tone and belligerence of the founding head, several board members resigned. A few stayed on, and the Striving School returned to its normal administrative structure. In this case, the model had trumped the mission; the Striving School still exists, but it never grew and never realized the potential of its mission.

During a week at Harvard Business School, I read the case of Willow Creek Church (Harvard Business School case number 9-691-102), now a famous example of a nonprofit whose leader, Bill Hybels, used business and marketing techniques to grow his organization at a phenomenal rate. In 1989, Willow Creek Church was the best-attended Christian church in America, serving close to 14,000 worshipers on the weekends and another 5,000 during weekday services. It had a volunteer work force of some 4,500 people who served in more than 6,000 positions performing more than 90 different services. The church's yearly revenue exceeded $12 million, and it had 147 full-time and 110 part-time employees on staff. Hybels achieved this magnitude of growth because he was willing to change and to abandon the traditional church service in order to maximize his mission, namely to convert as many people as possible to Christianity. He asked his potential customers (i.e., the unconverted or "unchurched" as he called them) how and when they would like to worship. Based on their feedback, he dismantled traditional models and practices, reassembled them, and gave birth to what today we call the mega-church. Willow Creek Church is perhaps the purest example of a mission trumping model.

I am not an Evangelical missionary, but the Willow Creek Case has haunted me for years now, because of its unadulterated vision of the primacy of mission. As headmaster of a traditional independent school, my most vexing challenges occurred when I attempted to try to change aspects of the school's model to better serve its mission. For example, part of my school's mission speaks to inclusion, compassion, and community. Our class day program included giving out awards that divided the class and left many students bewildered, saddened, or angry. Changing this ceremony to better serve our mission was a Herculean task unmitigated by the fact that everyone agreed on the meaning of the mission and the unhappiness of the award ceremony. (We eventually did change it, to everyone's eventual relief.) People get attached to their models, even misery-making models. What if schools were as in love with their missions but as flexible with their practices as Willow Creek Church? What would a school look like if it fixed its gaze solidly on its mission and cheerfully tinkered with its model, knowing that it was marching toward a more perfect embodiment of the vision of the school?

As a heuristic exercise, just take fifteen minutes to imagine the look of a school that had maximum model flexibility and whose core vision involved nurturing moral thinkers—which is essentially the core vision of every school mission statement. I would wager that you will envision a different organization than the typical U.S. school. For those of us who head schools, we must imagine what we would want our school to look like if we were the founder who enjoyed the full knowledge of the present conditions of the school. Let's call this the perfect founding position. Whenever we are troubled by an aspect of the model of our school, our vision about what ought to be done becomes clearer if we take this perfect founding position as a starting point in our deliberations. Ask yourself if you would have ever started an existing tradition in your school, if you had created the school in 1900 knowing what the educational conditions in 2007 would be. What would the public school system look like now from the perfect founding position vantage point? Certainly not what we have on our hands today.

To some, the founder-with-complete-knowledge perspective is just silly speculation. To others it is so far-fetched or impractical as to invite derision. Others might say that a school's model can be intellectually distinguished from its mission, but it cannot in reality be divided. Indeed, some may argue that Willow Creek did forsake its mission, namely converting the unchurched, because it strayed too far from its traditional model. Indeed, many faithful Christians are repulsed by the spectacle of mega-churches these days. If we are honest and fair, though, we have to concede that Hybels's achievement was remarkable and acknowledge that almost all denominations have tried to adopt at least some of his techniques. I have just been approached by a traditional, old Episcopalian Church to teach an adult education class about one of my favorite hobbies, finding the religious themes in the Simpsons cartoon series. You see, the church had discovered that many parishioners did not attend church because its services were scheduled at the same time as the cartoon. My class will, they think, co-opt these reluctant church goers. The lesson of Willow Creek for schools is that they must also start making the kinds of changes that are responsive to the current market and the contemporary needs of their students and families. This is not "selling out," but moving toward a greater dedication to the essence of mission.

The mission tells us how we *ought* to be and the model tells how we *are*. The model of a school is a combination of its buildings, its schedule, its calendar, its rituals, its dress code, its grading system, and so forth. Yes, disrespecting school models and too rapidly discarding them can entail negative consequences. When you read the case of Willow Creek, though, you notice that its leaders were never whimsical. They always strategically reflected on their ability to achieve the mission. They created rigorous feedback loops to ensure the integrity of their modular transformations. Our schools would do well to create similar feedback protocols in order to be able to change their ways of doing business to do a better job of doing business.

Feedback and evaluation should, though, be deliberately calibrated to measure mission success. Too often, the evaluation protocols begin to smother the mission and become another form of model worship. A school typically resembles, over time, the system its governing body establishes to benchmark success. If it is state-mandated testing, then no matter how inspiring the mission statement, the school will focus on preparing for the tests and that activity will permeate and change the mission and the culture of the school. Boards should be careful of what and how they measure their schools because they will inevitably get the kind of school they are measuring for. If you apply a melon baller to a melon, you will get melon balls and nothing more. If you sincerely and continually measure your school solely by its mission statement, then you should be prepared for a school that might look completely different in ten years, but one that is, indeed, fulfilling its mission. And fulfilling its mission is, truly, the measure of a school's success.

· 2 ·

Governance

Trying to Perfect

Eileen Shields-West

$\mathcal{T}$he English word "govern" derives from the Greek word *kyverno*, meaning "to steer a ship." For school systems, the image is apt, as all are grappling with ways to improve helmsmanship at the board level. For private schools, with their individual mission statements and particular focus, the goal of governance is leadership through partnership, or board business that is best performed by the board in concert with the head of school—a work still in progress. For charter schools, still fairly new on the educational landscape, the challenge is to juggle individual mission statements with the greater community's needs. Key is to find the right mix of public and private governance structures to take them from being start-up, facility- and fiduciary-focused organizations to becoming enduring choices within the broader framework of school reform. For public schools, the challenge is even greater. While lay governance of public education is a uniquely American tradition and something that is cherished, the poor overall performance of public schools is severely testing this concept. The result is increasing federal, state, and even mayoral influence in local educational governance. Where will all this lead?

Good to Great author and organizational guru Jim Collins set irreversible forces in motion when he published his 2001 book on why some companies make the leap to greatness and others do not.[1] At that time, he hoped that his message would be attractive not only to executives in the business sector but also to heads of nonprofits. His message, he said, transcended profit motives. Collins believes that "good is the enemy of great. We don't have great schools, principally because we have good schools. . . . The vast majority of companies never become great, precisely because the vast majority become quite good— and that is their main problem."[2] As it turns out, Collins's message is as popular with schools, churches, hospitals, police departments, and the like as it is

17

with corporations, but Collins is the first to reject the notion that the way to "great" for nonprofits is to become "more like a business."[3] In fact, he wrote and self-published an inexpensive online-marketed monograph in 2005 to accompany *Good to Great* called *Good to Great and the Social Sectors* to give nonprofits relevant guideposts.[4]

Collins specifically chose as a subtitle "Why Business Thinking Is Not the Answer" because he has come to the conclusion that it is naive to impose the "language of business" on the social sectors to get them to improve.[5] Instead, there must be a whole new language of greatness. To give one example: for businesses, profit is a perfectly realistic way of measuring performance; but for nonprofits, mission is pivotal. The question for a school then becomes: How effectively does it deliver on its mission and make a distinctive impact, relative to its resources?[6]

INDEPENDENT SCHOOL GOVERNANCE

In the independent school world, these ideas are defining new parameters of performance as schools look for ways to become even better at preparing students for an ever more challenging future. They are also generating a whole new list of dos and don'ts for governing boards. While trustees generally want to work within a school's culture to bring about change, they often become frustrated and even irritable when progress does not seem fast enough or change encounters resistance. School consultant Robert Evans, author of *The Human Side of School Change*,[7] is not surprised: "Schools are simply less suited to innovation than most organizations, and they adapt more slowly. . . . We can best help them fulfill their mission in new ways by meeting them on their own terms, tempering our expectations, concentrating our efforts, and celebrating their strengths."[8]

For some trustees, adapting to the school's terms is difficult, if not impossible. Trustees may demand that a poorly performing teacher be fired right away, but the head of school may argue that doing so would decrease morale and upset the sense of security among other teachers. Or trustees may push for merit pay, which often works wonders in the corporate world, but school heads may disagree, saying that teachers do not like that kind of competition with their colleagues.

With their lead and visible role, board chairs have to be especially careful. The National Association of Independent Schools (NAIS) stresses "Leadership through Partnership" between the board chair and the head of school. So one NAIS executive was completely astonished when he witnessed a board chair walk into a school and begin ordering about the school personnel. The board chair, a corporate CEO in his own right, obviously thought it was okay for him "to take charge" of the school.[9] In another instance, after an argument with the head of school, one board chair remarked that either he or she had to go.

Such behavior is shortsighted and sets up barriers to the proper working of boards. More and more, the real role of boards is seen as going beyond fiduciary oversight and strategic goal-setting to something now termed "generative" thinking.[10] In this new world of "governance as leadership," as it is called, it is more important than ever for staff and trustees to rise above petty differences and concentrate on making an institution the best it can be.[11] This focus does not mean overlooking glaring inadequacies, but rather using the long-standing procedures that are in place to deal with them. The head of school, and not the chair or any combination of trustees, is in charge of disciplining (and praising) school personnel. The chair can mention being upset with a particular faculty or staff member, but it is up to the head to decide whether to act or not. On the other hand, the head of school is the one employee who reports to and works for the board. Needless to say, though, it is the whole board in its most serious deliberation that hires and fires the head, not the chair alone.

Harvard professor Richard Chait, with co-authors William Ryan and Barbara Taylor, argues in *Governance as Leadership* that there is an increasing board problem. Too often, the authors say, trustees are spending more time on operational details and management issues than on the higher order of leadership and direction.[12] Chait comments, "Boards have become more regulatory, more compliance-based, more like a police officer than a member of a leadership team."[13]

One of the reasons for this shift in board direction is the series of corporate governance and accounting scandals that hit the news headlines in 2001 and 2002. The misdeeds of WorldCom, Enron, and Tyco executives led Congress to quickly enact the Sarbanes-Oxley Act, increasing the scrutiny of financial returns and audited records from publicly traded companies and broadening board members' roles in the preparation of those documents. Not to be caught off guard, nonprofits are following suit, and so board members feel a sense of urgency about their fiduciary responsibilities. To this end, independent school boards are establishing conflict of interest policies, requiring periodic review of investment policies and performance, and implementing term limits to remove the perception of undue influence resulting from long-term service.[14]

But governance experts like Chait worry that concentrating on fiduciary oversight, even if combined with strategic planning, will lead to unfulfilled boards. A remedy is generative thinking that goes to the core of an organization's mission. Generative thinking means asking questions of values, beliefs, assumptions, and organizational cultures. So, when a head of school comes to a board and says, "We have looked at all of the issues. Here is the problem. Does this solution work?" the question for the board becomes, "Do we have the problem right?"[15]

The best boards are those that can operate on all three levels: fiduciary, strategic, and generative. These boards foster a "fusion of thinking" instead of a division of labor between board and staff, and they can make a school more effective in meeting its mission and more accountable to its stakeholders.[16]

There are other ways, too, that boards can better themselves. Board-Source, a leading consultant on nonprofit governance with about 12,000 members, has devised twelve principles that power exceptional boards. While Jim Collins uses the moniker "good to great," BoardSource distinguishes between "responsible" and "exceptional" boards. President and CEO Deborah S. Hechinger explains that a responsible board is "capable and dutiful in carrying out its responsibilities," whereas an exceptional board "operates on a higher level that is both 'more' and 'different.'"[17]

BoardSource convened a group of governance experts and asked them to define the distinguishing characteristics of the best boards.[18] They came up with such traits as constructive partnership, mission driven, results oriented, strategic thinking, ethos of transparency, continuous learning, and revitalization.[19] While Hechinger says that she and her colleagues have seen boards with multiple exceptional characteristics, they have not encountered a single board that exhibits all twelve of them.[20] Sometimes the fault lies with the board members themselves; they come to board service because they believe in the mission of the school but do not necessarily know what the actual role of the board is and what their board responsibilities are. At other times, the fault can lie with the head of school who wants to use the board more for oversight than for strategic direction and leadership.[21] One thing is certain: good governance is a lot of work. As the late University of Chicago adult learning expert Cyril Houle was fond of saying, "A good board is a victory, not a gift."[22]

Good governance may also require experimentation. Some are suggesting, for example, that day school boards become more like boarding school boards by having fewer, but longer, meetings each year—maybe two or three days each. Longer meetings would allow more time for the robust discussion and participatory debate on strategic issues that need to happen at the board level.

CHARTER SCHOOL GOVERNANCE

Charter schools are the true experimenters of our time, mixing private and public elements of school design to offer parents and communities a viable option to traditional public schools. Governance is an integral part of that experimentation. As Paul T. Hill and Robin J. Lake state: "The debate over whether charter schools offer different or more effective instruction will go on for some time, but there is no question that chartering is an innovation in public school governance."[23]

Founded on the principle of self-governance exhibited by independent or private schools, yet tethered by accountability and performance standards to the public school system, charter schools are still trying to find their way in the governance arena, struggling with self-governance within limits. There is not yet a shake-down model.

In a way, charter schools' Achilles heel is that they do not own themselves; rather, the government owns them. As a result, there are several degrees of control when it comes to "self-governance." In fact, the major restriction, according to Hill and Lake, is that, except for a few states (Arizona, Colorado, Michigan, Virginia, and Wisconsin), legislatures require charter schools to be governed by nonprofit boards. They write, "Board melt-downs have de-stabilized many charter schools, and leadership and staff turnover due in part to conflicts with the board have been a major reason for charter school failure."[24] Some of these problems are to be expected in new organizations with start-up boards, which charter schools certainly are, and careful training of board members can help here. In addition, charter schools are likely to be founded by one or two visionaries with entrepreneurial skills who then have to learn how to transform their organizations into well-run, financially viable, competitive schools. Jeffrey Moredock, governance counsel for NAIS who has been involved in the start-up of several charter schools, recommends that founders take a year to learn about how a board operates even before they get into the minutia of where a school will be located and how to finance the facility. While this recommendation may be naive, Moredock wants to stress the importance of having good, even great, governance as a goal, as well.[25]

Once the board is set up, founders have to know when to relinquish control and let their boards do more of the work. Emily Lawson, founder and CEO of D.C. Preparatory Academy tells me that she is more of a "placeholder" and that if needed she will step off the board. "The big advantage," she says, "is that I was able to pick the original board—the personalities, the character—and define the working style of the board."[26] But now it should be the board's turn.

Charter schools also have to grapple with regulations and conditions placed on them by their authorizing authorities. For example, charter schools are usually required to have a certain percentage of in-state residents, a certain number of parents, and, in some states, an uneven number of board members. (Some charter school heads think the latter is rather silly because it seems to imply that boards will not be able to come to a decision without an odd number of board members.)

Probably the knottiest regulations have to do with head-board relations. In the charter school world, the evaluation of the head is much more closely tied to students' academic performance than in the independent school world, and this relationship can make the valued partnership between the board and head of school more difficult to achieve. But, in the end, charter school advocates say these restrictions are a small price to pay for the freedom to have their very own governing boards.

PUBLIC SCHOOL GOVERNANCE

The best way to describe what is happening in public school governance is to say it is revolutionary. Buffeted by two major course-correcting events—the 1983 publication of A *Nation at Risk*[27] and the 2001 legislation, popularly known as No Child Left Behind, that reauthorized the Elementary and Secondary Education Act—governance of public school systems generally has been in turmoil for the past two decades, with local, state, and federal officials scrambling for solutions and compliance at the expense of local school boards.

The mediocrity of American education and the threat that that posed to our nation, painted in A *Nation at Risk*, surprised many. David Gordon, editor of A *Nation Reformed? American Education Twenty Years after "A Nation at Risk,"* describes the 1983 report as having "wielded the rhetorical equivalent of [famed principal] Joe Clark's bullhorn and baseball bat" on public education, educators and parents.[28] The outcome was probably inevitable: further erosion of control by district school boards and principals themselves over schools. On top of that, President George Bush's signature domestic legislation, No Child Left Behind, with its requirements for mandatory testing of public school students in certain grades and its accountability measures, extended the hand of the federal government into schools as never before.

In the aptly titled book *Besieged*, editor William G. Howell states, "Today, professional politicians regularly drown out the voices and displace the visions of the individuals who have governed public schools for centuries: locally elected (and occasionally appointed) school board members."[29] He points out that throughout much of the nineteenth century, local school boards were practically the only game in town. For the most part, they hired and fired, set the curriculum, established the budget, and determined the length of the school day and year. But, then, because of consolidation and modernization trends in education, the number of local school boards declined from just about 119,000 school districts with 218 students each in 1936 to roughly 15,000 in 1997 with about 3,000 students each.[30] At the same time, there were more and more challenges to school boards' authority as a result of increased state and federal funding and regulations, and the continuous pressure to improve results. On the political side, candidates increasingly ran as "The Education Candidate" and a lot of them had takeover and other school reforms on their minds. By 2000, Peter Schrag observed in *The Nation*, "You are not a serious candidate these days without an education policy, which for most poll-conscious politicians, state and national, means higher standards, high-stakes testing, school accountability and tougher graduation requirements."[31]

In the 1970s and 1980s, it was often the governors who became involved in setting academic standards and in trying to prop up failing schools. Then, in 1991, Boston Mayor Thomas Menino started a trend among big city mayors by switching control of his city's schools from an elected board to a seven-member school committee chosen by him. Chicago's Mayor Richard Daley followed with a similar takeover in 1995, and New York City, under Mayor Michael Bloomberg, launched another mayoral governance model in 2002 that included eliminating smaller neighborhood school boards. To date, about a dozen of the nation's largest school districts are under mayoral control, and other cities, such as Los Angeles and Hartford, Connecticut, are in various stages of following their lead.[32]

It is not likely that mayors will get out of the education business any time soon. There is too much riding on it. The struggle for mayoral control reflects not only the discontent with low academic achievement and high dropout rates in many urban public school districts but also the belief that for cities to be competitive they need to provide good schools and an educated work force. Comments Stanford University education professor Michael Kirst, "It's not whether the mayors will be involved in city schools, but how."[33]

There is some evidence that mayoral takeovers are making a difference by raising academic scores, but the jury is still out about whether there has been sustained and substantive change for the better across the board in terms of lifting graduation rates and decreasing the number of high school dropouts. It is also important to note that cities such as Houston have improved scores with elected school boards after extensive reforms and that magnet schools generally do well, no matter the governance structure, because they are more focused and independent.

"There is no magic bullet," says former member of the District of Columbia School Board Robin Martin.[34] He does make the case, though, that less turbulence in governance is better for school systems and their students. In both Boston and Long Beach, California, for instance, where the mayors and school superintendents each served for at least a decade, there are results to show for it. He also argues, as do others, that under the best governance structure good schools would be given more discretion with their own management and with tailored, performance-based reward systems that benefit educators, parents, and especially students.

There is no doubt that the importance of good governance structures to sustainability, stewardship, and success in each of these educational models— independent schools, charter schools, and public schools systems—is more critical than ever. In all three cases, the effect of good governance should mean one thing: improvements in student achievement.

NOTES

1. Jim Collins, *Good to Great: Why Some Companies Make the Leap—And Others Don't* (New York: HarperCollins Publishers, 2001).

2. Ibid., 1.

3. Jim Collins, *Good to Great and the Social Sectors: Why Business Thinking Is Not the Answer* (Boulder, Colo.: Jim Collins, 2005), 1, www.jimcollins.com.

4. Ibid.

5. Ibid., 2.

6. Ibid.,

7. Robert Evans, *The Human Side of School Change: Reform, Resistance, and the Real Life Problems of Innovation* (San Francisco, Calif.: Jossey-Bass, 1996).

8. Robert Evans, "Why a School Doesn't Run—or Change—Like a Business," *Independent School* 59, no. 3 (Spring 2000):42–45.

9. Patrick Bassett, "Independent Perspective: Rethinking Independent School Governance," *Independent School* 61, no. 4 (Summer 2002):7.

10. Richard Chait, with William P. Ryan and Barbara E. Taylor, *Governance as Leadership: Reframing the Work of Nonprofit Boards* (Hoboken, N.J.: John Wiley & Sons, 2005), 79.

11. Ibid., 182.

12. Chait, with Ryan and Taylor, *Governance as Leadership*.

13. Richard Chait, interview by Manda Salls, Harvard Business School Working Knowledge, April 4, 2005, http://hbswk.hbs.edu/archive/4735.html.

14. David E. Ormstedt, *Holding the Trust: An Independent School Trustee's Guide to Fiduciary Responsibilities* (Washington, D.C.: National Association of Independent Schools, 2006).

15. Chait, interview by Salls.

16. Barbara Kreisler, "Governance as Leadership: A New Model for Nonprofits," *Bright Ideas* 24, no. 2 (Spring 2005): 45–46.

17. Deborah S. Hechinger, "From Responsible to Exceptional: Lessons in Good Governance," *Independent School* 66, no. 1 (Fall 2006): 30–36.

18. Deborah S. Hechinger, president and CEO of BoardSource, in discussion with the author, April 2007.

19. Hechinger, "From Responsible to Exceptional," 34.

20. Hechinger, in discussion with the author, April 2007.

21. Ibid.

22. Quoted in Hechinger, "From Responsible to Exceptional," 34.

23. Paul T. Hill and Robin J. Lake, "Charter School Governance" (paper presented at the National Conference on Charter School Research, Vanderbilt University, September 28, 2006), 1.

24. Ibid., 13.

25. Jeffrey Moredock, governance counsel for National Association of Independent Schools and former school head, in discussion with the author, April 2007.

26. Emily Lawson, founder and executive director of D.C. Preparatory Academy, in discussion with the author, April 2007.

27. United States National Commission on Excellence in Education, *A Nation at Risk: The Imperative for Educational Reform*, A Report to the Nation and the Secretary of Education (Washington, D.C.: National Commission on Excellence in Education, 1983).

28. David T. Gordon, ed., *A Nation Reformed? American Education Twenty Years after "A Nation at Risk"* (Cambridge, Mass.: Harvard Education Press, 2003), 2.

29. William G. Howell, ed., *Besieged: School Boards and the Future of Education Politics* (Washington, D.C.: Brookings Institution Press, 2005), 1.

30. Ibid., 4.

31. Peter Schrag, "Education and the Election," *The Nation* 270, no. 9 (March 6, 2000): 11.

32. Martha T. Moore, "More Mayors Move to Take Over Schools," *USA Today*, March 20, 2007, http://www.usatoday.com/news/education/2007-03-20-cover-mayors-schools_N.htm.

33. Ibid.

34. Robin Martin, District of Columbia School Board member 2003–2006, in discussion with the author, April 2007.

FURTHER READING

Conley, David T. *Who Governs Our Schools? Changing Roles and Responsibilities.* New York: Teachers College Press, 2003.

Epstein, Noel, ed. *Who's in Charge Here? The Tangled Web of School Governance and Policy.* Washington, D.C.: Brookings Institution Press, 2004.

McAdams, Donald R. *Fighting to Save Our Urban Schools . . . and Winning: Lessons from Houston.* New York: Teachers College Press, 2000.

Peterson, Paul E., and Bryan Hassel. *Learning from School Choice.* Washington, D.C.: Brookings Institution Press, 1998.

• 3 •

Financing Education

The Worm in the Apple

Peter M. Branch

𝒻rom the colonial era to the present, economic status has had a controlling effect on American education. In the beginning, education was the responsibility of the parent, the master, and the church. While it was agreed that knowledge was important to the worthiness of a child, a worker, and a parishioner, no expectation of universal instruction or of government funding prevailed until the mid-nineteenth century, and then only with the exclusion of critical segments of society. As a result, it was left to the most local of authorities, parents or their surrogates, to supply education as they could afford. Farmers taught their sons to be farmers. Craftsmen educated their sons and their apprentices. Mothers taught their daughters the household duties. Members of the gentry who wished more classical studies engaged tutors for their children, though mostly for their sons. A few private seminaries could take their sons' education further, to prepare them for professional life, principally as ministers, doctors, or lawyers. At the elementary and even secondary level, home schooling prevailed. Economic status controlled access and opportunity.

Following the establishment of the new American republic, occasional communal efforts to address literacy and morality for more than a few resulted in local schoolhouses sometimes funded by parents who even boarded the schoolmaster and sometimes funded by localities that levied taxes for this purpose on all householders. Thus began the dependence of public schooling on the taxation of property. With the coming of the industrial age and the desire of Progressive-era reformers for compulsory attendance laws to ensure the assimilation and literacy of growing foreign-born populations, states began to set requirements for sound and effective education. Funding still fell mainly on localities.

Despite the growth in the nineteenth century of publicly funded common schools, as they came to be called, there was still strong support for non-public education. Private academies continued to exist and prosper by meeting the college preparatory needs of the upper classes. Even female seminaries developed to serve the presumed special needs of young women. Moreover, with the rise of compulsory attendance laws, some religious groups, primarily the Roman Catholic Church, became concerned that the public schools were, at best, neutrally secular and, at worst, determinedly Protestant. To address this concern and to retain the loyalty and the souls of their adherents, religious groups established parochial schools funded by donations to the church by parishioners and fees from parents.

This education movement was seen by anti-Catholics as a form of separatism and a threat to a common democratic ethic and ethos. It was also thought that those who had their own schools would be unwilling to financially support the common schools through taxation. But religious, ethnic, and economic bigotry also played a critical part in the effort to stamp out parochial education. This effort came to a head in the Far West, where there was little tradition of private schooling. In 1922, by ballot initiative, Oregon voters approved a Compulsory Education Act which mandated that all students between the ages of 8 and 16 must attend the local public school or their parents would be punished by fine or imprisonment. In 1925, in *Pierce v. Society of the Sisters*, the Supreme Court ruled that

> the Act of 1922 unreasonably interferes with the liberty of parents and guardians to direct the upbringing and education of children under their control. . . . The fundamental theory of liberty upon which all governments in this Union repose excludes any general power of the state to standardize its children by forcing them to accept instruction from public teachers only. The child is not the mere creature of the state; those who nurture him and direct his destiny have the right, coupled with the high duty, to recognize and prepare him for additional obligations.[1]

In declaring the law null and void, the Court also stated that it would do irreparable harm to the business and property of private schools.

Pierce v. Society of the Sisters established the right of parents to choose the school they think is best for their children. In doing so, the Supreme Court also established the principle that the government did not have the right "to standardize its children by forcing them to accept instruction from public teachers only." A question might be asked today whether the government has the right to standardize its children by forcing them to accept instruction through a universal curriculum or through universal standardized testing under the threat of removal of federal funding for their schools. To the extent that some states require private schools to hire only public school certifiable teachers, to the extent that statewide curricula are imposed on nonpublic schools or that private school students have to pass state testing based on standard curricular expectations, to the extent that legislators' pet projects become mandated programs for all schools, true choice in education is denied. For many private schools, the threat of government interference has led to the rejection of any offer of federal or state financial assistance lest it lead to the imposition of external mandates. When money is given, strings are inevitably attached.

Choice in education is also chimerical if it is not affordable or available. Sometimes it is available but not affordable to certain individuals. At other times, it is affordable but not available. High-quality private education exists in many jurisdictions in the United States, but many private schools lack the financial resources to award the need-based financial aid that would allow families, regardless of economic status, to enroll their children. While many public schools offer excellent education, especially in jurisdictions with high tax bases, many others, especially in jurisdictions with low tax bases, lack the resources to fund good facilities and hire strong teachers. Even wealthy school districts may not offer the specialized services required by individual students with special needs. No Child Left Behind, the legislative effort to standardize educational performance adopted in 2001, gives children in failing schools the right to choose to move to a successful school. Yet in rural districts such a choice may not exist within a practicable distance, and in certain failing urban districts there may be few alternatives.

Economic status continues to dictate the equity and adequacy of American education to the detriment of the general welfare that the Constitution sought to establish. Where a child was born, where a child lives, who a child's parents are, what their circumstances are, and what a child's race, religion, ethnicity, and gender are determine his or her educational opportunity and achievement more than any inherent intellectual ability. The greatest correlation of high scores on most standardized tests is with parental economic status.

The financing of precollegiate education in the United States since the Second World War has been intimately connected with the movement to achieve, first, an equitable education; second, an adequate education; and, most recently, an efficient education for all children. In a largely immigrant nation founded on the belief "that all men are created equal" and, says the Declaration of Independence, endowed with inalienable rights including, "the pursuit of happiness," education was seen as essential to that pursuit. For social reformers, equity in educational opportunity was seen as essential to a just society and the lifeblood of a democratic polity.

It was therefore inevitable that those most excluded from equal access to educational excellence should seek redress. In the 1950s, the civil rights movement mounted a full-scale legal attack on the premise, established in the Supreme Court case of *Plessy v. Ferguson* (1896), that segregated schools could constitutionally exist as separate but equal entities. In a few jurisdictions, schools designated for African Americans may have been equal in funding, quality of facilities, and teacher salaries, but equality of such educational resources was largely lacking in segregated districts. When the Court ruled in *Brown v. Board of Education of Topeka* (1954) that racially separate schools were inherently unequal, not only were segregated schools ruled unconstitutional but the importance of equal schooling was raised as an educational necessity, if not a right.

As a result, other issues of educational inequity came to the forefront of policy debate, court review, and legislative action. Most prominent among these issues has been the issue of funding equity, based in the belief that inequity in financial support for a school or school district relative to others of similar character and size will yield the likelihood of a poorer education. With the movement of middle-class white families to suburbs and the concentration in rural areas of poorer whites and in the cities of poorer families of color, distinction within states of tax-base wealth, not to speak of the greater ability and willingness of wealthier districts to provide a higher percentage of income to school support, led to clear inequities in educational resources. (In states and districts where equalization of funding has been enforced, the parents in wealthier districts or schools have sometimes subverted its intent by providing additional monies through fund-raising, even setting up nonprofit foundations for support of special projects, sports teams, or additional staffing.) It is this dilemma of economic geography, imbedded in the historic reliance on state control of education and local provision of funding, that has roiled educational finance debates since the second half of the twentieth century.

For the individual parent living in a district suffering from a lack of adequate resources, there have been few choices. Participation in the effort to gain legislative or judicial relief has become a civil rights endeavor into which many have entered. However, the effort to achieve compensatory funding of some type—although increasingly successful in the courts—has been long and arduous. The federal government over time has responded with a series of acts to benefit students with specific economic or educational needs and schools with specific percentages of students with such needs. Clearly such efforts have been helpful, although the effectiveness and adequacy of this program continue to be questioned.

Many families could not wait or did not believe that the solutions offered would adequately serve their children. As a result, some sought relief in the private sector. In the late twentieth century, a number of traditional private schools, both religiously affiliated and secular, became beneficiaries of the search for a high-quality education, or in some cases, of the flight from failing schools. The mixture of motives, as different as those of parents dedicated to public schools but unwilling to sacrifice their own children's education and those of parents uneasy about or hostile to the increasing racial diversity of urban schools, has created a challenge to both the public schools they leave and the private schools they seek to attend. As a result, private schools with openings or with a desire to reach out to nontraditional private school applicants need to carefully define their mission and philosophy so that parents have the necessary information to choose schools that are the best fit for their children and their families.

Although private schools charge tuition, and the established independent schools charge significant tuition, families with economic need should not avoid applying for that reason. Many private schools have financial aid budgets that can support families whose children they wish to enroll. Few schools offer no-need scholarships, however, so all parents applying for financial support in the form of reduced tuition charges should be prepared to fill out forms similar to those filled out to get aid from colleges. Parochial school charges are typically on the lower end of private school fees and may be even lower for members of the church, synagogue, or parish. Those families able to contribute additionally on a tax deductible basis will usually be asked to give an annual gift to the school or a major gift, if possible, to a capital or endowment campaign.

In the 1980s and 1990s, at the same time that issues of educational quality linked to equitable funding were stimulating reflection on the educational uniformity of public education, concerns from a rising religious perspective provoked a revival of an old educational model. Where Catholics had fled the Protestant bias of nineteenth-century public education, religious conservatives from an Evangelical Protestant perspective, among others, began to protest what they saw as the loss of a faith perspective in schools. Hostile to the elimination of government-sponsored prayer in schools as a result of Supreme Court rulings upholding the constitutional separation of church and state, they were equally troubled by the teaching of the scientific-based Darwinian theory of evolution and other indicators of a secular education. Many enrolled in the fight for what they saw as majority or religious rights being abused by influential minorities or activist judges. Others sought refuge for their children from schools and a society gone wrong.

As a result, many religious conservatives began to home-school their children, and the movement caught on. Soon there were home-school organizations, conferences, and religiously based curricula. Stung by accusations that their children lacked social skills, some parents organized home-school teams, choruses, and other groups. In some jurisdictions, they have been able to persuade, or legally force, their local districts to let their children participate in extracurricular activities. With the exception of the oversight costs some states incurred in order to supervise home schools and the marginal costs of such students on public school teams, the greatest cost to public schools has been the loss of per pupil daily attendance fees in jurisdictions where this movement has had a significant impact.

The many education reform efforts of the last quarter of the twentieth century, from specific curricular changes, to changes in teaching methodology, to restructuring of administration, among many others, were a testimony to American optimism and idealism. But some reformers and not a few parents became discouraged at the lack of progress in the face of so many reforms and an ever-increasing demand for financial support. In either a new effort of reform or, in the view of their opponents, an effort to undermine and supplant the public schools, a creative group of advocates persuaded some states and even the federal government in the District of Columbia to authorize the establishment of what came to be known as public charter schools. As a financial design, this educational entity has the combined virtue of public school funding and private school independence. Established under the authority of an authorized educational entity, whether a school district, charter board, university, or other, these schools receive slightly less than the public school per child annual expenditure but are largely independent of the school district and need not employ a unionized staff. Many states and districts have resisted the charter school movement, but it has had an astounding growth as well as some spectacular failures due often to poor oversight.

Because public charter schools are a new movement and few schools have been in existence longer than ten years, parents must be cautious, as with any school, to investigate the financial stability as well as the mission, curriculum, and graduation rate, for example. But as a reform effort, charter schools have some real leverage since, as public schools, they are free and must accept students on a first-come, first-served basis. Any success they have can be a competitive model for the public school system. Unlike private schools, however, their lack of selectivity limits their ability to focus on a specific range of abilities or interests. The public school system, which has the same democratic challenge, may have a larger student pool and thus a greater financial ability to assign personnel to address specific student needs. Currently in those locations such as the District of Columbia, where there is a significant and growing charter school population, the public schools are threatened financially by the loss of clients, not to speak of the loss of support.

Tuition tax credits and vouchers for parents whose children are attending private or parochial schools have long been advocated for by some who wish to offset the cost of private education. While the National Association of Independent Schools has been critical of both devices and suspicious of the threat to the independence of their schools, Catholic and some other nonpublic schools have seen such possibilities as providing relief for schools whose families may not be able to afford the full cost of tuition and whose constituents cannot offset the cost with giving. In 2007, the Republican Congress and president authorized a $7,500 per student school voucher program in the District of Columbia for families meeting an income means test. With minimal limitation on the independence of private schools, it gained the participation of private schools across the educational spectrum. Schools with low enrollment and/or schools with tuition at or below the voucher, such as the Catholic schools of Washington, were the primary beneficiaries. With the loss of about 1,500 students, the D.C. public schools were the significant losers.

Ostensibly intended as a pilot reform program, the D.C. Opportunity Scholarship Program has been more a model of the continued controversy over whether such a market-driven private school choice program can have better results than the local public school. There have been no substantive studies of outcomes, and no significant differences in performance have been observed in any of the studies that have been undertaken. The latter findings are similar to findings from studies made in Milwaukee and Cleveland. Whether these outcomes are the result of poor testing methodology, the long-term educational disadvantage of economically deprived students, the lack of effectiveness of the schools attended, or the brevity of the period of enrollment remains to be seen. In any case, significant resistance to taking monies from the public schools to help students enroll in private schools, especially in religious institutions, makes this financing device one that few states will welcome. In the District of Columbia, the funding has been uniquely from the federal, not the local, treasury.

While the issue of educational financing may be seen as an issue of equity and adequacy in education, the nature of school financing may be seen as a determinant in outcomes. Indeed, the ways in which schools are funded have an important impact on their organization, their curriculum, their teachers, and their students. Public schools, funded by public monies, are subject to multiple institutional demands from local, state, and national levels. They may be induced, even coerced, by the power of the purse to adopt certain curricula, to impose specific certification requirements on teachers, and to respond to public pressures in regard to values education, employers' expectations, and the socialization needs of a democracy. Similarly, nonpublic schools, funded largely by tuitions, annual gifts, and, to some degree, donated endowments or religious support, have to be responsive to the expectations of the parents and donors or religious institutions upon whose support they depend. Principals of public schools grow weary of the parent who complains that "for what I pay in taxes. . . !" No more happily does the private school leader welcome the words, "For what I'm paying in tuition . . . !"

However, accountability to the local demand of the individual parent may be the best of all educational worlds. At least the parent is personally invested in what really matters—the education of his or her child. The complaint may or may not be justified, but the exchange can be productive and the response of the teacher can make a difference. The larger issue for parents is whether the money they pay through their taxes or tuition is being used well to make a difference in their children's education. As a matter of public policy, this financial question is at the forefront of the examination of public schooling in America today.

Some critics of educational practices have argued that money does not matter; that we are already spending too much, and that no amount of money would make a difference. This school of thinking believes that the system is broken and that a revolutionary, not evolutionary, change must be made.

Others students of educational systems, who are more optimistic, point to ways in which money does make a difference—in better facilities, more able individuals choosing to teach, greater attention to individual students due to lower class sizes and specialized instruction, adequate support staff, up-to-date technology, more diverse activities, and better communications between home and school. Whether public or private, schools that provide these effective services and programs will be sought after by parents. Families will reward such schools with loyalty and trust. All that most parents have to pass on to their sons and daughters are the skills and values that will make them competent, caring, responsible, and happy citizens of American society. To help their children achieve those goals, mothers and fathers will make most any affordable sacrifice. It is the obligation of the policy makers and educators of the United States to ensure that such sacrifices are equitable and well rewarded.

NOTES

1. *Pierce v. Society of the Sisters of the Holy Names of Jesus and Mary*, 268 U.S. 510 (1925).

FURTHER READING

Odden, Allan, and Lawrence O. Picus. *School Finance: A Policy Perspective*, 4th ed. New York: McGraw-Hill, 2008.
Wong, Kenneth K. *Funding Public Schools: Politics and Policies*. Lawrence: University Press of Kansas, 1999.

II

GENERAL CHOICES

· 4 ·

American Public Education

Paula J. Carreiro

$\mathscr{I}$n this democratic nation, our public schools shoulder the expectations of a demanding citizenry. They are responsible for the continuity of the American system of government, the health of its economy, and the perpetuation of its social values.[1] These megagoals exist, whether in spite of or because of the large numbers of people served by the public school system. In 2002, 86 percent of Americans between the age of 25 and 29 had graduated from public high schools.[2] This high rate of public school participation distinguishes the United States from many other developed nations.

When one compares the structures and beliefs inherent in American public schools to those of other countries, additional differences are readily apparent. Both control and funding of our schools occur primarily at the local level with oversight by individual states rather than the national regulation and funding prevalent in many other Western education systems. However, our schools must adhere to the Constitution of the United States. As a result, most religious instruction in public schools is banned, which is not the case for many of our European counterparts. Early on there was also a uniquely American belief in the school's capacity to solve social problems, although some would argue that such belief has diminished in the last few decades.[3] Nonetheless, most schools, whether public or private, permit or promote discussions of societal issues as well as the teaching of cultural values regardless of the inherent conflict surrounding these topics. Public schools are typically divided into three segments beginning with elementary school, which serves our youngest students from kindergarten through fourth, fifth, or sixth grade, depending on the individual school district's preference. Students then advance to junior high school or middle school (the most current designation). This educational experience begins where elementary school ended and usually continues through the eighth grade.

The high school years tend to be grades 9–12. Some very small school districts may operate a single school building that houses kindergarten through grade 12. Whatever the configuration, public schools have strived over the years to meet the academic and, more recently, the developmental needs of the students they serve as well as the demands of the greater society.

THE HISTORY OF PUBLIC SCHOOLS

In the era of the American Revolution, the founders of this country recognized that for a fledging democracy to flourish, citizens must have access to education. Thomas Jefferson was the first American leader to speak of this necessity. In 1779 he proposed a system to provide free education for the children in Virginia for three years; after that, the best and the brightest would continue their education at the state's expense. Although his plan was never enacted, his idea for a free education for the children of America did form the foundation for future public school endeavors.[4] From the beginning, both politicians and educators linked the success of the new republic to the education of its people.

Until the mid-1800s, education existed in a variety of forms but could hardly be called a system. There were numerous regional, local, and private institutions usually dependent on the resources of a town or city. Other schools were affiliated with religious institutions or trade associations and advanced a particular perspective. Most schools were created to educate the sons of the wealthy. Public voice or involvement in funding was rare.

Enter Horace Mann. His beliefs in common education were fervent. He envisioned a school system for this country that would be "available and equal for all, part of the birthright of every American child."[5] With his election to the Massachusetts board of education in 1837, Mann supervised the creation of a common school system that expanded throughout the state. He and other education reformers of the day fought for what was the beginning of our current public school system by successfully arguing that such a system could transform our nation and its capacity to compete with other countries by producing literate and virtuous graduates. Common school advocates further promoted free and public schools with an appeal to a state concerned with crime, poverty, and an influx of immigrants and thus ethnic tensions. Education, it seemed, could be the antidote to myriad woes. Massachusetts passed the first compulsory attendance laws for the elementary school years. New York soon followed, and by the end of the nineteenth century the common school advocates had largely realized success.

It is important to note that these compulsory attendance laws did not apply to secondary schooling for older students. In 1900, only 10 percent of American teenagers, aged 14–17, were enrolled in public school. For the most part, those attending a high school were the sons of the wealthy. By the year 2000, public high school enrollment had grown to 88 percent, as the need for secondary education became further recognized and public high schools proliferated.[6]

While it would be nice to wrap a bow around this educational package and deem it a gift to all Americans, we would overlook the fact that not everyone of school age was a recipient, at least in an equitable way. In the midtwentieth century, one's ability to benefit from the best educational opportunity proved to be directly related to income, race, gender, physical or mental handicap, place of residence, and family occupation. Most educational policy makers were not attentive to the plight of the poor, working-class immigrants, females, African Americans, or the disabled. Although there were attempts to address this inequality, the efforts were patchwork and the outcomes were spotty at best.[7]

In recent decades, we have seen increasing numbers of protest movements for social justice as it relates to American public school education. The probable catalyst for this movement was *Brown v. Board of Education of Topeka* in 1954. Many would say that we have made enormous progress on the equity front since that time; others would argue that the number of children "left behind" in 2007 is unconscionable. But everyone would agree that the need for equal access to high-quality educational environments for all of America's children remains one of the most critical issues facing our country today.

TODAY'S ISSUES

In past centuries, policy makers and educators faced daunting challenges, but they were not without laudable successes that benefited our current public school educational system. There are many issues today, however, for which there are no comparables, no standard set of blueprints from the past that necessarily apply. Schools are often the only stability in the lives of our children. Therefore, out of necessity, schools are asked to expand curricula to include those things that were once left to families, churches, and social organizations. Add to those demands the rising expectations of Americans that schools prepare our children with the values, behaviors, and skills needed to succeed in an increasingly complex society. Further, it is seen as the school's task to produce exemplary citizens who will contribute to the social stability in the country. Finally, thanks to some hard-fought legislative decisions, schools are required to create equitable environments among students displaying a wide range of economic, racial, social, ethnic, and physical and mental differences. These issues are all critical to the education that our children will receive but they constitute a huge responsibility. Increased demands on our public schools also come from other contemporary issues.

NEW TECHNOLOGIES

One demand relates to the use of new technologies. Evans Clinchy, senior consultant at the Institute for Responsive Education in Boston, has observed, "Insofar as the adoption of this new technology in our schools is concerned, the digital revolution is still in its swaddling clothes."[8] Although many educators would agree, computers and other digital technologies have been used in our schools for years. Just as there is hope in the capacity of technology to further transform our educational system, there is recognition that many wrong turns have been taken along the way. In addition, educators lack consensus on how technology can transform educational practice. These facts are of consternation to a tax-paying public and school administrators who must distribute scant resources. Not only does the purchase of the hardware systems, the ongoing expense of software to support the new technologies, and the cost of research, development, and replacement take a huge bite out of the funding pie, but the professional development necessary for implementation is formidable. On the other hand, there is real optimism that, with technology, schools can individualize instruction in ways never before possible and that students can have access to information to advance their research and understanding in a broad range of topics. Schools will also have to make some tough decisions on how to deal with the "digital divide" as they look to provide equitable access to technology for all students. Some schools have already been the beneficiaries of corporate gifts or other special funding sources. Although the media repeatedly warns of the danger of popular social networking sites and the many opportunities for misuse of technology, schools will no doubt continue to expand the use of new technologies as they are created. These are tools our students will need and use.

REFORMS

Public schools in the United States have been subjected to reform movements with head-spinning frequency. While many such attempts at overhauling the existing system have had some positive effects, far too many fail for a variety of reasons, not the least of which is the reluctance of a teaching force on whom great demands are already made to accept a "top-down" mandate. Such an approach, say Stanford University professors of education David Tyack and Larry Cuban, "slights the many ways in which schools shape reforms and teachers employ their wisdom of practice to produce pedagogical hybrids."⁹

The most recent reform efforts have focused on the issue of standards and accountability. The 2001 No Child Left Behind legislation is a current example of a national mandate that requires states to use annual testing to identify "underperforming schools" and then take action to improve test scores. Advocates of this approach believe that there is still too much local control over schools, while local school authorities in many states are demanding an end to this legislation and view such national involvement as interference. Teacher groups reasonably resent curriculum that is presented as "teacher-proof" at a time when high-stakes testing is limiting their ability to be creative and responsive to individual student needs and interests. The tension among state, local, and federal authorities and stakeholders is long-standing and likely to continue.

EXPANDED SCHOOLING

Societal changes in the United States have led to some new and interesting ways to think about how we use our schools. Schools that sat empty for months in the summer may now house summer school, summer camp, or community initiatives. With the increase in single parent households as well as dual income families, the need for child care at a much younger age has increased. Many public schools now use their facilities to provide programs for children in the early preschool years. Similarly, adult education classes, whether for a degree or to pursue a hobby, are increasingly prevalent. Sponsors are finding ready partners in many public schools that are available in the evening.

Since the design of many existing school facilities might not be equipped to handle a multiuse approach, Tom Donahoe suggests that schools consider a redesign of the building to accommodate the extension of the school day and the use of the school year-round.¹⁰ The implementation of this suggestion will no doubt depend on community support and the schools' capacity to increase the complexity of the current operating design.

FUNDING INEQUITIES

Historically, the funding as well as the control of public schools has been at the local and state level. Only in the late twentieth century did the federal government become significantly involved in issues aiming to redress funding equity. Because financing of the annual costs of schools has been largely based on property taxes, districts with high property values have had an advantage in raising the funds for support of their schools. Court action has found that such inequities in funding deprive students of an equal education and has required states to develop formulas to offset these imbalances. These issues, and offshoots such as the question of what funding is necessary for an adequate education, continue to challenge the school reform movement and threaten public support.

ADVANTAGES AND DISADVANTAGES OF PUBLIC SCHOOLING

The title of this section seems to suggest that there is an inherent option in most families' decision to send their children to a public school. For many that is simply not the case. And even if the decision to enroll in a neighborhood public school is a matter of choice among alternatives, there are many advantages to that choice. Proximity to school events and classroom friends certainly affect the quality of family life. It is also true that larger public systems are more able to support special programs such as those for the gifted and talented or to offer services to children with special needs.

The real truth is that the right school for an individual child has more to do with individual teachers, the quality of the curriculum, and the overall fit for the child and the family. Parents should ask to visit the school before a child enrolls. On that visit it is appropriate to ask about class size, opportunities for parental involvement, attention to the needs of individual learners, and the philosophy of the school. How often does the school communicate to parents and by what means? Are there courses in the arts, and, if the school is an elementary division, are the children regularly allowed to play outside? What extracurricular activities are available? Is there a focus on character development as well as academics? Are there high standards for both achievement and behavior? Is the environment safe for children both physically and emotionally? Are students able to assume leadership roles? What assessments are used?

The answers to these and other questions will offer insights into the educational belief system of an individual school. Depending on the response, families can create a partnership with the school their child attends. It could well be the local public school.

PUBLIC SCHOOLS IN THE TWENTY-FIRST CENTURY

If we were to create a report card for our public school system in the United States, the grades would be mixed. A large body of research links the quality of education in any given city with the tax base of its residents. If schools must rely on funding formulas that reward the wealthiest of districts, there will certainly be discrepancies in programs available to students as well as in the ability to recruit and retain teachers. If additional support and supervision are determined state by state, dramatic differences in expectations will persist across the nation.

Such variations in school districts complicate predictions for the success of public schools in the twenty-first century. Of course, predicting the future has always been an uncertain endeavor, but in this time of accelerating change, it is problematic at best. What we do know is that schooling should no longer be constrained by an agrarian calendar more appropriate to the nineteenth century. We also know that the school design and methodology developed to ensure student success in a twentieth-century industrial era will limit opportunities for today's students whose jobs in the future may not even exist at this moment. Yet these are the models familiar to policy makers as well as parents. The information age and beyond will need citizens ready and able to understand and contribute to our democracy. The need for literacy and numeric acumen will not decline. Science, the arts, and history, to name a few disciplines, will certainly endure and continue to contribute to the welfare of the individual as well as the nation. But our schools must expand the program horizon for the twenty-first century. We need to care more about integrity, about the ability to work with others across race, ethnic, and geographic boundaries, and about ingenuity and problem-solving skills than we do about test scores if our students are to thrive. Patricia Graham, professor of the history of American education at Harvard University, stresses that "what the country needs now is both the enhancement of the wit and character of the young, and such efforts should be at the heart of our institutional efforts."[11]

Concluding chapters of this book expand upon specific criterion schools should consider when looking at educational transformation in this twenty-first century, and I have no doubt that those suggestions will continue to spark public debate on the role of public schooling in America. And that is as it should be. This debate has always been at the center of shaping our schools as democratic institutions and, in turn, as shapers of our democratic society. As much as it is possible to grow frustrated at the challenges we face in ensuring that our public schools meet the needs of all our children, there is no fight more worthwhile. But because nothing is more inevitable than change, we must not curse the battle because it will always be with us. Giving up on public schools is not a national option because there is no other instrument or institution at hand with the capacity to address the many needs of our many children. For them, for our great nation, and for our ever smaller world, we must continue to struggle with the pursuit of educational equity and excellence.

NOTES

1. Patricia Graham, *Schooling America* (New York: Oxford University Press, 2005), 3.

2. *Microsoft Encarta Online Encyclopedia 2007*, s.v. "Public Education in the United States," encarta.msn.com.

3. Jonathan Zimmerman, *Whose America? Culture Wars in the Public Schools* (Cambridge, Mass.: Harvard University Press, 2002), 228.

4. Gordon C. Lee, *Crusade against Ignorance: Thomas Jefferson on Education* (New York: Teachers College Press, 1961), 66, 97–100.

5. Horace Mann, *The Republic and the School: Horace Mann on the Education of Free Man*, ed. Lawrence Cremin, Classics in Education 1 (New York: Teachers College Press, 1957), 8.

6. "Public Education in the United States."

7. David Tyack and Larry Cuban, *Tinkering toward Utopia* (Cambridge, Mass.: Harvard University Press, 1995), 22.

8. Evans Clinchy, *Transforming Public Education* (New York: Teachers College Press, 1997), 134.

9. Tyack and Cuban, *Tinkering toward Utopia*, 83.

10. Tom Donohoe, "Finding the Way: Structure, Time and Culture in School Improvement," *Phi Delta Kappan* 75 (December 1993): 301–10.

11. Graham, *Schooling America*, 253.

Independent Schools

Pearl Rock Kane

$\mathcal{H}$orace Mann, often referred to as the father of American public school education, argued that a democratic nation must have free, universal, nonsectarian education. Mann wanted a school that would be "available and equal for all, part of the birthright of every American child," for rich and poor alike.[1] The public school he envisioned was to be superior in quality to any comparable private school so that parents would choose public schools in the best interest of their child. Mann hoped that private schools would then simply go out of business. Horace Mann won his major battle—the public school became one of the hallmarks of American society—but he never achieved his goal of eliminating private schools. Parents continued to choose private denominational and nonsectarian schools that accorded with their values in his day. And they still do. There have always existed two parallel sectors of education in this country—public and private.

Since 1889, when the federal government started collecting private school statistics, private school enrollment has remained relatively stable, averaging 9 percent, except for a brief period after school desegregation (in 1954) when it jumped to 12–13 percent.[2]

Among the unaffiliated schools are the independent schools, the small group of nonprofit private schools that are the most well known and expensive. These schools call themselves independent to underline their freedom from state regulations though, at the secondary school level, they are popularly referred to as "prep" schools since their purpose is to prepare students for entrance into four-year colleges. In the 2006–2007 academic year, the National Association of Independent Schools (NAIS), the organization that represents independent schools, had 1,145 member schools, with an enrollment of 561,679 students nationwide.[3] The total enrollment represents only 1 percent of all students in the United States, but independent schools have exerted influence beyond the small size and historically rank among the most prestigious school institutions in the country.[4]

Apart from a few general regulations, mostly related to issues of health and safety that are mandated by local and state governments, independent schools operate relatively free of government regulation. They are also self-sustaining, funded almost exclusively by private monies and tuition. Most independent schools are reluctant to accept any state or federal money for fear that it would lead to government intervention and compromise their independence.

There is a great deal of diversity among independent school types. They include boarding and day schools; they may be coeducational or single gender. They may span different grades, kindergarten through grade 12, or focus on only a few grades at the elementary, middle, or high school level. Some have endowments that rival those of most private colleges; others barely cover their operating costs with tuition and rely on contributions. Some are highly competitive; others provide a nurturing environment for students who need a "second chance." Independent schools thrive in urban centers, hilly suburbs, and rural outlands. Some, such as Collegiate School in New York City and Roxbury Latin in Boston, trace their histories to pre-Revolutionary America; many prominent schools were founded after the industrial boom of the late nineteenth century; and a handful are so new as to have only graduated one or two classes.[5] Each is guided by its own mission. All relish their distinctiveness.

HISTORY

Beginning in the seventeenth century, there were a variety of quasi-private schools in this country. These schools were private in the sense of governance and ownership, but most depended on public funds for their survival. With the advent of the common school, which provided free education for all, these private schools lost their public support as well as their clientele. Yet some parents were willing to pay for education that they believed was more rigorously academic than that available in public or common schools or that reinforced their ethnic or religious values.

From these early schools, many of the independent boarding schools developed. They were modeled on European schools for upper-class students, incorporating a classical education and physical education. Independent day schools have their antecedents in proprietary schools (privately owned), town and church schools, and the country day schools that were designed to provide an education comparable to that offered in the best eastern boarding schools.[6] Schools founded in the Progressive era reflected the optimistic educational ideas of the age. In recent years, some have opened up in new locations to serve the increased populations in towns that have become new centers of business. The various ways that the schools have been founded shape their identities. As one scholar has observed, "The schools have histories, stories, and traditions that influence the behavior of students and teachers alike. There is a feeling that the past is important, and that precedents add authority to rules and procedures."[7]

PHILOSOPHY

Some independent schools began as proprietary schools, but those that have emerged as members of the NAIS are nonprofit, mission-driven institutions. Schools hold themselves accountable to their missions. Missions distinguish a school's purpose; they may, for example, connect the school to a religious philosophy. The mission drives the work of the schools, and state accreditation authorities hold schools accountable to their own missions rather than to an external set of standards like that imposed on public schools.

Most independent schools focus on a mission of developing the mind, body, and spirit. Character development is a pervasive goal in and outside of the classroom, reinforced by the prevalence of teachers who serve as advisers and coaches. Most schools require students to participate in athletic activities or co-curricular activities, and schools often have as many teams as they have interested players, with a full schedule of competition.

DISTINGUISHING CHARACTERISTICS

While independent schools pride themselves on their individuality, there are six distinguishing characteristics common to independent schools: small size, self-defined curriculum, self-selected students, self-selected faculty, self-governance, and self-support.[8]

Small Size

The general philosophy of independent schools may best be articulated as a belief in personalization, which results from a key characteristic of independent schools—their small size. Independent schools strive to remain small, and admissions officers often proudly announce their student-faculty ratios. The median class size of independent schools overall in 2006–2007 was sixteen.[9] Small size does not only mean that students receive more individualized attention in the classroom. In a small school, there are more opportunities for students to participate in extracurricular activities and to hold leadership positions. In a small, personalized environment, every student can find his or her niche, explore specific talents, and find strong role models.

Academic dean William Bullard points out that opportunities for close student-teacher relationships, while available at all schools, are characteristic of independent schools, where teachers work with students "in many different capacities"—as coaches, advisers, and leaders.[10] Researcher Arthur G. Powell concurs: "The heart of the independent-school method," he says, "has always been individual attention. It is the centerpiece of the schools' claim to educational distinctiveness and a key means to promote both community and standards."[11]

Parents are attracted to the nurturing environments of these schools, in which most students have advisers who keep close watch over their progress. Independent school parents receive frequent, detailed written reports about their children, and schools host a range of events to showcase student activities. One independent school teacher described the atmosphere this way: "Whether they're strong, weak, or in the middle, every student is well known and well cared for."[12]

The Self-Defined Curriculum

The notion that all students have potential for success is evident in the classroom structures as well, for independent schools generally resist sorting, or "tracking" students and require the same basic curriculum for all students. The commitment to small class size promotes personalized academic attention; teachers spend significant time with students outside of class, helping them to meet the demands of the curriculum. The absence of tracking contributes to the rigorous nature of the schools, for every student is held to high expectations.

Although some states require mandated courses such as American history, independent schools are free to develop curricula without the constraints of state standards. Independent school teachers do not have to spend classroom time drilling students for tests required by the federal No Child Left Behind legislation that have been imposed on public schools by most states. Independent schools choose texts that support their values, and the curricula at most schools are dynamic, responsive to the needs of the students and also often open to new understandings about learning theory. Above all, independent school curricula are characterized by rigor.

Yet the curricula of independent schools are not free from external pressures. These schools "prep" students for success in college,[13] and many parents choose them to give their children advantages in the college admissions process. The ever-increasing competitiveness of selective colleges has exerted pressure on independent schools. For example, many schools have expanded the staff in their college guidance offices and incorporate SAT preparation into the school day.

Nevertheless, the curricula of independent schools involve more than the work of the classroom. Powell claims that, until the 1950s "the development of character was [the] most important professed objective" of independent schools and religious training and athletics were perceived as important means for meeting this objective. Then, in the 1960s, attention to self-esteem and other forms of character and community development emerged as important values.[14] Today independent schools pay significant attention to character development, student self-esteem, and community building. Many schools have peer leadership programs, for example, which coordinate discussions between older and younger students about navigating social situations.

Independent schools strive to offer excellent co-curricular programming that provides opportunities for developing nonacademic goals. In 1977, Leonard Baird studied a range of "elite" independent schools and noted that "a number of campuses include art galleries, computers, radio and TV stations, golf courses, skating rinks, horse stables, and planetariums."[15] These campuses have grown even more impressive in subsequent years, especially with the explosion in technology. Each school strives to fill its campus with everything "state of the art."

Self-Selected Students

Students apply to independent schools; schools choose to accept—or not to accept—students. As author Otto Kraushaar has noted, "Both the patrons and the school have a stake in seeing that the contract is fulfilled satisfactorily."[16] Students know they must fulfill the demands of the school or risk being expelled. At the same time, the schools make deep commitments to students. Even the most sought after schools with waiting lists work hard to retain students and to meet their individual needs.

At the beginning of the twentieth century, prominent boarding schools were elite places; parents sent their children to schools such as Choate, Groton, and Exeter so that they might meet the "right people" and take their place in upper echelons of American society. Many of these schools, from their early days, offered scholarships and focused on their mission to form fine citizens, yet students of color were often excluded, and Jews experienced significant discrimination on campuses.[17]

Following the civil rights movement, independent schools began to seek diversity in their student bodies. Many schools have taken initiatives to bring underrepresented groups to their campuses. For example, in 1964, twenty-three independent schools developed Project ABC: A Better Chance, a program that continues to bring talented students of color to independent schools.[18] In the 2006–2007 academic year, 21.9 percent of the total enrollment in NAIS member schools were reported to be students of color. Enrollments in these schools were 5.9 percent African American students, 3.1 percent Hispanic American students, 7.0 percent Asian American students, .2 percent Native American students, 4.1 percent multiracial students, 1.6 percent Middle Eastern American students, and 2.6 percent international students.[19] Schools increasingly see themselves as preparing leaders for a diverse society and a global economy. They value diversity in the population of the school as well as in the curriculum, and they work to promote tolerant communities. Diversity work led to the founding of groups such as the first Gay Straight Alliance (GSA) at Concord Academy in 1988.[20] To prepare independent school graduates to be productive citizens in life and work, schools recognize the need to provide an environment that reflects the multicultural society that students will inherit.

Self-Selected Faculty

Independent schools set their own requirements for teaching at their schools. In most states, independent school teachers are not required to hold teacher licenses or to have credentials from teacher training programs. Instead, the schools seek teachers with strong academic records and believe that these teachers, armed with the knowledge in a discipline gained in selective colleges, will be most effective. Since the co-curriculum is an important part of independent school programs, the schools also seek young people with athletic ability or special talents who can serve as athletic coaches, yearbook editors, and theater directors. With the exception of teachers of lower grades, where pedagogy and knowledge of child development are valued, teachers learn how to teach "on the job." Some schools have instituted mentoring programs, and many sponsor professional development to help teachers succeed in the classroom.

As independent school leaders recognized the importance of creating a diverse student population, they began to actively recruit teachers of color to their schools. A diverse faculty not only provides students with a community that reflects the world that they are about to enter but also help provides students with role models who represent the many experiences that are a part of American life.

Although they often work for lower pay than public school teachers, independent school teachers express significant job satisfaction. Bullard points out that "a spirit of collegiality" prevails in most independent schools "because everybody in the workplace has similar responsibilities—division heads, deans department chairs, and teachers—teach, advise, coach, and work with parents."[21]

Contractual negotiations between the faculty and administration in independent schools are not as formalized as in public schools. Some schools publish salary scales; some guard salary information. With only rare exceptions, teachers at independent schools are not protected by unions and do not receive tenure. They work at the schools according to a mutual understanding, and teachers are often asked to perform extra duties not specified in their contracts. They generally perform these duties gladly, for the ethos of the independent schools is, as Bullard says, a "family ethos."[22]

Self-Governance

Boards of trustees are responsible for governing independent schools, and this structure, required by law for nonprofit organizations, also guarantees the schools' independent nature. Boards of trustees are responsible for holding the particular independent school "in trust." They have fiduciary responsibility and are charged with appointing and overseeing the chief school administrator—the head—who operates the school on a day-to-day basis.

Independent school boards in the United States differ from other nonprofit boards in that they are largely constituent based and self-perpetuating. Boards may include alumni and respected educators or professionals from the local community, but they are primarily made up of parents of current students. While this composition may create the problem of decision-making that is "present minded," it also fosters dedication and generosity in supporting the school. Nominating committees of boards often seek members who will lend their expertise as well as their financial support.

The autonomy of board governance allows the schools to act quickly. A board can respond to the needs of a particular school community without having to work through the cumbersome bureaucracies that govern public school districts.

Self-Support

Independent schools operate as nonprofit institutions. They are not eligible for government funding, save for some mandated services such as transportation. The schools rely "primarily on tuition for support, supplemented by gifts from parents, alumni and alumnae, foundations, corporations, and (for some) income from an endowment."[23]

The cost of operating schools with extensive facilities while maintaining small class size is high. The average median tuition at NAIS day schools in 2006–2007 was $15,763; at boarding schools, it was $32,594.[24] An average of 18.3 percent of independent school students receive some form of financial aid.[25] Still, most parents cannot afford these costs. Consequently, independent schools continue, by and large, to educate children of well-to-do families, though most have made significant efforts to attract students from diverse racial, ethnic, and socioeconomic groups.

INDEPENDENT SCHOOLS IN THE TWENTY-FIRST CENTURY

In "Reflections on a Century of Independent Schools," Powell points out that independent schools have become more connected to mainstream American education. No longer as elite and isolated as they once were, he argues, "Independent schools today operate very much in the real world." He also argues that independent schools ought to play a leadership role in American school reform.[26] The benefits of personalization achieved at independent schools can be a model for schools that seek to bring isolated young people into a healthy relationship with their communities. Moreover, the drive for high expectations for students and teachers that shape the culture at independent schools can set an example for improving flagging academic standards in American schools.

Independent schools are uniquely poised for preparing young people for the high-tech, multicultural, global community in which they will live. First, independent schools place a premium on teaching critical thinking, providing students with the skills to consider questions of the future. Second, independent schools are making significant strides toward building multicultural communities, discussing multicultural issues, and incorporating global considerations into their curricula. Most independent schools have long required students to learn foreign languages. Finally, independent schools often have access to resources that can offer students hands-on experiences beyond the classroom, bring technology to their campuses, and create international study opportunities. These and the comprehensive offerings and personalized attention independent schools provide through the curriculum and co-curriculum have a cost. The challenge facing all independent schools at the beginning of the twenty-first century is providing these distinctive features with income from tuition. That is the cost of independence. If Horace Mann were alive today he might argue convincingly that our nation would be stronger, not if private schools were eliminated, but if all students had the quality of education offered in independent schools.

NOTES

1. Quoted in Lawrence Cremin, ed., *The Republic and the School: Horace Mann on the Education of Free Man*, Classics in Education 1 (New York: Teachers College Press, 1957), 8.

2. U.S. Department of Education, National Center for Education Statistics, *Digest of Education Statistics, 2005*, NCES 2006-30, table 3, Enrollment in Educational Institutions, by Level and Control of Institution: Selected Years, 1869–1870 through fall 2015, http://nces.ed.gov/programs/digest/d06/tables/dt06_003.asp.

3. See the website of the National Association of Independent Schools, Facts at a Glance, http://www.nais.org/resources/statistical.cfm?ItemNumber=146713.

4. See the website for the National Association of Independent Schools, 2003–2004, www.nais.org.

5. Jeff Archer, "A League of Its Own," in *Lessons of a Century: A Nation's Schools Come of Age*, ed. *Education Week* Staff (Bethesda, Md.: Editorial Projects in Education, 2000), 219, http://www.edweek.org/ew/articles/1999/10/20/08andove.h19html?print=1.

6. Otto F. Kraushaar, *American Nonpublic Schools: Patterns of Diversity* (Baltimore, Md.: Johns Hopkins University Press, 1972), 56–68.

7. Leonard L. Baird, *The Elite Schools: A Profile of Prestigious Independent Schools* (Lexington, Mass.: D.C. Heath and Company, 1977), 1.

8. Pearl Rock Kane, "What Is an Independent School?" in *Independent Schools, Independent Thinkers*, ed. Pearl Rock Kane (San Francisco, Calif.: Jossey-Bass Publishers, 1992), 7.

9. National Association of Independent Schools, Facts at a Glance.

10. William Bullard, "On Teaching in the *Independent School*," in *Independent Schools, Independent Thinkers*, ed. Kane, 163.

11. Arthur G. Powell, *Lessons from Privilege: The American Prep School Tradition* (Cambridge, Mass.: Harvard University Press, 1996), 203.

12. Quoted in ibid., 204.

13. Kane, "What Is an Independent School?" 9.

14. Powell, *Lessons from Privilege*, 20, 25.

15. Baird, *Elite Schools*, 4.

16. Kraushaar, *American Nonpublic Schools*, 93.

17. Archer, "A League of Its Own," 219.

18. See the website of A Better Chance, About Us, www.abetterchance.org/AboutUs/AboutUs.html.

19. National Association of Independent Schools, Facts at a Glance.

20. See the website of the Gay, Lesbian, Straight Education Network, http://www.glsen.org/cgi-bin/iowa/all/about/index.html.

21. Bullard, "On Teaching in the Independent School," 156.

22. Ibid., 170.

23. Kane, "What Is an Independent School?" 8.

24. National Association of Independent Schools, Facts at a Glance.

25. Ibid.

26. Arthur G. Powell, "A Reflection on a Century of Independent Schools, in *Lessons of a Century,* ed. *Education Week* Staff, 226.

· 6 ·

Chartering Choices

A Strategy for Creating New Schools

Bruno V. Manno

The U.S. effort to create new public schools through the charter strategy began in 1991 when Minnesota passed the first law allowing charter schools. Since then, the number of charter schools has grown from one St. Paul, Minnesota, school that opened in 1992, enrolling 35 students, to more than 4,000 schools in forty states and the District of Columbia enrolling more than 1,135,000 students. Today, just above 2 percent of students in public school systems attend charter schools. Three states—Arizona, California, and Texas—have nearly 40 percent of the charter schools; three additional states—Florida, Michigan, and Ohio—have 20 percent of the schools.[1]

Charter schools are attracting considerable attention. They are popular with parents and—unlike school vouchers—elicit political support from a broad array of Democrats and Republicans. In urban America, they are fast becoming an alternative to the traditional school system, creating a new education marketplace for many American communities and emerging as a force for broader system reform.

For example, around 20,000 students, or about 27 percent, of the District of Columbia's public school children attend 71 charter schools. Dayton, Ohio, has 33 such schools representing around 30 percent of students enrolled in public schools. In Kansas City, Missouri, nearly 20 percent of public school students are enrolled in charter schools. New York City and Chicago are involved in district efforts to create new schools, many of which are to be chartered. In one of the most intriguing initiatives under way in American education, New Orleans is reinventing its public school system as a charter system, with nearly 70 percent of its public school students enrolled in charter schools.[2] There are also international examples of charter schools, including variants in Great Britain, Chile, Argentina, New Zealand, and Japan.

WHAT IS A CHARTER SCHOOL?

A charter school is an independent public school of choice, freed from rules but accountable for results. These schools are a new species, a hybrid, with similarities to traditional district public schools, some of the prized attributes of private schools, and crucial differences from both.[3]

As a public school, a charter school is open to all who wish to attend it, without regard to race, religion, or academic ability. It is paid for with tax dollars and has no tuition charges, with public dollars following the child to the school of choice. Finally, it is accountable for its results—indeed, for its very existence—to the "public" through a contract with an authoritative state recognized body (such as a state or a local school board or an entity created specifically to charter schools) and to the "market" of those enrolling (and teaching) in it. This approach to creating new schools aims to increase school autonomy, encourage innovation, and expand parental choice while providing new accountability mechanisms through both a contract with a government agency ("from above") and a social market ("from below").

Charter schools are different from standard-issue district public schools in at least five key features: they can be created by almost anyone; they are exempt from most state and local regulations and are essentially autonomous in their operations; they are attended by youngsters whose families choose them; they are staffed by educators who are also there by choice; and they can be closed for not producing satisfactory results.

Charter schools resemble private schools in two important respects. First, they are independent. Although answerable to outside public authorities for their results (far more than most private schools), they are free to produce those results as they think best. They are self-governing, nonprofit institutions, and, while held to the same academic expectations (standards, testing, yearly improvements in results) as district public schools, they have wide-ranging control over curriculum, instruction, staffing, budget, internal organization, calendar, schedule, and much more.

Second, they are schools of choice. Nobody is assigned against her or his will to attend (or teach in) a charter school. Parents select a charter school for their children, much as they would a private school, though with greater risk because a charter school typically has no long record of accomplishment. Charter schools, then, incorporate a market dimension to school accountability by giving families (and educators) the option of choosing the school that their child will attend (or in which they will teach).

THE CREATION AND OPERATION OF CHARTER SCHOOLS

The "charter" is a formal, legal document, best viewed as a performance agreement or contract between those who propose to launch and run a school—the operators—and the body empowered to authorize and monitor such schools—the sponsors or authorizers. The charter offers operators and sponsors an opportunity to create program and pedagogical innovations and an incentive structure different from that of public schools. The performance agreement is the legal basis for dispensing consequences to schools. If a charter school succeeds by meeting the terms of its performance agreement, it can reasonably expect to get its charter renewed when the time comes. If it fails, it may be forced to shut down. In addition, if it violates any of the unwaived laws, regulations, or community norms during the term of its charter, it may be shut down sooner. These conditions are different from the historic reward structure for schools in the district sector that will continue to exist whether or not students are learning. By 2005, nearly 440 charter schools had, for various reasons, been closed.[4]

While the contract is a legal document, it would be a mistake to think of it only in legal terms. Managing a charter school involves directing many relationships among a variety of actors and stakeholders who strive to add social value by operating a school. Operators may be a group of parents, a team of teachers, an existing nonprofit community organization such as a hospital, Boys and Girls Club, university or daycare center, nonprofit charter management organization (CMO), or even—in several states—a private for-profit firm known as an education management organization (EMO). Sometimes an existing district school seeks to secede from its local public system and become a charter school or, in a few jurisdictions, to convert from a tuition-charging private school to a tax-supported charter school. In a few instances across the country, charter school teachers have also organized themselves into a cooperative or other professional practice arrangement that then contracts for the school's operation.

The charter application spells out why the school is needed, how it will function, what results (academic and otherwise) are expected, and how these will be demonstrated. When the operator contracts with another entity—for example, CMOs, EMOs—to manage the school, the operator remains legally responsible to the sponsor.

The sponsor can be a state or local school board. In some states, public universities have authority to issue charters, as do county school boards, nonprofit organizations, a mayor, and city councils. If the sponsor deems an application solid, it will negotiate a detailed charter—the performance contract—for a period of time, typically five years but sometimes as short as one year or as long as fifteen years. During that period, the charter school has wide latitude to function as it sees fit, assuming its state enacted a strong charter law that does not constrain schools with many of the limitations and regulations under which conventional public schools toil.

WHAT DO CHARTER SCHOOLS LOOK LIKE?

Key features of the charter idea include waivers from most state and local regulations; fiscal and curricular autonomy; independence in making personnel decisions; responsibility for delivering the results that the charter pledges; and removing from school districts the "exclusive franchise"[5] they have to create and run public schools. While charter schools by law must be open to all students, many tailor their curriculum to specific student populations. There is no one model, therefore, of what a charter school looks like.

A recent effort to create a typology of charter schools identified fifty-five distinct subtypes within ten categories organized by instructional theme (progressive, traditional, vocational, general, and alternative delivery) and student populations served (at-risk, alternative, gifted, and special education).[6] In addition, charter schools mean different things in different states since how the law is written affects the framework for creating these schools.

SUPPORT FOR CHARTER SCHOOLS

Nationwide, one-third of charter schools are located in large urban districts, compared with 10 percent of traditional public schools. Thus they attract a large disadvantaged student population and have the potential to impact disproportionately the education of minority and low-income students.[7] Upward of 58 percent of students enrolled in charter schools are minority students, with 52 percent eligible for free and reduced lunch, compared to 45 percent and 40 percent, respectively, in regular district schools. Charter schools enrollment includes 11 percent special education students and 12 percent English language learners, compared to enrollment of 13 percent and 11 percent, respectively, in district schools. These figures vary by state and district.[8]

Charter school teachers are more likely to have master's degrees in fields such as business, arts, and science, though they are less likely to have full state certification in the subjects they teach than district teachers. But charter schools also differ from each other in teacher and leader hiring and recruitment practices when analyzed by number of years open, authorizer type, region, and other categories. On average, the student-teacher ratio is lower in charter schools (16.0 to 1) than in districts schools (17.2 to 1).[9] In about half the states with charter laws, all teachers in charter schools are required to have the same subject-specific licenses as teachers in district schools. The rest of the states allow their charter schools to hire at least some teachers who may not be licensed but have other relevant education or experience in the subject areas they teach.[10]

Although the vast majority of charter school teachers do not work under union contracts, some do. Some unionized charter schools operate under the same contracts that apply to district schools. Others negotiate school specific contracts. In a few instances, unions have supported the creation of charter schools in the interest of their members, though in most states, teacher unions are among charter schools' most vocal opponents and critics.

The general public is still unfamiliar with charter schools. Only 34 percent of registered voters accurately describe charter schools as public schools, though the more the public learns about these new schools, the more they support them.[11] For example, the public particularly appreciates that charter schools are smaller than district schools, have greater autonomy, and are school of choice. Early studies suggest that low-income parents use the same techniques and tools for making school choice decisions, and are just as satisfied with their decisions, as wealthier parents.[12]

THE SUCCESS OF CHARTERING

Chartering has changed the way that public education is delivered, creating an institutional innovation in public education. As a strategy, it offers potential school operators the opportunity to contract with a public entity to create a performance-based autonomous, public school of choice. It is useful to know if this new strategy is succeeding, as well as if the schools created by the strategy are succeeding. As Ted Kolderie, one of the architects of the charter idea, points out, "The schools and the strategy are different things . . . and each needs to be measured and evaluated separately."[13]

There is growing, positive information on the success of the strategy when it comes to creating new schools, catalyzing new ways of networking schools, growing their numbers, inspiring new approaches to governance, and stimulating pedagogical innovations.[14] There is little good evidence yet on the strategy's overall effectiveness in raising student achievement. But there are clear signs of potential, though more evidence is needed before robust conclusions about school effectiveness can be reached.

The one study to use randomization to examine the impact of attending a charter school found that students chosen by lottery to attend charter schools managed by the Chicago Charter School Foundation outperformed students on the school's waiting list who remained in traditional public schools.[15] Several analyses of student achievement conclude that, while the overall quality of available research was poor, the studies using more reliable methods show achievement in charter schools improving more rapidly than in traditional public schools.[16]

Charter schools have brought new blood into the teaching profession, as teachers in them are far more likely to come from selective colleges and to have majored in the arts and sciences, as opposed to education.[17] Moreover, these schools appear to be safer and have fewer discipline problems than traditional public schools.[18]

Chartering also provides an easy mechanism for creating small schools—a reform strategy many consider to hold great promise for raising achievement and graduation rates in urban schools. There is even some evidence that competition from charter schools has spurred traditional public schools to improve their performance—and no evidence that the presence of charter schools has had an adverse impact.[19]

OBSTACLES AND OPPONENTS

There are hints of problems that, if left unchecked, could limit the potential of the chartering strategy. While chartering has maintained bipartisan support in Washington and in a number of states, notable opposition comes from three directions: some state policy makers, many local school systems, and most mainline public education interest groups. This opposition works on many fronts, including stunting the growth of charter schools, weakening charter laws, limiting the funding charter schools receive, and preventing them from gaining access to facilities on equal terms with other public schools.[20] A recent study across sixteen states and the District of Columbia showed that charter schools receive about 22 percent less in per-pupil public funding, or $1,800, than the district schools that surround them. The funding gap is wider in most of twenty-seven urban school districts studied, where it amounts to $2,200 per student.[21]

Moreover, state caps on the number of charter schools or on charter school enrollment now constrain further growth in at least nine states.[22] Finally, some charter authorizers have proven to be ill-equipped to provide schools with sufficient support, and few authorizers seem willing to close bad schools for academic performance reasons, making clear one of the challenges to the accountability promise of these schools. A lax approach to charter granting and renewal threatens to allow the rotten apples in the charter crop (of which there are more than a few) to spoil the rest.[23]

REINVENTING PUBLIC EDUCATION IN THE TWENTY-FIRST CENTURY

Supporters of chartering often explain its primary contribution to reinventing public education by using the market metaphor: the strategy unleashes competition that alters incentives and requires that schools consider the desires of clients, consumers, and choosers. This is true. But is the market metaphor sufficient to describe how chartering works? I think not.[24]

A complementary—perhaps a more adequate metaphor—is the admittedly ambiguous notion of community along with the added notions of cooperation and citizenship. While there is truth to the notion that markets can create the infamous autonomous individual acting to maximize individual interest, it is also true that markets have the potential to create shared notions of community and what others call "social capital."[25]

Charter schools are created by choices—teacher, parent, and student choices—that produce voluntary associations—in this case, school communities. The choice metaphor is complemented by the community metaphor. In short, the notions of clients, choosers, consumers, and competition are a necessary but insufficient way to think about the value of the charter strategy: removing the exclusive franchise the district has to start schools creates a possibility for forging new cooperative communities of shared vision, shared interest, shared results, and ultimately shared citizenship.

Charter schools can be thought of as "reinventing public education." Traditionally, a public school is defined as any school run by the government, managed by a superintendent and school board, staffed by public employees, and operated within a public-sector bureaucracy. "Public school" in this familiar sense is not very different from "public library," "public park," or "public housing" project.

Now consider a different definition: a public school is any school that is open to the public (i.e., has an open admissions policy), paid for by the public (i.e., no tuition charges), and accountable via a performance contract to public authorities for its results. So long as it satisfies those three criteria, it is a public school and what is offered under its aegis is public education. Public education need not be run by government. Indeed, it does not matter—for purposes of its "publicness"—who runs it, how it is staffed, or how long each class meets. Public education is not primarily a set of particular institutions or operating models. It is an end to be achieved using whatever institutions and models best accomplish that purpose.

Within this context, the roles and responsibilities of local school boards would change. These boards—approximately fifteen thousand of them—are now charged with authorizing, financing, and operating public schools. Their new role would be to cede the operations function to independent organizations that would run individual schools or networks of schools through a managed competition process. The primary board functions would be to authorize and finance schools within the context of reasonable systemwide requirements for safety and health, equality of student and family access to good schools, and student literacy that would support adult success and well-being. The result would be a school board managing a portfolio of performance agreements with individual schools and networks of school providers.[26]

In short, charter schools are the farthest-flung example today of reinvented public education. However, it is important to bear in mind that they are part of a bigger idea: public education in which elected and appointed officials play a strategic rather than a functional role, leading to public support of schooling without governmental ownership or direct management of schools.

NOTES

1. Two primary sources are used for much of the data and other information on charter schools: the website of the National Charter School Research Project (www.ncsrp.org) of the Center on Reinventing Public Education, especially its annual report, Robin J. Lake and Paul T. Hill, eds., *Hopes, Fears, and Reality: A Balanced Look at American Charter Schools in 2006* (Seattle, Wash.: Center on Reinventing Public Education, University of Washington, December 2006), and the website of the National Alliance for Public Charter Schools, www.publiccharters.org.

2. See especially Todd Ziebarth, *Top 10 Charter Communities by Market Share* (Washington, D.C.: National Alliance for Public Charter Schools, September 2006); Paul Hill and Jane Hannaway, *The Future of Public Education in New Orleans* (Washington, D.C.: Urban Institute, January 2006).

3. Charter laws vary greatly from state to state, particularly on the degree of autonomy and fiscal equity charter schools have compared to district public schools. What is described here is what charter schools look like in states with stronger laws that allow a large degree of autonomy at the school level.

4. Center for Education Reform press release, Washington, D.C., February 27, 2006, http://www.edreform.com/index.cfm?fuseAction=document&documentID=2338 &SEctionID=55.

5. Thanks to Ted Kolderie for the phrase.

6. Dick M. Carpenter II, *Playing to Type: Mapping the Charter School Landscape* (Washington, D.C.: Thomas B. Fordham Institute, October 2005). For an examina-

tion of several high-profile charter schools, see Paul Tough, "Still Left Behind: What Will It Take to Close the Education Gap?" *New York Times Magazine*, November 26, 2006.

7. U.S. Department of Education, Institute of Education Sciences, National Center for Education Statistics, *America's Charter Schools: Results from the NAEP 2003 Pilot Study*, NCES 2005-456 (Washington, D.C.: National Center for Education Statistics, 2004).

8. Robin J. Lake and Paul T. Hill, eds., *Hopes, Fears, and Reality: A Balanced Look at American Charter Schools in 2005* (Seattle, Wash.: Center on Reinventing Public Education, University of Washington, November 2005). See also National Center for Education Statistics, *Characteristics of Schools, Districts, Teachers, Principals, and School Libraries in the United States: 2003–2004 and Staffing Survey* (Washington, D.C.: National Center for Education Statistics, April 2006), http://nces.ed.gov.

9. Lake and Hill, eds., *Hopes, Fears, and Reality: National Center for Education Statistics, Characteristics of Schools, 2003–2004*.

10. Lake and Hill, eds., *Hopes, Fears, and Reality, 2005: National Center for Education Statistics, Characteristics of Schools, 2003–2004*.

11. National Alliance for Public Charter Schools, *April 2006 Poll on Charter Schools* (Washington, D.C.: National Alliance for Public Charter Schools, 2006).

12. Paul Teske, Jody Fitzpatrick, and Gabriel Kaplan, *Opening Doors: How Low Income Parents Search for the Right School* (Seattle, Wash.: Center on Reinventing Public Education, University of Washington, January 2007).

13. Ted Kolderie, "Is Chartering, as a Strategy, Succeeding?" *Urban Ed: Magazine of the USC Rossier School of Education*, Fall 2006, 20.

14. Bryan C. Hassel, "Friendly Competition," *Education Next* 3, no. 1 (Winter 2003): 8–15.

15. Caroline M. Hoxby and Jonah E. Rockoff, "The Impact of Charter Schools on Student Achievement," November 2004, www.economics.harvard.edu/faculty/hoxbypa paper.

16. Bryan C. Hassel and Michelle Godard Terrell, "Charter School Achievement: What We Know, 3rd Edition," paper prepared for the National Alliance for Public Charter Schools, October 2006; Lake and Hill, eds., *Hopes, Fears, and Reality, 2005*; Todd Ziebarth, *Signs of Promise: Hispanic Achievement in Charter Schools* (Washington, D.C.: National Alliance for Public Charter Schools, 2006); Todd Ziebarth, *The Renaissance of Urban Education: Charter Schools in America's Cities* (Washington, D.C.: National Alliance for Public Charter Schools, 2006).

17. Caroline M. Hoxby, "Would School Choice Change the Teaching Profession?" *Journal of Human Resources* 38, no. 4 (Fall 2002): 122–45.

18. Jon Christensen, *School Safety in Urban Charter and Traditional Public Schools* (Seattle, Wash.: Center on Reinventing Public Education, University of Washington, 2007).

19. Caroline M. Hoxby, "School Choice and School Productivity: Could School Choice Be a Tide That Lifts All Boats?" in *The Economics of School Choice*, ed. Caroline M. Hoxby (Chicago, Ill.: University of Chicago Press, 2003), 287–341.

20. Andrew J. Rotherham, "Increasing the Supply of Public Schools," Public Policy Institute Briefing Paper, April 9, 2003; Bruno V. Manno, "Yellow Flag," *Education Next* 3, no. 1 (Winter 2003): 16–21.

21. Sheree Speakman, Bryan Hassel, and Chester E. Finn Jr., *Charter School Funding: Inequity's Next Frontier* (Washington, D.C.: Thomas B. Fordham Foundation, August 2005).

22. Todd Ziebarth, *Peeling the Lid Off State-Imposed Caps Charter Schools* (Washington, D.C.: National Alliance for Public Charter Schools, February 2007).

23. Andrew J. Rotherham, "The Pros and Cons of Charter School Closures," in Lake and Hill, eds., *Hopes, Fears, and Reality, 2005*, 43–52. On how quality authorizers should operate, see also the website of the National Association of Charter School Authorizers, www.charterauthorizers.org.

24. For a similar position, see John E. Brandl, *Money and Good Intentions Are Not Enough; or, Why a Liberal Democrat Thinks States Need Both Competition and Community* (Washington, D.C.: Brookings Institution Press, 1998).

25. James Coleman and Thomas Hoffer, *Public and Private Schools: The Impact of Community* (New York: Basic Books, 1987).

26. Paul T. Hill, *Put Learning First: A Portfolio Approach to Public Schools* (Washington, D.C.: Progressive Policy Institute, 2006).

The Ends of the Spectrum

A Comparison of Traditional and Progressive Schools

Richard P. Fitzgerald

In thirty years at independent schools, I have worked in two progressive schools and three traditional schools. My approach to these schools, as genres or as archetypes, is predicated, therefore, on experience as opposed to scholarship. That experience has given me insights into both the differences and the similarities between these seemingly opposite, end-of-the-spectrum types of schools.

During the summer of 2003, at an Oxford Round Table, I was struck by the controversial nature of the term "progressive education" and the name John Dewey. The reactions of some of the participants took me aback. I kept trying to point out to them all the ways that their own schools were employing the now long-accepted ideas of Dewey and Francis Wayland Parker and others. They would have none of it. For them, if a school called itself progressive it was, by pop-definition, a school that allowed all students to "progress" at their own pace, held to no academic standards, and allowed (probably encouraged) on-campus social practices of the most decadent variety. Yet to other participants, principals and heads of school at mainstream and middle-of-the-road schools, conservative and/or fundamentalist schools were, by definition, schools that emphasized a lockstep course of study over student interests, required an inflexible and mandated-from-on-high curriculum, treated teachers like assembly line workers, and restricted on-campus social practices.

Both views were wrong, full of untested hypothesis and needless speculation. As noted above, I have spent most of my academic life in traditional schools. There I learned about high academic commitment, dedication to scholastic excellence, and a selflessness that was as deeply ingrained as was the dedication to intellectual rigor. I have also spent significant time in progressive schools. There I learned about active learning, cooperative curricular planning, and an inspirational dedication to the individual student's education that testified to the ability of a single teacher's practice to make a substantial difference.

BACKGROUND AND HISTORY

In the mid-1980s, after twelve years as a teacher and administrator at Collegiate School in New York, I became the director of Little Red School House, one of the most historically significant progressive schools in the country. This school, which counted John Dewey among its founders, had been the first school in New York City to use the city-as-classroom, to unbolt the desks and carpet the rooms so that children could sit on the floors in reading circles, and to encourage learning-by-doing. In 1920, these were radical innovations, and they were greeted as such. Indeed, after a number of years as a "progressive" public school, Little Red School House was forced to become an independent school to preserve and develop its progressive experiments.

When I arrived in 1985, there was an air about the place of nearly reverential devotion to progressive principles. As the new director, I had, for a brief time, the fresh eyes capable of seeing it with some semblance of accuracy. And as I looked around, I saw practices that reminded me of Collegiate School, that bastion of traditional education. I also encountered some educational thinkers who profoundly changed the way I thought about education. These wonderful teachers and administrators taught me all about the city-as-classroom, invented spelling, and constructivist approaches to the classroom. I gained immeasurably from them and will be forever grateful.

And yet, I continued to see a lot of teaching that looked strangely familiar. Lower school teachers sat on the carpeted floors, in circles with their students, and read with (not to) their students, just as in Collegiate's lower school. Middle school teachers presented "challenges" in the science laboratories that asked students to experiment with no right or wrong answers expected, just as in Collegiate's middle school. The similarities were uncanny, but I did not dare note them to my new colleagues. However, it became increasingly clear that classic progressive teaching practices had entered the mainstream years earlier. What had once been radical at Little Red had become standard practice at Collegiate. Both the successful traditional school and the successful progressive school had, naturally, moved toward the center; each had adapted the best practices of the other.

The history of the movement that produced Little Red School House and Elisabeth Irwin High School is mostly unknown to the general parent public. I am constantly surprised, more than a hundred years after the beginning of the progressive movement, that so many thoughtful parents (and even many thoughtful teachers) do not take the time to understand the basic tenets and history of progressive education. Instead, the term has become a cliché that signifies a student-dominated classroom and the very name "John Dewey" is now a catchphrase for all that has supposedly gone wrong with American public education. Nothing could be further from the truth.

In fact, the progressive education movement was an outgrowth of a larger political movement of the late nineteenth century. The historian Lawrence A. Cremins writes, "Proponents of virtually every progressive cause from the 1890s through World War I had their program for the school. Humanitarians of every stripe saw education at the heart of their effort toward social alleviation." Cremins also notes that the progressive movement was notable for its "pluralistic, frequently contradictory character."[1]

Lynn Olson, a journalist who covers education, describes three strands of progressive education that have been identified by historians: pedagogical progressives, social progressives, and administrative progressives.[2] Each strand of progressive educators brought a distinctly different approach to the classroom. The pedagogical progressives were the proponents of the student-centered, interdisciplinary studies approach. Parker, often considered the "father" of the progressive education movement, was the primary advocate of this branch of progressivism.

The social progressives, including Dewey, believed, in Olson's words, that "schools in an industrial society must assume many of the functions increasingly abandoned by home and community and work to fashion a more egalitarian order." These educators "dared the schools to build a new social order." Though this approach fell out of favor by the 1940s, the impact of these educators on school programs can still be seen in community service programs, health education programs, and counseling and advising programs.[3]

The administrative progressives, as the third progressive alternative, says Olson, "sought to use new advances in scientific measurement and testing to bring greater efficiency to schools." They "sought to equalize educational opportunity by providing each student with a curriculum best suited to his or her interests and abilities" and thereby "prepare students for their places in society." The administrative progressives promoted "more frequent use of standardized tests, a curriculum differentiated for vocational and college-bound students, and the grouping of students by levels of ability."[4] It is evident, though not always realized, that common educational practices often thought of as traditional, if not conservative, actually gained traction because of the beliefs of a group of progressive educators.

Though the progressive movement of Dewey and Parker no longer exists, their experiments and innovations, from the student-centered classroom, to community service programs, to the use of scientific-based metrics to measure educational progress, have become part of our educational mainstream. It is obvious that the creative ideas and original theories of progressive education have enriched all our schools.

In 2002, I was appointed headmaster of Bentley School, a very traditional school in Oakland, California. When I arrived, I did not find what I had expected to find. I did not find a school obsessively focused on subject matter to the exclusion of the individual learner. Indeed, I found a school with a broad variety of teaching styles, a school less committed to a particular approach to teaching and more committed to helping students to learn well, by whatever methods worked. I found a school less insistent on ideology and much more insistent upon using a diversity of methods to promote learning in all disciplines. In short, I found a traditional school with students and teachers highly engaged in the process of learning, using methods from all over the spectrum. I was happily impressed by the manner in which progressive methods had been integrated into the curriculum in ways that made little of the ideology but much of the practical application.

Such schools as Bentley and Collegiate are the inheritors of an educational approach just as thoroughly rooted in the late nineteenth century as that of the progressive schools. Such schools look back to the Report of the Commission on Secondary School Studies (1893), prepared by the Committee of Ten that was appointed by the National Education Association and led by Harvard's president, Charles W. Eliot. Previously, traditional mainstream schools were anything but typical. The report indicates that when the researchers surveyed forty leading secondary schools throughout the country to find out "which subjects were taught and the total number of recitations or exercises allotted to each subject," they found that "the total number of subjects taught in these secondary schools was nearly forty . . . and that even for older subjects like Latin and algebra, there appeared to be a wide diversity of practice."[5] The report urged the establishment of a standardized curriculum for all high school students, regardless of whether they were terminating their studies at the end of high school or going on to college. In the words of historian and educator Jeffrey Mirel, the report concluded that "all high school students should follow a college preparatory curriculum."[6]

This report is significant, even today, for it established the curriculum that we think of as the traditional secondary school curriculum and that still flourishes in many public and private secondary schools. It made the eight-year elementary school and the four-year secondary school standard. The committee also recommended four basic curricula for high school study: the classical, the Latin-scientific, modern language, and English. Each curricular designation included foreign languages, mathematics, history, English, and science, a sequence of courses we continue to recognize today. In addition, the committee introduced the idea of elective courses, stressed the importance of Latin before Greek, and created the standard science sequence: biology, chemistry, and physics. Finally, it led, in 1900, to the establishment of the College Board Entrance Examination.[7]

The commitment of President Eliot and the Committee of Ten to a rigorous liberal arts education changed the nature of traditional education. Their approach is deeply rooted in the importance of the course of study versus the interests of the student, and it influenced, and continues to influence, all secondary schools, both traditional and progressive. At the very least, this traditional academic curriculum provides an understandable base into which progressive practice can be thoughtfully integrated.

CONCLUSION

Lynn Olson, writing about the differences between progressive and traditional schools, says, "At its simplest level, one could say that it's a debate between education broadly and narrowly conceived, between the primacy of the child and the primacy of subject matter, between spontaneous and formal approaches to schooling, and between education designed to transform the nation's cultural heritage and one designed to preserve it."[8]

Looking back at the century-long dichotomy, the so-called debate has become more of a constructive dialogue, each side benefiting from the core practices of the other. Progressive schools have been courageous pioneers undertaking advance-guard educational experiments in a manner that has allowed traditional schools to adopt the resulting best practices. Hence, were I a parent, I would look for that progressive school that has not just remained true to its progressive history but has developed a dedication to the incorporation the newest experimental pedagogy, progressive-based or not.

Traditional schools, in equal measure, have often been the places best able to adapt (not just adopt) new practices in a manner less controversial and, thereby, lend legitimacy to important teaching practices that might not otherwise have reached the mainstream. Hence, were I a parent, I would look for that traditional independent school with an ability to combine a dedication to its academic traditions with a corresponding commitment to the thoughtful adaptation of the most effective new teaching practices on behalf of the students.

As I look back on my experiences in traditional and progressive schools, I would argue that the most effective school model for this still-new century is the traditional-progressive school. Traditional-progressive schools—perhaps we should call them the generative schools—are schools capable of re-creating themselves through careful consideration of the best teaching practices available.

These thoughtful institutions combine the best aspect of both the progressive schools and the traditional schools. Stanford historian Larry Cuban says that these schools and their teachers practice "conservative progressivism."[9]

Both schools that call themselves traditional and schools that call themselves progressive, if they are "good" schools, display many of the characteristics of the generative school. The curriculum is sequential and developed in the school by teachers and curriculum-development specialists. However, this teacher-developed curriculum sequence offers sufficient flexibility for individual teachers to make midcourse corrections for specific students. In the generative school, the child is at the center of the curriculum but at that center the student is joined by a teacher-mentor. Testing is termed "assessment," and assessment methods combine both traditional practice (essays, research papers, mathematical proofs) and assessments with a high degree of validity (exhibitions, portfolios, group projects.) Grading is narrative but based on rigorous academic expectations. In short, progressive methodology is married to traditional scholastic values. The result is a school of great accomplishment and creativity, an institution where teachers and students stand at the core and where curricular innovation springs from profoundly serious academic values.

Were I a parent looking for the best possible school for my young child, I would look first for schools that display many of these generative qualities. I would think long and hard about whether this manner of school—given its ability to be both student-centered and academically rigorous—isn't exactly the right match for my child.

NOTES

1. Lawrence A. Cremins, *The Transformation of the School* (New York: Knopf, 1961), quoted in Lynn Olson, "Tugging at Tradition," in *Lessons of a Century: A Nation's Schools Come of Age*, ed. *Education Week* Staff (Bethesda, Md.: Editorial Projects in Education, 2000), 95.

2. Olson, "Tugging at Tradition," 95.

3. Ibid., 96–97.

4. Ibid., 97.

5. National Education Association, *Report of the Commission on Secondary School Studies* (Washington, D.C.: National Education Association, 1893), 4–5, www.archive.og/search.

6. Jeffrey Mirel, "The Traditional High School: Historical Debates over the Nature and Function," *Education Next* 6, no. 1 (Winter 2006): 2.

7. Diane Ravitch, *Left Back: A Century of Failed School Reforms* (New York: Simon & Schuster, 2000), 47.

8. Olson, "Tugging at Tradition," 94.

9. Larry Cuban, *How Teachers Taught* (New York: Teachers College Press, 1998), quoted in Olson, "Tugging at Tradition," 94.

· 8 ·

The Too-Long Summer Vacation

School Calendar Reform

Charles Ballinger

$\mathcal{T}$he reality of summer learning loss is well known to most educators. Experienced teachers acknowledge the loss each autumn when they have to extensively review the previous year's work. Educational research over the past twenty years has confirmed the loss as well.

It is surprising, then, to reflect on the indifferent attitude of many educators toward this detriment to student learning. Ordinarily, a hindrance to optimum learning would evoke considerable concern, even outrage, among educators, with abundant calls for change. Summer learning loss, however, has been so pervasive for so long that many educators simply resign themselves to what has always been, regardless of the consequences to students.

Tradition alone is not a reason to continue an administrative arrangement that was designed for yesteryear's social and economic circumstances and that is demonstrably harmful to so many American students. No longer do the nation's farms and ranches require young helping hands to ensure their survival. No longer do major corporations require American employees and their families to take vacations only in the middle of summer. Family vacations today occur in any season of the year, as parents find an opportunity for leave from their jobs.

Those who rhapsodize that summer out-of-school learning experiences will substitute for the time away from formal learning ignore real life, because a majority of America's students are not involved in structured summer learning experiences. Far fewer than half of America's students go to summer school. Even fewer—perhaps 15–20 percent—of America's students go to summer camp.[1] Since some of those going to summer school are also those going to camp, it is clear that a majority of students do not experience quality learning during the long—too long—summer vacation of the traditional American school calendar.

71

72 *Charles Ballinger*

SCHOOL CALENDAR REFORM

One way to mitigate summer loss is, of course, to reduce the length of the summer vacation. American schools' summer vacation of ten to twelve weeks compares unfavorably, from a learning perspective, with the summer vacations of five to eight weeks experienced by European and Asian students. A considerable amount of learning loss can occur in the additional four to five weeks of vacation that American students receive. How long does the summer vacation really need to be? Three weeks? Six weeks? Surely, though, not the current ten to twelve weeks offered by most American schools.

The school year can be reorganized in a number of ways. The current 180 instructional days required by a majority of state legislatures can be rearranged so that summer vacation is reduced while other common vacation times are expanded. For example, the Christmas–New Year's holiday period can be lengthened to three or four weeks, making it a true "winter" holiday. In addition, spring vacation can be two or three weeks rather than just one, and a fall vacation can be two or three weeks. By modifying the traditional school calendar to include the vacation periods just described, the traditional long summer can be reduced to four to seven weeks, depending on the length of other vacations in the year.

Another way to reduce the summer of forgetting is to lengthen the school year from the usual 180 days of annual instruction to 200 or more days. The longer year is being considered and implemented by a growing number of American schools, in response to concerns raised by national leaders about the increased political and economic competition coming from both friendly and not-so-friendly countries around the globe. A reduction of summer vacation by just three weeks annually for twelve years, in conjunction with the longer instructional year, would offer a student an additional year of learning time. Since American students in their prime of their working life twenty years from now will compete with the world's better students, that extra year of learning can be an important asset for students and their future.

There is more flexibility in a year than usually envisioned. As figure 8.1 demonstrates, there is a flexibility of sixty days with which to design a school calendar that takes into account learning patterns, avoidance of learning loss, and parental and staff concerns.

365	days per calendar year
−180	days of legislatively mandated instruction annually
−104	weekend days (Saturday and Sunday)
−10	winter holidays (Christmas, New Year's)
−11	other legal holidays
60	**remaining optional/flexible days**

Figure 8.1. School-Year Flexibility

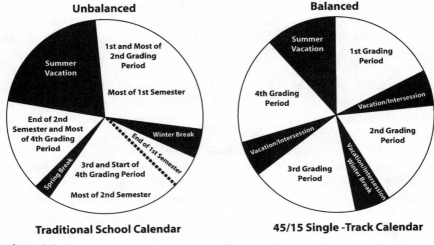

Figure 8.2.

The circle graphs in figure 8.2 clearly demonstrate the imbalance of the traditional calendar and the greater balance of a modified, or year-round, calendar. It is important to remember that the traditional school calendar is not primarily a learning calendar, nor was it designed to be.

Calendar restructuring efforts reflect the desire to improve student achievement. School districts that have already altered the school year refer to the revised calendars as modified, or balanced, calendars. Others speak of alternative, community, or year-round calendars.

EDUCATIONAL REASONS FOR CALENDAR MODIFICATION

Whatever the name, the philosophy and intent behind the proposed calendar change is constant: improved educational circumstances for America's students. Robust studies and research syntheses reveal the positive impact balanced calendars have on students' academic achievement. Carolyn Kneese and Stephanie Knight's 1995 study, for example, compared the academic performance of students following a year-round calendar to those following a traditional calendar from the same, dual-track schools and using the same curriculum and course of study. The analysis, which also controlled for socioeconomic factors, prior achievement levels, days of instruction, and class size, showed that students on the year-round calendar demonstrated a statistically significant academic advantage over their classmates on the traditional calendar.[2]

Kneese published a research review in 2000 that synthesized individual studies which met certain methodological standards. Overall, 71 percent of sign test findings showed positive impact for balanced calendars, 17 percent showed negative impact, and 12 percent showed mixed results.[3] Finally, a more exhaustive research review published in 2003 in the *Review of Educational Research* revealed that a majority of school districts reported that students following a modified calendar academically outperformed their classmates following a traditional calendar. The researchers noted that the modified calendar appeared to be particularly helpful for disadvantaged students and that recently implemented reforms demonstrated considerably improved results.[4]

These research results testify to the benefits to students of year-round schools. Explanations for these results are elaborated below.[5]

Balanced calendars can effectively maintain student interest in learning. When periods of teacher-student interaction in the classroom are followed by scheduled vacations, interest remains high throughout the learning period because students can contemplate a coming vacation. The vacation period, however, is not so long that students lose skills previously taught. Nevertheless, refreshed by the break, teachers and students return ready to work.

The typical traditional school calendar begins its year after a nearly three-month layoff. It struggles through the year by almost, but not quite, finishing the first semester before a two-week winter holiday period. Then the semester resumes for just three weeks after the holidays before it is completed. Once the first semester ends, teachers typically are given two or three days to grade semester final exams, record the grades, and plan—with negligible time available for thoughtful revision—the beginning of the next, or second, term.

The typical second semester is little better. Teachers, staff, and students begin it with a rush. A customarily short spring break of one week or less is scheduled about halfway through the semester. After the break there is a long slide in student interest in learning as the student contemplates the long summer vacation ahead. The traditional calendar has little rationale for learning.

Different types of student learners require different time configurations. While acknowledging this truism, many educators—in practice—actually adhere to another quite opposite learning principle—that one calendar fits all students. In addition, they seem to be in denial about summer learning loss. Consequently, school leaders ignore the warning of the National Education Commission on Time and Learning that there is an unacknowledged design flaw in school time schedules. This flaw can be corrected with a rethinking of how time for learning is provided.[6]

Intersession classes provide faster remediation and advanced enrichment. After several weeks of class work in modified calendar schools, students have a scheduled vacation, called intersession. During intersessions, remediation and enrichment can be offered. If an elementary student is struggling with fractions, or a secondary student with algebra, intersession provides a welcome opportunity to take immediate corrective action. If the intervention is successful, struggling students can resume class work at a level comparable to that of their classmates when instruction begins again. Intersession can also be a period for enrichment and creativity. Year-round and modified calendar schools have developed exciting one- to three-week classes in standard subjects along with the arts, advanced science, and computers, as well as independent study units.

Students learning a second language can benefit from a modified calendar. With students arriving at schools with increasingly diverse backgrounds, a greater variety of languages is heard in the school. A long summer away from language instruction is not helpful to students learning English as a second language. In fact, it is not helpful to any student learning a second language.

Co-curricular and extracurricular activities can take place throughout the year and can reinforce previous learning. Students remember material best when they have an opportunity to apply what they have learned. A school calendar with intersessions allows them this opportunity. Intersession intervals can offer a time for science projects, independent study, subject-focused camps, and preparation for music events, SAT or ACT exams, or academic decathlons. Fall and winter intersessions are good times for high school students to visit prospective college campuses. Student-athletes can use intersessions in at least two ways: to concentrate on their sport or to remediate academic problems and retrieve good standing.

Teachers can take advantage of year-long opportunities for staff development. In a balanced-calendar school, staff development is continuous and available throughout the year rather than just in the summer months. This in-service schedule is similar to that in professional fields such as medicine, law, and engineering.

Teachers' fears that an alternative calendar will prohibit them from pursuing advanced degrees have not been realized. When teachers need in-service or graduate training, universities provide it. In areas where several teacher institutions vie for graduate students, the institutions compete vigorously to provide classes at times convenient to teachers.

OTHER REASONS FOR CALENDAR REFORM

Buttressing the educational reasons for calendar modification are social, economic, and political forces that increasingly encourage calendar modification.[7]

Social

An increasingly urban and technological America gives rise to concerns about the productivity of young people during the summer months. Of what value is it to society to have hundreds of thousands of America's youth largely unoccupied, unemployed, or unsupervised for up to three months each year? Those who see social dynamite building in such circumstances are particularly eager to see the length of summer vacation reduced.

Economic

Better use of educational facilities is a matter of importance in growing communities unable to cope with the influx of school-age children. Currently, school buildings are generally used only nine and one-half months of each year, five days of each week, and ten to twelve hours of each day. Unused capacity is costly to any enterprise. Optimum use of facilities all twelve months makes economic sense. With resistance to new taxes or increased fees a reality in many communities, economic pressure grows to utilize fully what schools already have: capacity to educate.

Political

Elected officials generally respond to community forces that promote a given solution to an identified problem. To a large degree, calendar modification is entering that stage of an idea whose time has come. It is becoming increasingly easy for elected officials to advocate a reduced summer vacation to reduce summer learning loss and to promote better use of available facilities.

CONCLUSION

As noted in the beginning of this chapter, some educators are reluctant to confront the seriousness of summer learning loss. Gerald W. Bracey refers to it as the phenomenon no one wants to deal with.[8] A discussion of calendar modification disturbs the status quo. Nevertheless, the discussion is important in the unending quest to seek better ways of educating students in the hopes of their retaining greater amounts of information and attaining higher levels of achievement.

In conclusion, consider this question: If year-round education were the traditional school calendar and had been so for one hundred years or more, and if someone came along to suggest a "new" calendar wherein students were to be educated for only nine months each year, with another three months free from organized instruction, would the American public allow, or even consider, such a reform?

NOTES

1. American Camping Association official, personal communication with author.
2. Carolyn Kneese and Stephanie Knight, "Evaluating the Achievement of At-Risk Students in Year-Round Education," *Planning and Changing* 26 (1995): 71–90.
3. Carolyn Kneese, *Year-Round Learning: A Research Synthesis Relating to Student Achievement* (San Diego, Calif.: National Association for Year-Round Education, 2000).
4. Harris Cooper, Jeffrey C. Valentine, Kelly Charlton, and April Barnett, "The Effects of Modified School Calendars on Student Achievement and School Community Attitudes: A Research Synthesis," *Review of Educational Research* 73, no. 1 (2003): 1–52.
5. The following discussion is abridged from Charles Ballinger and Carolyn Kneese, *School Calendar Reform: Learning in All Seasons* (Lanham, Md.: Rowman and Littlefield Education, 2006), 6–8.
6. National Education Commission on Time and Learning, *Prisoners of Time: Schools and Programs Making Time Work for Students and Teachers*, ED 378686 (Washington, D.C.: Government Printing Office, 1994).
7. The following discussion is abridged from Ballinger and Kneese, *School Calendar Reform*, 45–47.
8. Gerald W. Bracey, "Summer Loss: The Phenomenon No One Wants to Deal With," *Phi Delta Kappan* 84, no. 1 (2002): 12–13.

FURTHER READING

Kneese, Carolyn. "The Impact of Year-Round Education on Student Learning: A Study of Six Elementary Schools." *ERS Spectrum* 18, no. 1 (2000): 20–26.
———. *Year-Round Learning: A Research Synthesis Relating to Student Achievement*. San Diego, Calif.: National Association for Year-Round Education, 2000.
National Association for Year-Round Education website, www.nayre.org.
Roby, Douglas E. "Comparison of Reading and Math Achievement in West Carrollton School District under Two Types of School Structure—YR vs. TC." Ph.D. diss., University of Dayton, 1992.

III

PARTICULAR CHOICES

· 9 ·

The Preprimary Schools of Reggio Emilia

Pam Oken-Wright

Do nothing without joy.

—Loris Malaguzzi

$\mathcal{R}$eggio Emilia is a city of about 142,000 people in the region of Emilia Romagna in northern Italy. It is the birthplace of the Italian flag, the origin of the wonderful Parmigiano Reggiano cheese we import, and the home of a world-class system of public preprimary schools. The more than thirty infant-toddler centers and preschools in Reggio Emilia have garnered worldwide attention for the high level of work done by children and teachers, for extraordinarily beautiful school environments, and for the tremendous community support the schools enjoy. Many educators in the United States first learned of the schools of Reggio Emilia from a Newsweek article published in 1991, in which the preprimary schools of Reggio Emilia were acclaimed as the world's best in early childhood education.[1] In 1998 Howard Gardner described the schools of Reggio Emilia as

> a collection of schools for young children in which each child's intellectual, emotional, social, and moral potentials are carefully cultivated and guided. The principal educational vehicle involves youngsters in long-term engrossing projects, which are carried out in a beautiful, healthy, love-filled setting. . . . Nowhere else in the world is there such a seamless and symbiotic relationship between a school's progressive philosophy and its practices.[2]

This essay offers a brief history of the schools of Reggio Emilia, an overview of the guiding principles of the Reggio philosophy, and some examples from personal experience as I work to adapt those principles to our American context.

81

A BRIEF HISTORY OF THE PREPRIMARY
SCHOOLS OF REGGIO EMILIA

At the conclusion of World War II and the end of Fascist dictatorship in Italy, a group of determined parents in Reggio Emilia began to build, with their own hands, a school for their young children. That is where Loris Malaguzzi, the "guiding genius" of the Reggio philosophy,[3] found them and where a collaboration between educators and parents began and endures to this day. In the 1950s and 1960s Reggio teachers, led by Malaguzzi, embraced a goal of innovation in education, inspired by the thinking of John Dewey, Jean Piaget, and Lev Vygotsky. The desire to put current learning theory into practice has endured throughout the history of the preprimary schools in Reggio Emilia, including the theories of Jerome Bruner, Howard Gardner, and others. In the 1960s the preprimary schools of Reggio Emilia became municipally supported.

A QUICK LOOK AT THE SCHOOLS OF REGGIO EMILIA

The preschools and infant-toddler centers of Reggio Emilia offer full-day programs to children from all socioeconomic backgrounds; children with disabilities, referred to as children with special rights in Reggio Emilia, have priority in placement. The schools do not have directors; the teachers share the responsibilities of running of the schools. Two teachers work as equal collaborators in each classroom, supported by a pedagogical coordinator (*pedagogista*), who may travel between two or more schools, and a studio teacher (*atelierista*). Teachers and children stay together for three-year cycles: three in the infant-toddler centers (ages 0–3) and another three in the preschools (ages 3–6).

The schools, each with its own identity, are "amiable" places[4] that emanate "welcome" to children and parents. Light and transparency, living plants, natural materials, and peaceful colors lend the spaces a serene, inviting atmosphere. Documentation panels line the walls. These exquisite displays with photographs of children working, accompanied by text of teachers' and children's thinking about the experience, make the teaching and learning in the school visible to all who enter. Children's work in many media, often accompanied by their reflection or by that of their teachers, is everywhere. The children in the Reggio schools are engaged, self-directed, and collaborative. They consider themselves and are considered by others to be agents of important work. In every preschool and infant-toddler center I visited in Reggio Emilia the teachers' beliefs about children, teaching, and learning were clearly apparent in their interaction with the children and in the environment, even without benefit of translation from the Italian in text or discourse. Those beliefs form the basis for a set of principles that inform all practice in the Reggio schools.

GUIDING PRINCIPLES OF THE REGGIO EMILIA PHILOSOPHY

As far as I know there is no "definitive" list of Reggio principles. Indeed, a study of the literature reveals many variations, often including the same ideas but with slightly different organization. In fact, the Reggio Emilia philosophy is organic, with each "principle" weaving in and out of the others; thus it defies the very categorization that might help us understand it better. So, as you read this set of principles, or similar ones, notice how each affects the other; imagine them as threads woven into whole cloth, rather than a list of distinct and separate ideas.

The Image of the Child

Every child is considered competent, resourceful, full of potential, in search of relationship with others and ideas, and an active agent in his or her own learning from birth. Teachers' interactions with children are, therefore, highly respectful of the children themselves, of their experiences and culture, and of their work. Teachers also trust that, given a chance, children will gravitate toward that which challenges them and is worth knowing.

The School Environment

Most who enter an infant-toddler center or preschool in Reggio Emilia for the first time are struck by both the beauty of the school and the way that the children's presence is apparent in the space whether the children are physically there or not. Visible throughout the building are images of the children and their work, as well as evidence of children's families, culture, and experiences.

The educators of Reggio Emilia refer to the environment as "third teacher." They recognize that a school environment can invite children to work collaboratively or alone. It can invite self-sufficiency and interdependence or dependence on adults. It can invite harmony or discord. It can exhaust or energize. The teachers of Reggio Emilia set up school environments to foster collaboration, self-sufficiency, harmony, joy, and energy. They prepare the environment carefully and intentionally to call the children to intellectual pursuit through what they call "provocations." A provocation might be a question or challenge, or it might be a new, intriguing object or a change in the environment, offered to children as an invitation to discovery, investigation, and joy.

Collaboration

Collaboration is "the backbone of the system" in Reggio Emilia.[5] It is, to a large degree, what makes the remarkable results of the Reggio schools possible. Each classroom has two teachers who work as equals, collaborating to plan, facilitate, document, and research. Children collaborate with each other toward shared goals in play and project work. Teachers collaborate with children in the course of investigation. Children may bring an idea to teachers or teachers may bring one to children, but, however an investigation begins, children and teachers work together to figure out what aspect of the idea speaks to the children and how they might develop a deeper understanding of the idea. This principle may be one of the most elusive of the Reggio Emilia philosophy, as learning is not directed by either children or teachers. Rather, children and teachers work together, constructing the experience of studying a topic as they go along, creating together the path the investigation will take.

Reggio teachers consider the education of the child to be a collaborative venture among teacher, child, parent, and community. Parents assume many roles in the collaborative process, including serving on advisory councils. Teachers and parents of children engaged in a particular project may meet together to explore opportunities and possibilities for supporting the children's inquiry; they may meet together to create a surprise for the children or work together to enhance the school environment. When they are in the school parents can read documentation of children's ongoing and recent experiences. The schools of Reggio Emilia enjoy a remarkable level of support from parents. Lilian Katz suggests that this support may be due to the high quality of experiences the schools offer to their children.[6]

Most of the project work in Reggio schools is done in small groups. According to recent research about the relationship between group learning and individual learning, children learn better with the perspectives of others than when alone. In addition, the individual contributes to the collective knowledge of the group, knowledge greater than any of the group's members could have constructed alone, and which they all share.[7] In a Reggio or Reggio-inspired classroom children seek each other out in order to collaborate in play, solve problems, and exchange ideas. Teachers use many different strategies to support this rich exchange; for example, they may refer a child to another child who has solved a similar problem in the past or who has expertise in a particular area (from tying shoes to writing); encourage children to invite collaboration; help children work together to solve problems while refraining from solving problems for children; and invite children to join small groups for project work. Even the way the environment is arranged encourages group work.

The Teacher's Roles

A teacher's role in Reggio Emilia is complex. There are no scope and sequence to follow: there are no manuals. Each investigation with children is new, negotiated from the beginning by teacher and children together.

As children work and play in an environment arranged with care to encourage collaborative, thoughtful endeavors, teachers observe and document. They are alert about when to step in to offer materials, techniques, or tools, whatever they think will support the children's work, without doing it for them. Observers in Reggio schools are sometimes surprised that teachers become as involved as they do in children's projects. The difference between enough and too much intervention seems to lie in teachers' ability to listen intuitively to the child and read the situation, rather than focusing on the adult's agenda. If a teacher intervenes with respect for the child's vision and with the intention of helping him accomplish what he is trying to do or take his idea a step further, the child's vision remains intact and he is inclined to continue toward his goal.

Teachers in Reggio Emilia listen with more than their ears. They value listening as a whole-mind, whole-heart endeavor. When they intervene in children's play and representation they do so with considerable intention, perhaps asking themselves, What are the children trying to do? Are they satisfied with the way it's going? Is there something I can do to help them pursue their goal according to their own vision? If so, what would be of most help without interrupting the flow of ideas?

The teachers also act as memory keepers for the children. To help them to carry an idea through to fruition, a teacher may hold the children's current ideas for them until the next time they can meet; then she may invite the children to reflect on those ideas further and consider the topic anew. The documentation a teacher creates can also be a "memory keeper" for the children; children can peruse documentation of a shared experience, using it as a bookmark of sorts so that together they can revisit their work and proceed from there.

The Reggio teacher is a researcher of children; she is a researcher of the particular children in front of her; and she is a researcher of learning theory. She conducts her research through documentation, which involves not only gathering data and creating a history of the investigation at hand and the experiences she and the children have shared, but also interpreting those data to understand the children's thinking and learning as deeply as possible.

Documentation

Documentation is the visible trace of children's experiences, thinking, learning, and process and the teachers' interpretation of the meaning of those experiences. Teachers take notes and photographs of children's learning processes, collect the children's representations or images of them, tape-record children's conversation and thinking, and collect artifacts of project work. At the end of a project they organize all documentation data collected, add narrative (the story of what happened), and interpretation (what they hypothesize it means), and they create beautiful and insightful displays. The displays can take many forms, among them panels on walls, notebooks, books, videos, and the children's own artifacts. This documentation, visible everywhere one goes in the school, serves to inspire children to remember and revisit experiences, to inform parents and visitors of the process and meaning of a project as seen by teachers, and to support teachers' understanding of the meaning of the project.

The creation of documentation products is only one step in a much larger process of understanding children's learning and relationships, and it may come fairly late in the life of an investigation or project. Much important documentation goes on long before a wall panel is ever created. Teachers document daily; they are as likely to record one child's process while making a painting as they are to document the process of a major investigation. Years ago, inspired by a triptych with teachers' notes and illustrative drawings that were posted outside the classrooms in a Reggio Emilia preschool, I began to make daily logs in our Junior Kindergarten at St. Catherine's School in Richmond, Virginia. Each day, I compile documentation data into a log that reflects the experiences important to the group. Each log contains narrative, illustrative photographs of children's process, children's work or images of it, transcripts of any important conversations, an occasional video clip, and, where appropriate, reflections about the meaning the children or I construct from the experience being documented. The daily log is published on a webpage, and I send the link to parents via e-mail. I also print out a copy and keep it in the classroom, accessible to children and teachers. It is this initial documentation that helps me to see the meaning of what happened on a particular day and consider next steps—whether to sit tight and observe a little longer, offer a new provocation, or take the children's ideas back to them for more conversation. Periodically I review the daily logs, looking for patterns in children's thinking and interests and considering possibilities. I may use them to pull an entire investigation together to make a more permanent form of documentation.

Documentation is fundamental to the Reggio Emilia approach, for it serves all who are involved in the children's learning: children, teachers, parents, administrators, and often the community. At its best documentation makes children's learning visible in ways conventional assessment tools cannot. It also makes teaching transparent. Documentation can be of use to teachers and administrators when seeking funds, when making the school and its work known in the community, and when trying to turn the attention of the community toward the needs of its children.

Symbolic Representation

Young children have powerful ideas—ideas so expansive and elusive that they often cannot represent them to their satisfaction with verbal language alone. But they can make their most profound ideas visible through drawing, painting, sculpting, constructing, moving, making music, and other graphic and temporal media. In Reggio Emilia educators refer to all the ways in which children can represent their ideas as "the hundred languages of children." They make multiple media available to the children from a very early age— many kinds of pens and paints, potter's clay, materials for collage and construction, wire for sculpting, and looms for weaving, for example. Teachers support the children's learning about what the media can do and what the media let the children do, so that the children have many ways to make their ideas visible. Through representation in all these media, the children are able to delve more deeply into topics that interest them, and they also learn to translate their ideas from one medium to another. For example, a child might paint a picture of a tree, draw it, sculpt it in three dimensions, and engage in conversation with others about its multiple aspects to arrive at an understanding of "tree" that is satisfying to him or her.

All Reggio teachers work to support children's learning through representation. Small groups of children also work in the atelier with an *atelierista* to explore and learn about media, to work on collaborative projects, and to represent their ideas through multiple media. In addition each classroom has a mini-atelier, in which small groups of children can work on ongoing projects in the context of their classroom.

Children's Co-Construction of Theory

Children construct theories about how the world works all the time. Teachers in the Reggio schools encourage children to explore those theories together through conversation and representation. An example of co-construction of theory in the context of a project from our Junior Kindergarten class follows.

After a particularly big snowstorm the children were full of images, conversation, and emotion about their experiences within the snow-covered world. The teacher observed the children's interest and excitement and when they sat down together at morning meeting she asked, "Tell me about snow." The children were used to having conversations as a group in which they posed theories about questions that intrigued them, and they quickly began wondering about the source of the snow. The teacher recorded and transcribed the conversation. She then studied the transcript looking for and discovering that there were, indeed, patterns in the children's theories. Most held that the source of snow was magic, with either God or Santa Claus an agent of that magic. Later the teacher took those theories back to the children, inviting them to consider them a little more. Again she listened to the conversation for other understandings and ideas. For several weeks the children continued to think about snow, representing snowflakes in paint, clay, found objects, blocks, and so forth. They continued to wonder about the source of snow. The teacher invited the children to draw their ideas about the source of snow and to articulate their theories several times over the course of the project. At one point, the children thought that if they were able to make snow themselves they would discover the source of the snow that falls from the sky. The teacher helped the children gather what they needed, clarify their thinking, and express their ideas to each other when necessary. She offered support to work through stumbling blocks as the children experimented, failed, and tried again. But she did not scoop up the idea herself and take it on. She respected the children's agenda regarding snow, worked hard to understand what they were really trying to do, and supported them in their efforts to come to an answer that satisfied them. When the children's experiments did not make snow, the children regrouped and decided that they needed to refer to experts. The fifth-graders, they thought, would know how to make snow. With the teacher's help, they interviewed the older children. As it turned out, the fifth-graders' theories were not much more sophisticated than those of the young children. However, the 5-year-olds' sustained work of figuring out how it snows eventually led them to a theory that satisfied them: Snow starts as a tiny speck of ice and, in six stages (inspired by the six sides of a snowflake?) develops arms and detail and size, until it is a snowflake.

As often happens when 5-year-olds "live" with a question long enough, their theories evolved from highly magical to increasingly plausible and, finally, to close to accurate. Had the teacher told the children from the beginning what she knew about the source of snow, the children would have transformed that information into theories that made sense to them (often no more accurate, and maybe less than they would have constructed on their own). But they also most likely would have stopped constructing theory about the question once they perceived that they had been told "the truth" by an adult. So, that first bit of theory constructed from the teacher's information would have been as far as the investigation went. Perhaps even more significant was that in working together over time to figure out how it snows the children learned how to engage in inquiry. Furthermore, when children have grappled with an idea long enough, working together to grow theories that satisfy them, any information about the topic that crosses their path seems to become instantly theirs. They remain open to inquiry about the question for a long time, setting a far more receptive stage for learning in the future.[8]

A Dynamic "Curriculum"

Curriculum is a poor word for the learning that goes on in the schools of Reggio Emilia. The Italians have called the particular way of flexible planning for learning that teachers do *progettazione*. George Forman and Brenda Fyfe have called it negotiated learning,[9] rather like negotiating a slalom or a winding road. Instead of working from scope and sequence, teachers observe and document; study the documentation to try to really "hear" what the children are meaning in their play, conversation, and representation; and plan "next steps" accordingly. There is a marvelous flow to all of this, a sort of organic quality and a connectedness. The "next step" in the study of a topic is not likely to come out of the blue from the children's perspective, because that next step is determined in response to what the children themselves just said and did.

This approach requires a rather different disposition toward time than we in the United States traditionally have held. Deep understanding never comes in a hurry, and it never obeys a timetable. In Reggio Emilia, a project may last a day or a year. A teacher's goal is to help children maintain their enthusiasm and engagement in an investigation as long as they can. Sustained investigation takes time, of course, but from it children learn not only more about a topic than they could in a conventional early childhood curricular "unit," but they also learn how to collaborate to co-construct theory, how to pursue an idea that interests them, how to express their ideas and theories to others, how to consider the ideas of others in the light of their own theories and experiences, how to have cognitive conflict without emotional conflict, how to reason in more and more sophisticated ways, and how to set a goal and to develop a satisfaction bar for oneself in meeting that goal—all dispositions that in essence create the inclination to live the life of a learner. In a Reggio classroom time is the learner's friend and teacher. Children have long periods of time in which to play and work during the day. Teachers try to limit the number of interruptions to this work. Work that is not finished to the child's satisfaction can be continued the next day.

THE REGGIO EMILIA APPROACH AND AMERICAN SCHOOLS

The educators of Reggio Emilia caution us not to interpret their experiences as a teaching method. The approach cannot be "transported" or "adopted." But we do have much to learn from the experiences and reflections of the educators in Reggio Emilia. The principles that guide practice in the Reggio schools offer us insight and inspiration. The reflection that makes teaching a dynamic, alive process (reflection informs practice, which inspires further reflection) might inspire us to reconsider our current assumptions, as might such a high level of representation and thinking from such very young children.

Although interest in Reggio Emilia among early childhood educators in the United States is widespread and growing, the approach challenges American educators in some unique ways. There is no "how to" regarding the Reggio Emilia approach, as it is not a method but a philosophy and set of guiding principles. Teachers must be comfortable with not knowing in advance the topics of study, the paths investigations will take, or the end points. They must embrace the role of group learning. They must expect children to be capable of profound thinking and remarkable symbolic representation. They must embrace collaboration with colleagues and with parents. They must also be willing to invest time—time *with* children, time *for* children (interpreting documentation or collaborating with colleagues, for example), and time for their own learning. A deep understanding of the Reggio philosophy can take many years to develop. Like children constructing an understanding of how it snows, teachers in a school work together to construct a place where children and teachers learn with joy and passion, in relationship and with mutual respect, reflective of their particular culture and context.

There are many ways in which interested educators or parents can learn more about the schools of Reggio Emilia. The set of traveling exhibits, *The Hundred Languages of Children*, offers stunning panels and videos showing children in Reggio schools who are engaged in projects from beginning to end, including teachers' and children's reflections.[10] Study tours are held each year in Reggio Emilia, and few who visit there emerge unchanged. Observing firsthand the beauty of the schools, the relationships among children and between teachers and children, and the evidence of the tremendous capabilities of young children is a moving experience.

American schools whose educators have studied the Reggio philosophy and whose work is influenced by its principles hold delegation days, so that other educators can see the philosophy in action, including some schools for older children, as the principles are applicable to education at all ages. Opportunities to visit American reference points and to attend seminars and conferences nationwide are published in each edition of *Innovations* and on the Merrill-Palmer Institute (MPI) website.

To those considering such an education for their young children, I urge you to reflect on the principles and use them as reference points when observing in a "Reggio-inspired" school. You might also want to consider the relationships you perceive among children and between children and teachers in the schools. To those longing to create such a school for children, I invite you to study and learn and reflect, to find others who are on a similar journey, to embrace the complexity of this approach, and to realize that part of the beauty of the experience is that it asks of us, as adults, to always be learners.

NOTES

The author thanks Lella Gandini and Judy Kaminsky for their advice and encouragement.

1. "The 10 Best Schools in the World, and What We Can Learn from Them," *Newsweek*, December 2, 1991, 50–59.

2. Howard Gardner, "Complementary Perspectives on Reggio Emilia," in *The Hundred Languages of Children: The Reggio Emilia Approach—Advanced Reflections*, ed. Carolyn Edwards, Lella Gandini, and George Forman (Norwood, N.J.: Ablex, 1998), xvi.

3. Ibid., xv.

4. Lella Gandini, "Foundations of the Reggio Emilia Approach," in *Next Steps toward Teaching the Reggio Way: Accepting the Challenge to Change*, ed. Joanne Hendrick (Upper Saddle River, N.J.: Pearson/Merrill Prentice Hall, 2004), 16.

5. Ibid., 18.

6. Lilian Katz, "Images from the World: Study Seminar on the Experience of the Municipal Infant-Toddler Centers and Preprimary Schools of Reggio Emilia, Italy," in *Reflections on the Reggio Emilia Approach*, ed. Lilian Katz and Bernard Cesarone (Urbana, Ill.: ERIC, 1994), 12.

7. Project Zero and Reggio Children, *Making Learning Visible: Children as Individual and Group Learners* (Reggio Emilia, Italy: Reggio Children, 2001), 292.

8. For more about the investigation, see Pam Oken-Wright, "Embracing Snow," in *Next Steps toward Teaching the Reggio Way*, ed. Hendrick, 175–96.

9. George Forman and Brenda Fyfe, "Negotiated Learning through Design, Documentation, and Discourse, in *Hundred Languages of Children*, ed. Edwards, Gandini, and Forman, 240.

10. Information about current venues for "The Hundred Languages of Children" exhibits is available in the periodical, *Innovations in Early Education: The International Reggio Exchange*, and on the Merrill-Palmer Institute (MPI) website, Reggio resources section, http://www.mpi.wayne.edu/innovperiodical.htm.

FURTHER READING

Cadwell, Louise. *Bringing Reggio Emilia Home*. New York: Teachers College Press, 1997.

The Catalogue of the Exhibit: The Hundred Languages of Children. Reggio Emilia, Italy: Reggio Children, 1996.

Lella Gandini, Lynn Hill, Louise Cadwell, and Charles Schwall, eds. 2005. *In the Spirit of the Studio: Learning from the Atelier of Reggio Emilia*. New York: Teachers College Press, 2005.

· 10 ·

The Right Place

Nursery School in the Twenty-First Century

Gay Cioffi

It is my earliest memory: I approach the building feeling my mother's hand clutching mine. We walk up the stairs to the front entrance. I notice the stone benches on either side of the door as my mother rings the bell. In my memory, the nursery school—playing with wooden toys and puzzles, hearing the teacher read aloud—was the answer to my childhood dreams. I remember the easels and paint set, the books, the dolls, the blocks. When I look back, these memories are like treasures that I take down from the shelf and turn over and over in my mind.

I was enrolled at the nursery school in the small town of Williamsport, Pennsylvania, for just three weeks. I was three years old, and though it seems impossible that at such an early age I would have thought that I was in the right place, that was how I felt and that is how I have always remembered the nursery school. The environment was safe, nurturing, creative, and intellectually exciting, and I remember longing to return. Much to my regret, my days at the nursery school were all too brief. The year was 1953 and my mother, who had enrolled me at the school so that she could work part-time at the local factory, was overcome with guilt at the thought of leaving me in the care of others. It was a time when most mothers were "stay at home," and she believed that leaving me at the school was irresponsible.

Though nursery schools, originally called "infant schools," have been operating in Europe since the late 1700s, they did not become popular in the United States until the 1960s. The first U.S. examples were set up by universities in the 1920s and subsidized by the federal government to provide employment for teachers during the Great Depression.[1] Slowly, international consensus developed around the idea that early schooling was an important part of an overall educational system. The growing research that supported

93

this consensus, coupled with cultural shifts such as the increased participation of women in the workplace, accelerated the growth of nursery schools throughout the United States. The establishment of Project Head Start, a program of free early childhood education, as part of Lyndon Johnson's War on Poverty in 1965, marked the culmination of this trend.

Many years passed before the memory of the nursery school fully returned to me. It came back when I first walked into the Little Folks Nursery School in Washington, D.C., and saw the small tables and chairs, the wooden toys, and the layout of the playroom. The year was 1979, and though I had no way of knowing it at the time, this feeling of being in the right place would lead me to remain at the school as a teacher director for the next twenty-eight years.

I begin this essay with my own nursery school experience because even though the world has changed significantly in the last half-century, the needs of young children have not. Much of what makes the Little Folks School the right kind of nursery school for the twenty-first century was in place here thirty years ago and even present in the nursery school I attended briefly in 1953.

As I attempt to describe the Little Folks School, I will be referring to a 2000 study by the National Research Council entitled Eager to Learn: Educating Our Preschoolers,[2] which evaluated a broad range of behavioral and social science research on early learning and development of young children. The conclusions and recommendations of the study closely reflect the program that has been designed and implemented for children at the Little Folks School.

The Little Folks School, located in Washington, D.C.'s Georgetown neighborhood, is a small, independent nursery school for children ages 2½–5. Founded in 1972, it has a total enrollment of forty students and a staff of six teachers, including me. Little Folks is small by design. Young children's first experiences away from home should be in an environment where they know everyone's name and they feel as though their school is a part of their extended family. Research shows that children who feel a secure emotional attachment to their teachers are better socialized and able to "exploit learning opportunities."[3] This emotional attachment happens more easily in an environment where turnover among staff is infrequent and teachers are highly trained and experienced. Though it is extremely unusual in the field of early childhood education, four of the six teachers on our staff have been working at the Little Folks School for twelve years or longer.

The philosophy of the Little Folks School is based on meeting the needs of the whole child; all activities are assessed on their potential to develop the cognitive and intellectual, the physical (both large and small motor), and the social and emotional needs of children. As the National Research Council reports, "Cognitive, social-emotional (mental health), and physical development are complementary, mutually supportive areas of growth, all requiring active attention in the preschool years."[4]

Our program is play-based with a significant emphasis on the arts. We believe that experiences in the arts have intrinsic value in their own right and also help children develop skills necessary for future learning. The school has enjoyed a collaboration with the Wolf Trap Performing Arts Foundation that for many years has placed performing artists in seven-week-long classroom residencies with twice weekly engagements. Our arts-rich curriculum is a tremendous vehicle for whole child development. Our open-ended art projects promote fine motor skills, visual discrimination, hand-eye coordination, and spatial understanding. In addition, experience in the arts, visual as well as performing (music, movement, and drama), promote the ability to express and understand language, listen, follow directions, and concentrate—all important for early childhood development.

In a world in which students take Advanced Placement college-level courses in high school and high school subjects like algebra and biology in middle school, the pressure for more academics is felt even in many kindergartens and nursery schools. Little Folks is not one of them. Our approach is influenced by the teaching of John Dewey, who believed that children learn best by a process of discovery and exploration. At Little Folks School, children learn by interacting with materials, other children, and teachers. Though there is a definite structure and routine to the day, there are also built-in blocks of time that allow children to become immersed in play. Play is powerful, says David Elkind, author and distinguished professor of child development at Tufts University:

> It is vitally important to support and encourage self-directed activities by the young child. Even if those activities appear meaningless to us, they can have great purpose and significance for the child. These activities are not random and have a pattern and organization in keeping with the child's level of mental ability. Allowing the child time and freedom to complete these activities to her personal satisfaction nourishes that child's powers of concentration and attention. We run the risk of impairing these powers if we don't respect and value the young child's self-initiated activities.[5]

Pediatric learning specialist Mel Levine recently described a research report on brainstorming that provides specific evidence: when all things are equal—IQ, SAT scores, grades—the difference between young adult students who were able to brainstorm and those who were not was explained by the amount of time they had spent as young children in imaginary play.[6]

A child's day, even at the preschool level, is often overscheduled or dominated by "screen time"—time spent in front of television (now built in to many cars) and computers. There is often little opportunity for self-directed, imaginary play. A 2006 Kaiser Family Foundation Report documenting how much time infants, toddlers, and preschoolers spend with media, the types of media they are using, and the role media are playing in their environments, reported that 83 percent of children age 6 and under spend close to two hours using screen media on a typical day.[7] While the research about the long-term effects of this viewing has not kept pace with the increased use of technology, educational psychologist Jane Healy believes that not only does this screen time subtract from more concrete experiences that children need for healthy brain development but, "since virtually all parts of the brain are active during these early years," it also "will have profound and lasting effects" because it "limits appropriate experiences [and] sets up undesirable emotional/motivational patterns."[8] While early childhood educators continue to assess the value of computers in the nursery school environment, computers are not present in Little Folks School classrooms.

I remember my professors in the Department of Education at Pennsylvania State University in the 1960s predicting the information explosion that we currently witness. Their advice that the most important things to teach children were how to learn, how to problem-solve, and how to be critical thinkers remains pertinent today. A child's ability to gather information and process it in a creative and critical way begins in the early years, and an early childhood learning environment should provide numerous opportunities to practice these skills.

Although the National Research Council report states that, "No single curriculum or pedagogical approach can be identified as best," there are principles of learning that should be incorporated into the early childhood environment.[9] The ideas that learning is progressive and that young children can build on their concrete experiences when they are actively engaged with materials, other children, and staff are central themes. "If there is a single critical component to quality, it rests in the relationship between the child and the teacher, and in the ability of the adult to be responsive to the child. But responsiveness extends in many directions: to the child's cognitive, social, emotional and physical characteristics and development."[10] Such relationships are created by highly qualified and well-educated professionals in the field of early childhood education. To attract such individuals, it is important to provide worthy wages and benefits, something that is problematic in many early childhood centers.

On any given day, visitors to the Little Folks School or to other high-quality early childhood programs could enter a classroom or playground area and witness children busy at play. They would observe a well-organized room, full of beautiful open-ended art projects created by the children. They would notice various interest areas, such as, at Little Folks, the dollhouse, Duplo table, train set, or sand/water table. Although books are present in every area, even the playroom and outdoor playground, they would notice a library. They would see a corner rich with musical instruments and shelves stocked with various manipulatives. In addition to these open-ended materials, there would be shelves lined with puzzles and other learning materials that require preset solutions. They would see materials that children can use alone as well as equipment that encourages cooperative play.

If the visitors arrived at Little Folks on the first Thursday of the month, they could join in Sandwich Patrol, when the children make ham and cheese sandwiches. For young children, making a sandwich is like a construction project. Applying mustard and mayonnaise to bread, putting sandwiches into ziplock bags, and counting the results is a multitask project loaded with learning. The biggest lesson learned by all involved, however, and one of the key principles of our school, is that we take care of one another, whether the other is a family member, friend, or member of our community. This project grew from children's encounters with homeless people in Georgetown in the early 1990s. I would be frequently asked for money as I walked with children to area parks. When children asked why I was being asked for money, I explained that the people asking did not have enough to eat. It seemed logical that a project that involved the children in making food for the homeless would give them a very concrete experience with the concept of sharing, something that every teacher strives to impart. This approach to developing prosocial behavior is one of many projects in place at the Little Folks School. Parents and children alike have responded very favorably to Sandwich Patrol and our other community service projects. Parents and teachers appreciate these very real activities that provide an excellent altruistic model for young children.

At other times, visitors to Little Folks would see children actively creating, using, among other things, unit blocks (large and small), various art materials, and even recycled junk. The children's interaction with their teachers and each other would be rich with language as they describe the structures they have built, the pictures they have made, or the adventures they are embarking on. Teachers would be supporting the activity with meaningful questions and encouraging remarks. Children would be encouraged to "reflect, predict, question and hypothesize."[11] Children might eagerly document their adventures with a drawing, and the narrative would be added by the teacher. Questions by children or staff might prompt a visit to the library to gather information. Visitors would observe children who are independent and self-directed and who view themselves as learners. The children they see would be problem-solvers, building a foundation for the future they will inherit in the coming years, a future that will require imagination and creativity. Visitors would witness a certain harmony as well-trained teachers nurture young children as they navigate their way through the rapidly changing world of the twenty-first century. They would see children in the right place.

NOTES

1. *Britannica Student Encyclopedia*, s.v. "Kindergarten and nursery school," http://www.britannica.com/ebj/article-203436.

2. Barbara Bowman, M. Suzanne Donovan, and M. Susan Burns, eds., *Eager to Learn: Educating Our Preschoolers* (Washington, D.C.: National Academy Press, 2001).

3. Ibid., 307.

4. Ibid.

5. David Elkind, *The Power of Play: How Spontaneous, Imaginative Activities Lead to Happier, Healthier Children* (Cambridge, Mass.: Da Capo Press, 2007), 92–93.

6. Mel Levine, *A Mind at a Time* (New York: Simon & Schuster, 2002).

7. Victoria Rideout and Elizabeth Hamel, *The Media Family: Electronic Media in the Lives of Infants, Toddlers, Preschoolers and Their Parents* (Menlo Park, Calif.: Kaiser Family Foundation, 2006), 7.

8. Jane Healy, *Failure to Connect* (New York: Simon & Schuster, 1998), 207.

9. Bowman, Donavan, and Burns, eds., *Eager to Learn*, 307.

10. Ibid., 307.

11. Ibid., 308.

The New (Old) Vision

Montessori Education in the Twenty-First Century

Maura C. Joyce

*M*ore than a century ago, Dr. Maria Montessori (1870–1952) addressed the same issues in education that we face today. The advantages of the educational program she developed have now been the choice of several generations in the United States and worldwide. This program of education looks at the whole child and how education can provide assistance in the process of development. In Montessori's words, this education is "an aid to life."[1]

Montessori was also concerned with the preparation of children for the future. Like educators today, she, too, spoke about the issues of self-esteem, basic literacy, intellectual work, and social functioning. More important, she was interested in creating an atmosphere of peace for the future of the planet. During her lifetime she witnessed the collapse of world order with two world wars and the threat of the atomic age. She regarded children as the last agent available for stabilizing society. She wanted a plan of education that would allow for the development of a strong character, equipped with the power of adapting itself quickly and easily to the world at hand. "It is necessary that the human personality should be prepared for the unforeseen," she wrote, "not only for the conditions that can be anticipated by prudence and foresight."[2] The rapid pace at which the world is changing today makes preparation for an unknown future paramount. Montessori focused not on *what* students should learn. She focused on teaching students *how* to learn.

A BRIEF HISTORY OF MONTESSORI EDUCATION

Dr. Maria Montessori did not set out to become a pioneer in the field of education. She regarded herself as a scientist involved in research.[3] As a trained medical doctor, she spent years observing children in order to understand human development. Montessori based her method on human nature, those behaviors that children repeat over and over again, hundreds of times, from culture to culture, from generation to generation. Through research and her own observations, she noted that all children adapt to their environment—good or bad, healthy or unhealthy. The young child has the power to incorporate language and culture simply by being a part of his surroundings. No formal lessons are necessary, as the child does all the work himself.[4] According to Montessori, education should aid the child in this process. "It is Nature . . . which regulates all. . . . If we are convinced of this, we must admit as a principle the necessity of not introducing obstacles to natural development."[5] What she called a prepared environment was the key to healthy growth of the human being from infancy through adulthood.

Montessori's first experiment began in Rome, Italy, in 1907 with about fifty children, 3–6 years old. She called her classroom the Casa dei Bambini or "Children's House." Her goal was to provide the means for the children to become "civilized" and to adapt to the culture in which they lived. The room was filled with practical activities for self-care, such as hand washing, hair combing, lacing, and buttoning, and for care of the environment, such as sweeping, dusting, polishing, washing, and scrubbing.[6] She also had toys in the classroom for the children to play with. Montessori would introduce an activity to a child and leave him alone to choose to do it of his own free will. In a short time, she observed that the children were attracted to the practical activities and ignored the toys. They liked to work on things with a real purpose, and as they repeated and repeated these tasks, their ability to concentrate increased. Montessori included children of several ages in her experiment, to create a small society: the Children's House "is open to children of different ages from three to six years, who all live together as members of a family who, therefore, have need of different occupations."[7] This feeling of community created a safe environment for them to follow their inner urge— to work. These tasks with a purpose motivated their efforts.

The concept behind the creation of the Casa was to make sure that the environment was set up for the children to command. In time, Montessori determined that several components were vital to the prepared environment:

- *Accessibility* was paramount to building independence and self-esteem. All things in the room were child-size to fit the tiniest of hands.
- *Real objects*, like those that adults used, were made from wood and glass and were breakable. These materials provided natural consequences to movement and promoted coordination and practice.
- *Order* was paramount to creating a feeling of security and ownership. All things had a place, and their orderly placement facilitated the or-

ganization of information for the child. An organized environment created an organized picture in the mind.

- *Purposeful activity* meant that every activity had a purpose and provided an opportunity for real work. Children enjoyed the immediate feedback of a job well done.
- *Aesthetics* were important, and the environment was beautiful in its simplicity and practicality. Pleasing and inviting to the child, it was conducive to work and concentration.
- *Learning apparatus* was developed by Montessori after witnessing children using practical life materials to establish the ability to concentrate. She then introduced other developmental and academic materials. The Montessori apparatus, unchanged and still in use today, is the concrete representation of ideas and concepts. Items are "materialized abstractions" that bring qualities to the child's hand. Beautiful and brightly colored, the materials invite the child to touch them:
  - The *sensorial* materials were those Montessori had used in her earlier work with the mentally handicapped. These materials engaged the use of the senses to convey abstract qualities in the environment, such as dimension, length, odor, sound, and texture. The children responded to the activities with great interest, and learned to discriminate visual, tactile, and auditory subtleties.
  - There were many opportunities to develop *language* skills. Activities included vocabulary enrichment, speaking, writing, and reading.
  - Materials using beads, tiles, boards, and charts introduced *mathematics* and the concepts of quantity, symbol, and the decimal system.
  - An abundance of engaging activities brought more *cultural subjects* to the children. Extensions of the work with the senses and the language materials introduced geography, biology, music, and art.
- *Mixed-ages*, with children in three-year increments, created a community with heritage. "Nothing is duller than a Home for the Aged," Montessori said. "To segregate by age is one of the cruelest and most inhuman things one can do, and this is equally true for children."[8]
- *Teaching*, as such, disappeared in Montessori's classrooms. The teacher was reconceived as a "guide" who presented materials. The child worked with them, repeated the process until perfection or mastery, and then was able to abstract the concept. Only in the initial contact with the material was the adult involved.
- *Freedom to work* made the journey and the discovery the child's work. The guide was there only in order to provide the roadmap. The use of the hand was paramount in intellectual growth. The manipulative materials allowed for "auto-education" in which the child discovered on his own, not just taking the word of others to be true. Mario Montessori

(1898–1982), Maria Montessori's son, who collaborated with his mother in her work, said, "It is he [the child] who has to discover. It is of little benefit to his development if the discoveries are taught to him by somebody else. . . . The difference between being taught and discovering for oneself is like the difference that exists between eating a good meal and having somebody describe the delicious dishes of a dinner which he once ate."[9]

- *Socialization* was an important emphasis, as the children interacted with each other freely, respecting the boundaries of community and the individual's right to work peacefully.

With these concepts in place, at the end of the three-year cycle, the child had acquired physical independence. The 6-year-old cared for himself and his immediate environment and expressed his needs clearly. This child had absorbed the environments of his family and the classroom. He had arrived— but only at a point of departure.

DIFFERENT STAGES NECESSITATE DIFFERENT MODELS

After several years of working with young children, Montessori recognized that this early time was but one of a series of distinct stages in life. As Kay Baker, director of elementary training at the Washington Montessori Institute at Loyola College, has described, "Montessori identified four well-defined periods of life during which adaptation to society and the world and . . . construction of the personality are accomplished."[10] These four planes of development, as Montessori called them, are each characterized by particular needs, interests, and goals of the child. The first plane covers infancy, from birth to 6 years of age. The second plane is the period of childhood, ages 6 to 12. Next comes the adolescent, from ages 12 to 18, and finally the emergence of the adult takes place from ages 18 to 24. These four planes necessitate four plans for education.[11]

Turning her attention to the elementary child, 6–12 years old, Montessori found that new psychological characteristics posed new challenges. He had an insatiable appetite for knowledge and was eager to explore. No longer satisfied with his place in the small community of the family and the preschool classroom, the child sought the answers to questions about his place in the universe. Questions turned from "what" to "why."

To answer the new questions for the older child, Montessori found that the basic elements of the Casa still worked. The components of the Montessori classroom described above are intact for the elementary child, with an expanded curriculum for his greater intellectual capacity. Adaptations needed to be made:

more group lessons for increased socialization; the use of stories, pictures, and experiments to appeal to the powers of imagination and abstraction; and access to the outside environment—nature, libraries, and museums. Montessori teachers refrain from just answering questions; rather their work revolves around guiding students toward finding answers. Montessori saw traditional methods as ineffective. "How can the mind of a growing individual continue to be interested," she asked, "if all our teaching be around one particular subject of limited scope, and is confined to the transmission of such small details of knowledge as he is able to memorize?"[12] The teacher as guide works as an "enlightened generalist," giving lessons across a wide curriculum that leads students toward research, discovery, and a deeper understanding of concepts. As in the Casa, repetition of work, use of manipulative materials, and the freedom to explore drive students toward progress. Whereas the younger child learned to concentrate, the elementary child learns to problem-solve and think critically.

Montessori continued to grow her methods to match the growth of the child. Adolescence was a critical and sensitive stage, which, Montessori felt, had long been ignored. She saw this age, 12–18 years, as a parallel stage to the first plane, where an immense amount of physical and emotional growth takes place. This is the period of transition, when the "child" prepares to play his part in society as an adult. As in the Casa, this child was again in need of purposeful activity, but this activity meant more than just using appropriately sized utensils and props; it meant real work.[13]

The same components appear again at this level, again with modifications to suit the characteristics of the stage. The apparatus is replaced with opportunities to learn from experts and real experiences. Purposeful activity and freedom to work are essential at this level to promote self-confidence and self-worth. The Montessori adolescents have opportunities for "real practice" in society, including practical use of their skills, such as tending gardens, running a business, or apprenticing with a craftsperson. Lessons are in seminar format to give the student practice in discussion, reflection, and debate. Academics are rigorous, but based on research and the acquisition of skills, thus continuing the preparation of an individual able to adapt to an unknown future.

PREPARATION FOR THE
TWENTY-FIRST CENTURY: NEW (OLD) VISION

How can a 100-year-old method provide a new vision? How can it possibly be relevant in a world in stark contrast to the previous century? Last, and most important, how can it prepare the child for the future?

Montessori is "timeless" in that it has been successfully in practice for nearly a century with no change to its curriculum or method of instruction. It is universal, catering to children in any cultural, social, or economic setting. Rather than being based on trends in curriculum or style or on mandated content standards, Montessori education is based on the nature of the human being. It relies on those characteristics common to all humans, regardless of placement on the globe or placement in history.[14] Its objective is the development of the personality and the realization of human potential. It prepares the child for the future by allowing him the opportunity to adapt to his environment and culture. At the end of the education process, the adult human person needs the power to adjust to the world at hand. Education, Montessori says, needs to be the process of acquiring those skills required for an unknown future.[15]

In the United States, Montessori education became rooted in the alternative education tradition in 1959.[16] Montessori teacher training moved to the United States in the mid-1960s, and with it the number of schools began to increase. The first public Montessori school, begun as part of the desegregation movement, opened in 1968. By 1982 there were Montessori classes in more than fifty schools and districts. By 1996 the number had increased to two hundred.[17] In the last decade, the charter school movement has been a successful vehicle for implementing more Montessori settings with public funds. Current estimates indicate there are more than 4,500 Montessori schools in the United States, approximately 250 of which are within the public school system.[18] Clearly, a part of the public sector has embraced Montessori as a workable alternative.

This growth of Montessori settings is attributed to many factors, not the least of which is the results of implementation: students who are able to work independently, collaborate in a group, know how to learn, are responsible and accountable for their achievement, and are socially secure and adaptable. Another reason for growth is that Montessori provides a method of education that prepares the mind for success in today's world. Among the success stories are many who credit their Montessori education for preparing them to be great business leaders today. Most prominent are Larry Page and Sergey Brin, who founded Google. These men have shared publicly that their Montessori education taught them to be self-directed and self-starters, a must for success in this ever-changing world.[19] Montessori provides a model that is vastly different in pedagogy and methodology from traditional educational settings.[20] In a Montessori school, there is a new focus, a new vision of the child and how to prepare him for the future.

THE MONTESSORI ALTERNATIVE

Montessori is a time-tested and successful alternative to traditional education models. It promotes the necessary habits, skills, and values that adults will need in order to meet the demands of the future. The U.S. Department of Labor agrees. The Secretary's Commission on Achieving Necessary Skills (SCANS) was appointed in 1991 by the secretary of labor to determine the skills needed to succeed in the world of work. Its report makes a plea to educators to change curriculum and instruction to enable students to develop high-performance skills. It identifies necessary skills for high-performance work places: basic literacy, computational skills, thinking skills necessary to put knowledge to work, ability to manage resources, ability to work amicably and productively with others, ability to acquire and use information, ability to work with a variety of technologies. More important, the commission found a need for personal qualities that make workers dedicated and trustworthy. It wants workers who are responsible, who have self-esteem, who are sociable, and who can manage their time.[21]

Although proficiency in academic areas was also noted in the study, interpersonal and thinking skills are given much more emphasis. Creativity, decision-making, and problem-solving are critical tools for the workplace of the future.[22] The educational system needs to provide opportunities for students to participate as members of a team, to teach others new skills, and to exercise leadership. Certainly these goals were part of Montessori's original vision, and her method is proving itself as a viable option to achieve them. Studies have shown that Montessori students perform better on standardized tests of math and reading than their non-Montessori peers and that these students are better prepared for higher levels of education.[23] The journal *Science* reported the findings of a study that compared academic and social scores of Montessori students with other elementary school education programs. The results showed the benefits of Montessori education. Montessori children performed better on standardized tests of reading and math and exhibited more positive peer interactions and advanced social cognition.[24]

IS MONTESSORI FOR EVERYONE?

Every child can benefit from a Montessori education because of its basis in universal developmental characteristics. The students who benefit most from a Montessori education are the ones who begin in Montessori by the age of 3 or 4. It is more difficult to introduce Montessori to an older child, say of upper elementary age, in grades 4 and 5. Montessori only works when the family wants the benefits of a Montessori education. Reinforcement of the ideals—independence, freedom with responsibility, and social collaboration—at home make the most of Montessori education.

EDUCATION AND PEACE

As for Montessori's ultimate goal of a peaceful future for humankind, Ian M. Harris, professor in educational policy and community studies at the University of Wisconsin, Milwaukee, provides an interesting note. He conducted a study of peaceful pedagogy in the Milwaukee Public Schools, which has a Montessori school in its district. Some of the key questions in his study were: Is the classroom democratic? Does the teacher promote self-esteem? Does the teacher model peace? Do the students mediate their conflicts? Are students tolerant of each other? Are they compassionate with each other? The Montessori school scored statistically higher on all these questions.[25] In the current world political climate, it is hard not to agree that this goal of Montessori's is most important for our children.

NOTES

1. Maria Montessori, *The Absorbent Mind* (1949), trans. Claude A. Claremont (Oxford, England: Clio, 1989), 15.
2. Maria Montessori, *From Childhood to Adolescence* (1948), trans. Montessori Educational Research Center (New York: Schocken, 1973), 61.
3. E. M. Standing, *Maria Montessori: Her Life and Work* (New York: Hollis & Carter, 1957), 67.
4. Both men and women take up the role of teaching, and there has been a wonderful mix of both genders in the Montessori community. Both private and public Montessori schools admit children with no discrimination as to gender. For no other purpose than clarity in this essay, Montessori teachers are referred to as "she" and the child, as described by Dr. Montessori and the author, is referred to as "he."
5. Maria Montessori, *Spontaneous Activity of the Child* (1918), trans. Florence Simmonds (Adyar, Madras, India: Kalakshetra, 1965), 5.
6. Standing, *Montessori*, 46.
7. Maria Montessori, *The Discovery of the Child* (1948), trans. M. Joseph Costelloe (New York: Ballentine, 1967), 82.
8. Montessori, *Absorbent Mind*, 226.
9. Mario M. Montessori, "Keys to the World of the Child" (1948), reprinted in *AMI Communications*, 1998, no. 4: 12.
10. Kay Baker, "Optimal Developmental Outcomes for the Child Aged Six to Twelve: Social, Moral, Cognitive, and Emotional Dimensions," *NAMTA Journal* 26, no. 1 (2001): 73.
11. Dr. Montessori went back to formulate a plan of education for the child from birth to 3 years old. The idea of the prepared environment became even more crucial at this early stage. Additionally, she felt that if the child was developmentally served

in the first three planes, the university provided an appropriate setting for the fourth plane, ages 18–24. This essay focuses only on the planes of development that coincide with the American public school system, preschool through grade 12.

12. Montessori, From *Childhood to Adolescence*, 67.

13. Ibid.

14. Montessori, *Absorbent Mind*, 9.

15. Montessori, *From Childhood to Adolescence*, 61.

16. David Kahn, "The Montessori Mission," in *Implementing Montessori Education in the Public Sector*, ed. David Kahn (Cleveland Heights, Ohio: NAMTA, 1990), 10.

17. Bretta Weiss Wolff, "A Brief History of Public *Montessori*," excerpt from *Montessori School Management Guide* (New York: American Montessori Society, 1997), reprinted in *Public School Montessorian* 11, no. 1 (1998): 12.

18. *Montessori Community Resource* (Minneapolis, Minn.: Jola Publications, 2006).

19. "Larry Page and Sergey Brin, Founders of Google.com, Credit Their Montessori Education for Much of Their Success," *International Montessori Council News*, December 5, 2005, also on the website of the International Montessori Foundation, http://www.montessori.org/enews/barbara_walters.html.

20. David Kahn, "Is Public School Montessori an Educational Reform or Just Another Trend?" *Children's Post* (Rockville, Md.), December 1994, 19.

21. U.S. Department of Labor, *What Work Requires of Schools: A SCANS Report for America, 2000* (Washington, D.C.: Government Printing Office, 1991), viii.

22. Ibid., ix.

23. *Outcomes for Students in a Montessori Program: A Longitudinal Study of the Experience in the Milwaukee Public Schools* (New York: Association Montessori Internationale—USA, May 2003), 3.

24. Angeline Lillard and Nicole Else-Quest, "The Early Years: Evaluating Montessori Education," *Science* 313, no. 5795 (September 29, 2006): 1894.

25. Ian M. Harris, "Research Update: Montessori, Peace Education, and the Public Sector," *Montessori Public School Consortium Update* 3, no. 1 (1995): 1.

· 12 ·

Multiple Intelligences

Capitalizing on Strengths

Thomas R. Hoerr

$\mathcal{I}$ndependent schools are, by definition, unique and independent. Each school has its own mission, and each can choose to pursue that mission as it wishes—subject, of course, to laws and regulations. While this independence is sometimes reflected in staid schools that adhere to traditions and practices of yesteryear, it is also reflected in schools that seek to use new evidence about how children learn and grow. Compared to just a score of years ago, for example, magnetic resonance machines have given us insights regarding which parts of the brain are responsible for which kind of behaviors. We also know a great deal more about how attitudes are formed and how children learn. This is where today's New City School story begins.

In 1988 I read Howard Gardner's seminal book, *Frames of Mind: The Theory of Multiple Intelligences.*[1] I chose the book because I wanted a better understanding of the different strengths that children possess and how we might use them in our teaching. Schools do a good job of educating the bright and traditional learners, I knew. I wanted a model that would allow us to cast a wider net in creating student success. Simply put, there are many people who find success in the adult world—however that success is defined—but who were relatively unsuccessful in school. This disparity indicates that the pathway to success in school may be too narrow. The more I read, the more I recognized that Gardner's work offered insights that would be very relevant to creating a setting in which more students could achieve, and in which all students could achieve more.

New City School was founded in 1969 as an Open Classroom School. Indeed, its founders approached the St. Louis Board of Education with a proposal to create and run a public school but retain control over curriculum and selection of the head of school. (Today, of course, this arrangement would be called a charter school.) The Board of Education declined their request, and consequently an independent school was formed in the City of St. Louis. The founders wanted an experiential setting, they sought "joyful learning," they valued the arts, and they wanted to enroll a diverse student body in which respect and care was the norm.

Nineteen years later, as head of New City School, I was struck by how much the theory of Multiple Intelligences (MI) supported these original goals. Recognizing that all of us are smarter than any of us and appreciating the power of collegiality, I convened a faculty committee to read *Frames of Mind* and talk about its potential at New City School. It was a voluntary committee, meeting after school and over the summer; about one-third of our faculty joined it. From the start, it was clear that MI supported our principles. Recognizing MI meant believing that each child has strengths, that the arts are important, and that who you are is more important than what you know. The first two beliefs stem directly from MI theory; the third emanates from our faculty's value of the personal intelligences (sometimes also called "emotional intelligence," from Daniel Goleman's book of the same name).[2] Indeed, as we look to preparing our graduates for the uncertainties of the twenty-first century, it is imperative that they know their own strengths and weaknesses and that they can work with others, others who are both similar to and different from themselves.

As we read, going chapter-by-chapter through *Frames of Mind* and sharing responsibility for teaching and learning, we began to look at practices we were already doing that supported MI as well as new strategies which would help us becomes a more MI-friendly school. Candidly, we did not reflect on how this approach might affect our marketing or enrollment; rather, we felt that strategies which caused us to be more child-centered and help students learn must be beneficial in every way. (Fortunately, almost a score of years later, we were right!)

The theory of MI approached intelligence from a very different orientation. Rather than looking at intelligence as a score on a paper and pencil test, Gardner defines intelligence as solving a problem or creating a product that is valued in a culture. The implications of the terms "product" and "culture" are enormous. "Product" encompasses not only works of art but creating teams and building relationships. "Culture" captures the interplay between cultural mores and what is perceived to be of value. Too often in our status-driven society, for example, we equate intelligence with the talents that are financially lucrative. Gardner's point is that intelligences are problem-solving abilities, irrespective of whether they lead to high salaries; that relationship is often culturally dependent.[3]

From this definition, Gardner identifies seven different intelligences: *linguistic* (sensitivity to the meaning and order of words); *logical-mathematical* (the ability to handle chains of reasoning and to recognize patterns and order); musical (sensitivity to pitch, melody, rhythm, and tone), *bodily-kinesthetic* (the ability to use the body skillfully and handle objects adroitly); spatial (the ability to perceive the world accurately and to re-create or transform aspects of that world); *interpersonal* (the ability to understand people and relationships); and *intrapersonal* (access to one's emotional life as a means to understand oneself and others). Subsequently, he added an eighth intelligence, *naturalist* (the ability to recognize and classify the numerous species, the flora and fauna, of an environment).

In my book, *Becoming a Multiple Intelligences School*, I refer to the linguistic and logical-mathematical intelligences as the "scholastic intelligences."[4] These are the intelligences that are typically most valued in schools and the ones to which and through which most teachers teach. High-powered schools often develop their reputations by enrolling students who are strong in the scholastic intelligences and focusing on their development. (The No Child Left Behind legislation has exacerbated this trend, and while most private schools are not subject to this legislation, its presence has affected the dialogue on student growth and standardized testing.) In the kind of school I wish to lead, however (indeed, in the kind of school in which I want to enroll), the path to success is broader than just that paved with the scholastic intelligences. Students do need to read, write, and calculate well; there is no question about that. But we should view these outcomes as the floor, not the ceiling. Students should also be able to develop their talents in other intelligences; students should be able to use their strongest intelligences in learning; all students should become skillful in the personal intelligences.

Our faculty's pursuit of MI was never linear nor sequential. We began by listing those practices we already used that supported MI, and we then listed those strategies we might use to become more of an MI school. At one point, a group of us traveled to the Key School in Indianapolis, the first school to use MI (New City was the second school to do so). We spent some time there and learned from its approach. Throughout our journey, we reflected the collegiality described by Roland Barth in *Improving Schools from Within*.[5] Barth defines collegiality as educators working and learning together. If children are to learn and grow, he says, the adults must learn and grow, too. He describes the components of collegiality as teachers talking about students, teachers developing curriculum, teachers teaching one another, and teachers observing one another. I add a fifth collegiality component, teachers and administrators working together on committees.

As we began to pursue MI, it became a vehicle for faculty collegiality. We engaged in each of the behaviors that Barth described; we learned with and from one another. Teachers asked, shared, listened, and observed. Over the course of our MI implementation we have had an array of MI-focus faculty committees to help us do this. The Talent Committee read *Frames of Mind*. Other committees have included the Assessment Committee, the Parent Communication Committee, the MI Push and MI Pull Committees, the Portfolio Committee, the Genuine Understanding Committee, the MI Library Committee, the MI Institute Committees, and a committee now in existence, called simply the MI Committee.

In addition, as part of our quest for MI, we have had voluntary reading committees, and we have chosen to read *Emotional Intelligence* (Goleman), *The Unschooled Mind* (Gardner) and *A Whole New Mind* (Pink) among others.[6] In addition, MI has been a topic of many, many faculty meetings. Sometimes the focus is directly on MI, and we share strategies and ideas. Other times MI becomes the backdrop for discussing other educational issues, from preparing for standardized tests, to designing our open house, to talking about our extended day program, to planning our graduation ceremony.

At first, teachers would try to incorporate as many intelligences as possible into a lesson. We quickly realized that this approach was unrealistic and fair to neither teachers nor students. Some lessons lend themselves quite well to MI, while others are less conducive; moreover, the planning required to incorporate each intelligence in every lesson is prohibitive. Instead, we learned that teachers need to think about how to incorporate the intelligences as they plan units and themes; looking longer-term makes it a bit easier to figure out how and where to incorporate the nonscholastic intelligences. Oftentimes MI is an integral part of a lesson; sometimes its incorporation is obvious while other times it is subtle. That range is appropriate because MI is such a part of our philosophy and identity.

We went through a phase of inserting cute and fun MI activities into our lessons, whether or not they moved us closer to our instructional goals. MI is a tool, however, not a goal, so we always need to be sure that MI is helping us achieve our ends. Because MI can be so engaging for students, we have to remind ourselves that it is not enough for instruction to be fun and for students to enjoy school. Fun and enjoyment must go hand-in-hand with acquiring skills, knowledge, and understanding.

As part of our quest to make our classrooms and instruction more MI friendly, teachers also became aware of their own MI profiles. Each of us has a range of intelligence strengths, and we rely on our predominant strengths in teaching and eliciting information from students unless we consciously work to do otherwise. Ameliorating this tendency begins with a teacher reflecting on his or her own MI profile and then observing how it is manifested in planning and teaching. Sometimes teachers work to balance their presentations and focus, and at other times they make a concerted effort to work together so they can benefit from one another's intelligence strengths.

We tried two ideas that we gathered from the Key School. Flow time is a period in which students can pursue whatever intelligence they wish. Based on the work of Mihaly Csikszentmihalyi,[7] the goal is for students to get lost in time as they engage in their strongest intelligences. While there is no doubt that this idea has merit, we could never find a way to schedule it to work within the school day.

We also tried PODS (Personal Opportunities for Developing Strengths), times in which students elect to pursue an intelligence under the guidance of an adult (a teacher, administrator, or volunteer). These options range, for example, from PODS for board games (representing the logical-mathematical intelligence), creating cartoons (spatial intelligence), or tending in our school's garden (naturalist intelligence), to writing and performing a play (linguistic and bodily-kinesthetic) or singing in a choir (musical). Our students certainly enjoy these times, and so do the adults.

Grant Wiggins, consultant on educational assessment, says that "what you measure is what you value," and we have learned that assessment is a key consideration in implementing MI (as it is with every kind of pedagogy). If we truly believe in MI and if we really want it to be used regularly in classrooms, then we need to ensure that MI is part of assessment. That is, in addition to demonstrating their learning through the scholastic intelligences, students also need to be able to show what they know through their other intelligences. We achieve this aim by giving students intelligence options or by making it possible for them to use many different approaches. In explaining the causes of the Civil War, for example, fifth-grade students not only write about what happened, they become characters from the North and South and depict how these protagonists might view the upcoming conflict, and why. Students also do spatial and logical-mathematical timelines of the path to war, showing what was happening in the North and the South.

Similarly, as a culmination to their yearlong unit on the body, kindergartners build a life-size human body that works. A juice-box (heart) and plastic bags (lungs) demonstrate how the heart and lungs are connected, for example. Colored yarn depicts hair, veins, and arteries. First-graders show their knowledge of the parts of a plant and plant growth by becoming a life-size plant. Construction paper, straws, and felt are used to show the components of a plant and how it functions. Second-graders create 3-dimensional national monuments that should have been created but were never built (for example, the Golden Spike Railroad Museum). Third-graders build dioramas to show how Native American tribes lived and the rituals in which they engaged. Fourth-graders become the famous individual they have studied and are displayed in the Living Museum; they dress up in character and come alive to explain their life story. Fifth graders produce a huge quilt that captures both their personal identity as well as events in the Revolutionary War. Our sixth graders create a giant mural that addresses a form of discrimination or prejudice. These are just a few examples of how we use MI in assessment and presentation. Many, many more opportunities exist. All are accompanied by presentations in which students exhibit and explain their project, diorama, or mural to an audience that typically includes students from other grades, teachers and administrators, and parents. These presentations enable students to hone their interpersonal intelligence. In addition to creating each of these MI-laden projects, students also write a paper or report that shows their understanding in a very linguistic way. Often new technology, such as videocassettes, DVDs, audiotapes, or digital images, are used to capture students' non-scholastic intelligences. A spring portfolio night, when students review the contents of their portfolios with their parents, presents another opportunity to view progress in all of the intelligences.

Continuing on the idea that "what you measure is what you value," we knew that MI needed to be reflected on and in our students' report cards. Doing so would reinforce the role and value of MI to all of our constituencies: students, students' parents, and our faculty. We make a point of explaining and reporting on the various MI assessments, often using rubrics to show students' proficiency. We also make a point of using MI terms throughout our written narrative, referring to a student's "linguistic skills" or "interpersonal strengths." And because we place so much value on the personal intelligences, the entire first page of our report card is devoted to the intrapersonal and interpersonal intelligences. Yet after all these years, we still have not created a page that specifically addresses MI for our report card. When we tried such a page it seemed to shift too much focus onto MI, moving it from being a tool to becoming a goal. The reporting issue is one that we will continue to visit, however.

Our MI library is perhaps the capstone of our work with MI. It opened in December 2005, and Howard Gardner joined us to cut the ribbon. The 4,200 square foot library is filled with books, but that is only the beginning. It is designed to be visually attractive and to entice students. There are two fish tanks, one for freshwater and one for saltwater fish. Puzzles and board games abound on shelves. A music center contains cassettes related to curriculum, and earphones. A circular room with a metal wall and tile floor is designed for the spatial intelligence. Collections allow students to pursue the naturalist intelligence. Tables and seating support both collaborative learning and alone-time. Beyond the setup of the library, we offer weekly MI centers, times when teachers bring their classes to the library so that students can pursue particular intelligences. Over time, we plan to focus the centers to support the curriculum being taught in the various classrooms.

Gardner's model of intelligence has touched many educators around the world. Thousands of educators have visited the New City School to learn about our implementation of MI, and I receive hundreds of e-mail inquiries each year. Good teachers find that MI supports their efforts to find each child's strengths. However, MI has most often been implemented in individual classrooms; while there are schools framed around MI, they are the exception and not the rule. It is not surprising that such schools are few when one considers the energy required to move an entire school community down the MI road.

MI is not a panacea. As with any other tool, it can be well used or executed badly. However, our score of years with MI show that it enables teachers to personalize learning experiences. It supports creative curriculum design and experiential learning, and it offers many more ways for students to succeed. In our MI setting, students, teachers, administrators, and parents all learn.

NOTES

1. Howard Gardner, *Frames of Mind: The Theory of Multiple Intelligences* (New York: Basic Books, 1983).

2. Daniel Goleman, *Emotional Intelligence* (New York: Bantam Books, 1995).

3. For this discussion, see, generally, Gardner, *Frames of Mind.*

4. Thomas R. Hoerr, *Becoming a Multiple Intelligences School* (Alexandria, Va.: ASCD Press, 2000).

5. Roland Barth, *Improving Schools from Within: Teachers, Parents, and Principals Can Make the Difference* (San Francisco, Calif.: Jossey-Bass, 1990).

6. Goleman, *Emotional Intelligence*; Howard Gardner, *The Unschooled Mind* (New York: Basic Books, 1991); Daniel Pink, *A Whole New Mind: Why Right-Brainers Will Rule the Future* (New York: Penguin Group, 2005).

7. Mihaly Csikszentmihalyi, *Flow: The Psychology of Optimal Experience* (New York: Harper & Row, 1990).

· 13 ·

Schools for Gifted and Talented Students

Virginia H. Burney

Schools for gifted and talented learners are found in both the public and private school arenas. There are magnet programs within a single public school district, public residential high schools drawing students from an entire state, charter schools, specialized programs within universities, programs within schools, and independent schools with the specific mission of gifted education. While each school or program may differ in governance, funding, geographic district, and the particular criteria used to determine which students qualify as gifted and/or talented, they all serve those children who perform or have the potential for performing at a level far above their age mates in the domain or domains the school is designed to address. Some programs may be for those with extraordinary ability in the visual or performing arts; others are for those likely to be exceptional in one or more academic areas; and still others may include multiple domains of high potential or performance. The focus of the program or services dictates the identifying criteria used to select the students who participate.

These schools have been established because of the specialized nature of the curriculum and instruction that is needed to develop the potential of those with exceptional abilities. It has also been found that in addition to greater academic and work habit gains, gifted learners are more likely to thrive socially and emotionally when their academic needs are met and they are among others with similar abilities or interests. Some publicly funded schools have found that gathering these students in one place is a more efficient and cost-effective way to provide them with appropriate educational options than when they are scattered throughout a district or across a region or state. Some private schools have emerged because of the lack of sufficiently challenging options within the local public schools. Regardless of the reasons, in these times of focus on minimal competency and the competition of the global marketplace, there is an in-creased need for schools and programs that specialize in developing an often-overlooked segment of the student population—those who can perform well beyond what is required for grade-level standards and whose academic needs cannot be met through the confines of grade-level curriculum. This essay will provide a rationale for why these programs are important, the components of such programs, how they differ at each level of elementary, middle, and high school, and the benefits to students in terms of academic, social, and emotional needs and study skills.

NEED FOR GIFTED EDUCATION

Some schools claim that they are differentiating instruction for all learners or, in the case of some independent schools, that their curriculum is "college-preparatory," rigorous, or otherwise outstanding. However, the majority of in-struction in all schools is whole-class; the majority of curriculum is based upon grade-level standards; the majority of schools group students based upon their chronological age. Gifted learners, by definition, are able to as-similate new information at faster pace, can master greater depth of content than is usually available, and are able to reason at a higher level sooner than their age mates. Some excerpts from the research include:

- Differentiation within the regular classroom is not sufficient. Research in 1993 indicated that most teachers use one lesson plan to teach a di-verse group of students. In core subject areas, students with high abil-ity received no differentiated experiences in 84 percent of classroom activities. Ten years later, the results were the same in spite of the fact that the one-size-fits-all approach to teaching is ineffective and there has been much emphasis in the interim on differentiation.[1]
- The Templeton National Report on Acceleration warns, "Schools pay lip-service to the proposition that students should learn at their own pace; in reality, for countless highly able children the pace of their progress through school is determined by the rate of progress of their classmates. In the majority of our classrooms, an invisible ceiling re-stricts the progress of academically gifted students."[2]
- Gifted and talented elementary students have already mastered from 35 to 50 percent of the curriculum to be offered in five basic subjects before they even begin the school year.[3]
- Teachers play a vital role in the identification of students with gifts and talents. Teachers without training tend to overlook disadvantaged, underachieving, and culturally different gifted and talented students.[4]

- Children who are gifted and talented and who receive quality services have higher achievement test scores, higher high school graduation rates, and higher college graduation rates than gifted students who did not receive such services.[5]
- There are eighteen types of acceleration ranging from continuous progress to curriculum compacting, from early admission to subject-matter acceleration. The Templeton Report observes that acceleration "is strongly supported by decades of research, yet the policy implications of that research are widely ignored by the wider educational community. . . . The research on acceleration is expansive and consistent; and we are not aware of any other educational practice that is so well researched, yet so rarely implemented."[6]
- Students need to have had experience with academic challenge prior to advanced coursework at the high school level to develop the strategies needed for success in advanced work.[7]
- Education writer and analyst Thomas Toch has explained, "There is, perversely, no incentive in the law (i.e., No Child Left Behind [NCLB]) for schools to focus on their more capable students. Indeed, research by value-added advocate William Sanders has shown that the rate of progress for high-achieving students in low-performing schools in Tennessee has actually declined since the implementation of NCLB."[8]

What is clear is that the standard fare in America's schools does not meet the academic needs of gifted learners. Special schools or programs devoted to a higher level of instruction can help gifted students develop academically, personally in terms of habits of self-regulation, and socially.

IDENTIFICATION OF THE GIFTED

Definitions of giftedness and the underlying theories of different definitions generate discussion that is beyond the scope of this essay. Furthermore, for the sake of simplicity and because schools for the arts are covered elsewhere in this volume, the discussion here will be restricted to programs for those who are academically gifted; this is the usual domain of giftedness served by these specialized schools and programs. A somewhat common view of exceptional cognitive ability or performance includes those who score two or more standard deviations above the norm on a standardized measure of intelligence or achievement; this group would include about the top 2–3 percent of the population. If also including those with specific academic aptitude, or allowing for the standard error of measure, the group could include around 5–10 percent of the general population. These can be local norms or national norms.

Even if the focus is narrowed to a small percentage of the total student population, it would be erroneous to conclude that students in such a school or program would then be alike in their academic abilities or needs. When discussing giftedness and its identification, recognition must be given to the limitations of the instruments, to the fact that previous opportunity affects school-related knowledge, and to the understanding that "exceptional" cognitive function is a relative term when considering the environment of an individual child. Group tests of academic ability have serious limitations, including the reliance on facility with English, reported bias, low ceilings, and a lack of validity and/or reliability for use as an identifier of those at the highest level or from specific populations. All programs should use multiple measures to find all students of high potential. Tests administered individually by clinical psychologists are preferable, but rarely practical, especially for screening large numbers of students. While instruments to measure the upper ranges are few and there are few individuals functioning there upon whom to generate data, there can be a range of intelligence of 50 points or more within the gifted population itself using traditional measures alone. Furthermore, an individual gifted student may have far greater aptitude for one subject than for another. Tests of intelligence have limitations and are used here only to illustrate the point that all gifted children are not alike or equally adept at all subjects. Schools or programs for the gifted need multiple criteria for admission, flexible options, a range of services, and differentiated instruction in order to meet the differing needs of individual students within the program.

CURRICULUM AND INSTRUCTION

Gifted learners acquire new information with far fewer repetitions and at a faster pace than their peers of more average ability. Their abilities indicate a need for acceleration in their curriculum. Indeed, acceleration is the most effective intervention method for these students, but they also need content of greater depth and complexity than is usually found in grade-level curriculum. They need instruction in all subjects all the time that encourages inquiry, analysis, debate, and the development of the independent learner. It is not enough to provide a third-grade text to a second-grade student; nor is it enough to provide random enrichment options without acceleration. It is not enough to provide occasional accommodations for the gifted child and say needs are being met. True gifted education is more than the sum of a list of field trips, accelerated classes, independent studies, or academic competitions. These students require a systematically planned set of experiences that will develop their ability to think abstractly, work independently, process information quickly, manage their time, organize their ideas, analyze alternatives, and present their understandings to others in a clear and professional way. Done well, this curriculum is carefully articulated from grade to grade and level to level. Whenever possible and certainly through elementary and middle school, this curriculum is built upon big ideas and is full of interdisciplinary connection and challenge. Gifted education, done correctly, is rich and complex, deep and wide, rigorous and stimulating.

Some components for a strong program of gifted education include:

- A written philosophy and goals and/or outcomes for gifted students.
- An identification procedure in place that matches strengths identified with services provided. There must be multiple criteria used to address limitations of particular instruments and to assist in identifying students from traditionally underrepresented populations.
- Teachers and program administrators trained in best practices in gifted education.
- Modified scheduling and differentiated staffing to achieve its goals.
- Flexible service models that respond to the needs of the individual learner in the particular setting.
- Curriculum planned and articulated in a systematic way to build and span all years.
- Advanced content taught at a greater depth and at a faster pace.
- Instruction that includes teaching of creative problem solving, higher-level thinking skills, and critical thinking.
- Students who are pre-assessed for mastery of basic skills and knowledge. Alternate material is compacted, accelerated, and enriched.
- Acceleration options, including early entrance, grade skipping, subject skipping, dual enrollment, and early matriculation.
- Parent, counselor, and teacher education included with an attention to social and emotional needs.
- Multiple strategies used to assess student performance. Examples include standardized and criterion-referenced achievement tests, questionnaires, checklists, observation scales, interviews, and performance-based measures.
- All components of the program periodically reviewed by individuals knowledgeable about gifted learners and who have competence in the evaluation process. The results are used for continuing program development.[9]

The greatest service a school can provide is to demand that students think critically, produce high-quality products, and tackle material of significant depth and difficulty. Self-esteem is acquired through meeting and conquering a worthwhile challenge. Self-efficacy is earned through mastering difficult content. That confidence in one's own competence and independence forms the foundation for a craving for new academic challenge. Strong gifted education is what can unleash this power in a productive direction. Without it, a gifted student can systematically be taught to underachieve through being awarded good grades for high performance on work beneath capability and can lose the opportunity to develop advanced academic skills that will be necessary in college.

TEACHER PREPARATION

This type of education requires specialized training for those who write and those who deliver the curriculum for these students. We recognize that teachers who teach children with emotional or cognitive disabilities require special training to learn how to modify content, level, and pace of instruction. Teachers of those at the other end of the learning spectrum must also gain an understanding of gifted children, their characteristics, and their needs to effectively teach these students. Most states have a teacher license or endorsement for teachers of the gifted.

Teachers must have knowledge of curriculum writing for the gifted in order to develop what will undoubtedly be different from the traditional or adopted text. Teachers require professional development in how to compact curriculum and how to develop critical, creative, and higher-level thinking. Teachers need assistance with finding materials that can be used off-level to instruct and to assess. Teachers need to differentiate within their gifted classes in order to simultaneously accommodate those with differing needs and differing abilities. Some who have never taught such children think such an experience must certainly be easy, the students well-behaved, and the rewards unending. Indeed, teaching bright students can be wonderful and rewarding, but it requires passion, experience, knowledge, special training, and energy to challenge these learners to develop their potential. Parents and others who are investigating programs for the gifted must pay special attention to the curriculum and the training of faculty to be sure that the program is truly designed to develop higher-order thinking and is not just more work, not just acceleration, not just random unrelated experiences, or not just enrichment activities.

AFFECTIVE ISSUES

One of the greatest benefits of special schools and programs for the gifted is in the social and emotional realm. Because a child has advanced cognitive ability, he or she is likely to have some interests that are different from those of others of the same age. He or she may enjoy reading at a younger age, have a longer attention span, have a more advanced vocabulary, and be able to work more complex puzzles or play chess with greater sophistication than others of the same age. These abilities may result in having friends who are older or, in some cases, friends who are younger and can be directed in made-up games. Much is written about the greater likelihood of people with high ability to be introverted and to have greater intensity and perhaps greater sensitivity than those with more typical cognitive abilities. These differences can also result in a greater likelihood of conflict for the gifted child. Society does not deal well with being different, and the questions or comments from others about being different may elicit the question from the gifted child as to whether it is "OK" to be who he or she is. While these comments may not be intended to be pejorative ("My, that's a big word for such a little girl!") a message is sent that the child is different. When a child always knows the answer, always gets a high grade, always finishes early and easily, the child soon notices that not everyone has a similar experience. Our society is anti-intellectual, and the messages of lack of acceptance begin early. There is nothing wrong with the gifted child, but a constant reminder of being different, coupled with a lack of academic challenge, can soon make school an unpleasant place to be.

The situation may intensify in middle school. The adolescent longs to be a part of the gang, to be just like everyone else, to fit in, to belong, to be "normal." Couple the greater sensitivity of the gifted with the feelings of difference and the emotional time of early adolescence, and it underscores the importance of their being together in an appropriate academic environment. When gifted kids are together in school, their academic needs are met, and they can find others to whom they feel similar intellectually, socially, and emotionally. Instead of being forced to choose between achieving and belonging, adolescent gifted students can do both when in a school designed to meet their intellectual needs.

DEVELOPMENT OF SELF-REGULATORY BEHAVIORS

Another major benefit and purpose of grouping gifted students in a special program is to teach them study and time management skills. When in a program designed for learners who require multiple repetitions to learn something new, the gifted learner needs to do little to earn high grades. The gifted child can partially listen to the teacher explain or can skim new material or complete the homework correctly on the bus ride to school and gain high marks and high praise for little or no effort. When others are learning note-taking strategies or outlining or making vocabulary cards in order to study for a test, the gifted child is receiving a good grade without using those techniques. For many high-ability people, the need to actually study to learn new material was not required until late high school, college, or even graduate school, when the time for learning study skills was long past. If gifted children grow up thinking that if one is smart one does not need to study, then, when the wall is inevitably encountered, they may conclude that they must not be smart after all. At that time, the flailing for strategy and the loss of confidence can be very destructive at that time. Gifted students who have successfully mastered organization and time management, however, can conquer high school and college with confidence and success. These are the students who will fill the advanced and innovative positions needed in a globally competitive market; their talent must be developed.

SECONDARY OPTIONS

By the time students reach high school and college, there is usually some choice available in coursework so that gifted students can self-select into more advanced courses. Dual enrollment at a local college with the student earning credit for both the high school and college should be explored. Credit by examination, instead of required "seat time," should be requested. Early graduation can gain a gifted student an opportunity to get started early on the long road of college and graduate or professional school. Advanced Placement or International Baccalaureate programs are rigorous and will allow a student to earn advanced standing when entering most colleges. Distance-learning options are usually available for advanced high school students. These are all options that are frequently found in the local environment. However, depending upon the size, location, and resources of the local environment, courses that are advanced enough may not be available.

State public residential high schools for gifted students are available in fourteen states at the time of this writing, and they are able to provide rigorous programming for students, many of whom are from rural areas with limited advanced options. One example is the Indiana Academy for Math, Science, and the Humanities. Some universities also have full-time programs specifically for students who are younger than is typical, and they may provide some additional support or separate housing to assist younger students in the college environment. While there is no one comprehensive source for up-to-date information about particular schools for the gifted, the Davidson Institute's site lists state policies for gifted education; Hoagies Gifted webpage has a list of links to schools for the gifted; and the National Association for Gifted Children website has links to state affiliate chapters that can provide some guidance.[10]

Summer programs for the gifted have been great resources for students. Regional talent searches deserve special mention as they have proved to be the connection for gifted students to each other and to quality programming for those like themselves. These programs began with the Johns Hopkins Study for Mathematically Precocious Youth in the 1970s and have expanded to Northwestern, Duke, Iowa State, and Denver universities. Program goals include finding advanced ability, usually through making above-grade-level testing available to elementary and middle school students, and then providing information and opportunities to those students. Students typically take tests such as the SAT or ACT in seventh or eighth grade in order to demonstrate their level of curricular readiness.

CONCLUSION

Parents can work with the local school principal, superintendent, school board, state agency, and state legislators to advocate for the creation of appropriate services not only for their particular child but for all those who have advanced academic needs. If parents never tell policy makers of the needs that were not met, the schools and the governing bodies may never recognize the need to provide something different. When public schools do not provide appropriate options for gifted students, parents must investigate other possibilities, including independent school options, and seek their own solutions. While some families will have the means to seek nonpublic alternatives, including home schooling, all children should have the right to an appropriate education according to their needs. Schools and programs for the gifted are extremely beneficial for gifted learners, filling a need that cannot be met within the regular school program.

NOTES

1. F. X. Archambault Jr., K. L. Westberg, S. W. Brown, B. W. Hallmark, C. L. Emmons, and W. Zhang, *Regular Classroom Practices with Gifted Students: Results of a National Survey of Classroom Teachers*, Research Monograph 93102 (Storrs, Conn.: National Research Center on the Gifted and Talented, University of Connecticut, 1993); K. L. Westburg and M. E. Daoust, "The Results of the Replication of the Classroom Practices Survey Replication in Two States," *National Research Center on the Gifted and Talented Newsletter*, Fall 2003, www.gifted.ucon.edu.nrcgt.html.

2. Nicholas Colangelo, Susan G. Assouline, and Miraca U. M. Gross, *A Nation Deceived: How Schools Hold Back America's Brightest Students*, Templeton National Report on Acceleration (Iowa City: University of Iowa, 2004), 2:1, http://nationdeceived.org.

3. Sally Reis and Jeanne Purcell, "An Analysis of Content Elimination Strategies Used by Elementary Classroom Teachers in the Curriculum Compacting Process," *Journal for the Education of the Gifted* 16, no. 2 (1993): 147–70.

4. G. D. Schack and A. J. Starko, "Identification of Gifted Students: An Analysis of Criteria Preferred by Preservice Teachers, Classroom Teachers, and Teachers of the Gifted," *Journal for the Education of the Gifted* 13, no. 4 (1990): 346–63; Jean S. Peterson and Leslie Margolin, "Naming Gifted Children: An Example of Unintended 'Reproduction,'" *Journal for the Education of the Gifted* 21, no. 1 (1997): 82–100.

5. K. B. Rogers, *Re-forming of Gifted Education: Matching the Program with the Child* (Scottsdale, Ariz.: Great Potential Press, 2002); J. A. Kulik, *An Analysis of the Research on Ability Grouping: Historical and Contemporary Perspectives*, RBDM 9204 (Storrs, Conn.: National Research Center on the Gifted and Talented, University of Connecticut, 1992); C. L. Tieso, *The Effects of Grouping and Curricular Practices on Intermediate Students' Math Achievement*, Research Monograph 02154 (Storrs, Conn.: National Research Center on the Gifted and Talented, University of Connecticut, 2002);. C. Tieso, "Ability Grouping Is Not Just Tracking Anymore," *Roeper Review* 26, no. 1 (2003): 29–36; Colangelo, Assouline, and Gross, *Nation Deceived*.

6. Colangelo, Assouline, and Gross, *Nation Deceived*, 1:11.

7. George Wimberly and Richard Noeth, *College Readiness Begins in Middle School*, ACT Policy Report, 2005, www.act.org/research/policy/index.html.

8. Thomas Toch, "Measure for Measure," *Washington Monthly* 37, nos. 10–11 (October–November 2005): 29.

9. National Association for Gifted Children, *NAGC Pre-K–Grade 12 Gifted Program Standards* (Washington, D.C.: National Association for Gifted Children, 1998).

10. Davidson Institute, www.geniusdenied.com; Hoagies Gifted, www.hoagies gifted.org; National Association for Gifted Children, www.nagc.org.

FURTHER READING

Cross, Tracy. *On the Social and Emotional Lives of Gifted Children: Issues and Factors in Their Psychological Development.* 2nd ed. Waco, Tex: Prufrock, 2004.

Rogers, K. B., *A Menu of Options for Grouping Gifted Students.* Waco, Tex.: Prufrock, 2006.

Sanders, W. L., and S. P. Horn, "Research Findings from the Tennessee Value-Added Assessment System (TVAAS) Database: Implications for Educational Evaluation and Research." *Journal of Personnel Evaluation in Education* 12, no. 3 (1998): 247–56.

Van Tassel Baska, Joyce, and Tamra Stambaugh. *Comprehensive Curriculum for Gifted Learners.* 3rd ed. Boston: Pearson, 2006.

Webb, J. T., J. L. Gore, E. R. Amend, and A. R. DeVries. *A Parent's Guide to Gifted Children.* Scottsdale, Ariz.: Great Potential Press, 2007.

Westburg, K. L., D. E. Burns, E. J. Gubbins, S. M. Reis, S. Park, and L. R. Maxfield, "Professional Development Practices in Gifted Education: Results of a National Survey." *National Research Center on the Gifted and Talented Newsletter*, Spring 1998, 3–4.

14

Home Schooling

Merrill Hall

In the early years of America, home schooling—that is, the teaching of one-self at home or being taught by someone else at home—was perhaps the first and most common form of childhood education. Long after Benjamin Franklin established the first private academy in Philadelphia in 1751, if children, especially the children of the common folk, were to be educated, it often happened at home. If the families were wealthier, tutors might be brought into the home.

Famous home-schooled children include the likes of George Washington, John Quincy Adams, Abraham Lincoln, Thomas Edison, Robert E. Lee, Booker T. Washington, Mark Twain, Andrew Carnegie, Woodrow Wilson, Franklin Delano Roosevelt, and Margaret Mead. Thousands of less famous people, both boys and girls, were taught at home as well, especially before public schools blanketed the land and schooling was made compulsory in the late nineteenth century.

I am not suggesting that home schooling in the early years of our country and home schooling today are the same. We have, however, been conditioned over the years to think that learning can only happen in schools and in classrooms led by certified teachers, and that learning beyond the schoolroom venue is somehow impossible or unnatural. It is not. Many would argue that it is the other way around.

As late as the first half of the twentieth century, public schools did not generally assume responsibility for the education of ill or handicapped children. Some of these children had to be educated at home. It was not until 1975 that Public Law 94-142, known as the Education for All Act, provided some assurance that these children would receive a formal education. Even then, some of these children were taught at home, either by their parents or by the school systems that were required to take on that responsibility. Local school systems sometimes sent teachers into the homes.

In the late nineteenth century and first part of the twentieth, American missionary families living in remote parts of the world taught their children in their temporary homes in foreign countries, most frequently in Africa, South America, and Asia. Itinerant preachers in the United States often taught their own children as they traveled from church to church, bringing religious teachings to remote places in the United States. Some, no doubt, still do.

In recent times, children in families on the move, Olympic athletes, children in the entertainment business, and children living on remote farms where school buses did not travel or where the ride to a school was simply too far, needed to be educated outside of school. The children of families who went overseas after the two great wars, often to participate in the occupation or the rebuilding processes, needed to be educated, too. In many of these places international schools did not yet exist, and where they did exist, they were often fully enrolled. These students were taught at their home away from home. After a year or two they returned to their schools in America.

For all of these children, schooling at home, usually by the mother, was not only an option but a necessity. Most often, the sources of the education received were derived from what parents had learned as children and thought their children should know, and the lessons learned and taught by those who had gone before. Missionaries, some of whom wrote books about their experiences, were often the best sources for how to educate a child at home. Early missionary writers such as Charlotte Mason and Susan Shaeffer McCauley gave sage advice to parents who found it necessary to educate their children at home, whether the home was in America or abroad. One school in Baltimore was distributing its own courses for home schooling as early as 1907.

THE RECENT PHENOMENON OF HOME SCHOOLING

While home schooling as we know it grew in numbers, albeit slowly, throughout the early twentieth century, it was not until the 1980s, that the numbers accelerated. Coincidentally, in 1983 the National Commission on Excellence in Education published *A Nation at Risk*, informing anyone who cared to read it what many Americans already knew: that children in the United States were receiving, in general, a very weak education. The report focused on high school education but was instigated in large part by "the widespread public perception that something is seriously remiss in our educational system."[1]

Slightly prior to *A Nation at Risk*'s publication, a grassroots movement had begun in reaction to many of the inherent facets of American public ed-

ucation: large class sizes, relatively poor control of student behavior, and secular points of view, the latter being by far the most influential factor. In the
opinion of some, American society had slowly been moving away from
church, away from neighborhood schools, and away from what many called
family values. American schools are a reflection of American society, and a
small but vocal minority of parents did not like what they saw. Raymond
Moore, a psychologist, teacher, and former minister, and Dorothy Moore
published *Home Grown Kids*, and a year later, *Home-Spun Schools*, citing the
examples of many parents who were already successfully home schooling their
children.[2] Moore and Moore's writings appealed particularly to families who
sought a religious emphasis for their children's education.

In the 1960s, John Holt, a teacher in the Boston area, put a secular twist
on home schooling. He took issue with the way children were taught in
schools in his first book, *How Children Fail*. His thesis was that public schools
and their teachers were failing children, especially those children who tended
to do less well in school. He accused the schools of being insensitive, impa-
tient, inefficient, and dishonest. His third book, published in 1969, was titled,
The Underachieving School. He then wrote a series of books in the 1970s, all
of which moved toward the solution of "unschooling"—that is, educating
children without the traditional school, in the home or in groups designed for
this purpose. His final book, *Teach Your Own: A Hopeful Path for Education*,
was published in 1981 and revised in 2003 as *Teach Your Own: The John Holt
Book of Homeschooling*, with Patrick Farenga.[3]

In the late 1970s and early 1980s the number of children being schooled at
home was between 10,000 and 15,000. By 1988 that number had grown to between 150,000 and 300,000, and to between 250,000 to 350,000 in 1990.[4] Current estimates, as of 2004, range from 800,000 to 2.1 million children being
home-schooled in the United States, depending on which sources are consulted.

POLITICAL AND LEGAL CONSIDERATIONS

Until the early 1980s, not a great deal of attention was paid to home schooling. Although John Holt had attracted some attention with his books on unschooling and his encouragement of alternative teaching strategies and paths,
numbers were still small and the economic impact of children not enrolled in
school was minor. As the number of home-schoolers began to grow, however,
fueled largely by parents who wished a more religious orientation for their
children's education, some local school districts began to be concerned about
the teaching and monitoring being afforded to home-schooled children.
School officials were also increasingly concerned about the monies lost due to

lack of enrollments. In many cases, the states sent money to local school jurisdictions based on the number of enrollments. Lower enrollments meant lower income for the local school district.

Some of these districts attempted to exert authority in the form of home inspections and examinations of educational records. Some districts wanted to inspect and/or approve the family's educational plan, the textbooks used, and the daily lesson plans. Some districts wanted to insist that all home-school teachers be certified teachers. Some jurisdictions used truancy laws to bring parents of home-schooled children to court.

In *Home-Spun Schools*, Moore and Moore detail a number of state court cases in the 1970s and 1980s that put the home schooling of children for religious reasons on a firm footing.[5] In 1972 in *Wisconsin v. Yoder*, the Supreme Court supported a parent's right to have some significant say about his or her child's education. The Court upheld the right of an Amish family to refuse to send its children to the local public school on religious grounds, citing the Free Exercise Clause of the First Amendment. Still, in 1980, home schooling was illegal in thirty states.[6]

In 1985, a group of Texas families filed a class action suit against Texas school districts as home-schooling families were beginning to come under pressure from the Texas Education Agency (TEA). Texas state law required children to be educated in a public, private, or parochial school. The TEA had declared that educating a child at home could not possibly be an acceptable substitute for in-school instruction. Local districts began to prosecute home-school families for truancy violations. The families sought a declaratory judgment from the court that home schooling did, in fact, meet the statutory definition of a private or nonpublic school. The court found in favor of the families, as did the Texas Court of Appeals, and as did the Texas Supreme Court in 1994. Texas, once considered a state hostile to home schooling, is now considered to be home-schooling-friendly. This case took more than nine years from its beginning to its final resolution.

Still, truancy cases against home-schooling families continued. Growing numbers of parents believed strongly that the state had little or no responsibility or role in their children's education. These parents struggled against the state's assumed authority. They formed associations to help publicize their struggle and to lobby their elected officials. By the late 1980s, almost every state contained at least one home-school organization that hosted meetings and curriculum fairs, provided information and the path to legal advice, and shaped the communication between families and elected officials. These organizations became a powerful lobby. By 1993, home schooling was legal in all fifty states,[7] though some states do continue to monitor attendance, lessons, and test scores of home-schoolers.

THE PROFILE

In 1999, half of those parents participating in the National Household Education Survey Program (NHES) indicated that "giving the child a better education" was one reason for choosing home schooling. "Religious reasons" was given by 38.4 percent of the responders. "Poor learning environment at school" was given by 26 percent of the responders. Lesser percentages gave a host of other reasons.[8]

According to the same survey, the typical home-schooled child tends to be a white, non-Hispanic male or female child, in a family of two or more children, and often more than two children. This is not to say that home-schoolers are not of all races, nationalities, and religions. They are.

A large percentage of home-schooled children live in two parent homes (80 percent) where only one parent is employed outside the home (52 percent). For non-home-schooled children, these two percentages were 66 percent and 19 percent, respectively, in this survey. Because in many home-schooling families only one parent is involved in the labor force, and perhaps for other reasons as well, 64 percent of home-schooling family incomes were under $50,000 annually, which is almost identical to non-home-schooling family incomes, in this survey.

In this survey, one category in which a significant difference between home-schooling families and non-home-schooling families was observed was parents' highest educational attainment. Almost half of home-schooling parents had attained a bachelor's degree or higher, while only 33 percent of non-home-schooling parents had. Only 19 percent of home-schooling parents had not completed any schooling beyond high school, while 37 percent of non-home-schooling parents had not completed any schooling beyond high school.

ACADEMICS AND ACHIEVEMENT

A report published in 1995 stated: "Virtually all the available data show that the group of home-schooled children who are tested is above average."[9] The qualification to note here is "who are tested," because not all have been or will be tested, and not all states require annual testing. One must consider which home-schooled children have, over time, come forth to be tested. One must also read the original studies before drawing conclusions. Nevertheless, as of 1999, some populations of home-schoolers were testing above average, and, from my personal experience, I have no doubt that this is generally true.

SOCIALIZATION

The first comment of most persons unfamiliar with home schooling usually relates to socialization of the student. How will home-schooled children learn to get along with others if they do not go to school? How will they learn to understand people who are different from them if they do not encounter them at school? How will they learn manners and poise? How will they learn to handle themselves in social situations?

In my experience, the socialization of home-schoolers beyond the immediate family generally takes place after school and during weekends, at church, in scout groups, in choirs, on outings with other home-schoolers, and in neighborhood play. Home-schooled children associate with other children of all ages, not just with those in their age group (grade) at school. They associate with adults much more than children who go to school do. My impression is that they suffer much less peer pressure than non-home-schooled children do.

ADVANTAGES OF HOME SCHOOLING

In 1980, there were just a handful of curriculum providers and advice givers. Now there are thousands: from the large national publishers to the mom-and-pop shops where citizenship tapes are produced and later sold individually at annual, statewide curriculum fairs and educational sessions. Subscriptions to "how to do it" magazines are also available.

Consider that home schooling takes much less time than regular school. Those forty-five minute academic periods in school can be shrunk to twenty or thirty minutes at home. The entire school day can be completed in two and one-half to four and one-half hours. Consider that in a shorter time frame, the home-schooled student will have answered every question in every lesson. This concentration is a critical point. In my opinion, and in the opinion of others who have studied home schooling, the one-on-one nature of the instruction makes a great difference in the quality of the educational experience. Home schooling is akin to being in a classroom but being the only student, held responsible for every answer for every problem and for producing the only composition to be read and graded by the teacher. In some classroom settings, a student could go for days without answering a question or participating in a discussion.

On the other hand, in a home-school setting, reading class can last two hours. Any subject—science, history, math—can last two hours. When the student is interested and on fire with excitement and curiosity, there is no need to stop for recess, or lunch, or even the next class. When the space shuttle is lifting off or the president's inauguration is on television, it is possible to watch the historical moment and have conversations about it, too. Students may also experience the unexpected joy of seeing kittens being born and catch up on schoolwork the next day.

A FINAL WORD

As it always has, home schooling continues to evolve today. States and parents are finding ways to compromise. Home-schooled children find themselves attending school field trips and availing themselves of other school services. Parents are finding ways to have their taxes cover some of the cost of their children's home-school experience. Some children routinely alternate between school and home school, perhaps while traveling. Home-school groups are more common and more accepted than in the past. Technology is improving both instruction and management. Home-schooled students are routinely admitted to mainstream colleges and universities. Home schooling has come out of the cabin and has outlasted the one-room schoolhouse, and even the magnet school.

NOTES

1. United States National Commission on Excellence in Education, *A Nation at Risk: The Imperative for Educational Reform*, A Report to the Nation and the Secretary of Education (Washington, D.C.: National Commission on Excellence in Education, 1983), 1.
2. Raymond Moore and Dorothy Moore, *Home Grown Kids: A Practical Handbook for Teaching Your Children at Home* (Waco, Tex.: Word Books, 1981); Raymond Moore and Dorothy Moore, *Home-Spun Schools: Teaching Children at Home—What Parents Are Doing and How They Are Doing It* (Waco, Tex.: Word Books, 1982).
3. John Holt, *How Children Fail* (New York: Pitman, 1964); John Holt, *The Underachieving School* (New York: Pitman, 1969); John Holt, *Teach Your Own: A Hopeful Path for Education* (New York: Delacorte Press/Seymour Lawrence, 1981); John Holt and Patrick Farenga, *Teach Your Own: The John Holt Book of Homeschooling* (Cambridge, Mass.: Perseus Publishing, 2003).
4. Patricia M. Lines, *Homeschoolers: Estimating Numbers and Growth* (Washington, D.C.: National Institute on Student Achievement, Curriculum, and Assessment, Office of Educational Research and Improvement, U.S. Department of Education, 1999), 1, online edition, www.ed.gov/offices/OERI/SAI/homeschool.

5. Moore and Moore, *Home-Spun Schools.*

6. Patrick Basham, "Home Schooling: From the Extreme to the Mainstream," *Public Policy Sources*, no. 51 (2001), http://www.fraserinstitute.ca/admin/books/files/homeschool.pdf.

7. Ibid.

8. Stacey Bielick, Kathryn Chandler, and Stephen P. Broughman, *Homeschooling in the United States* (Washington, D.C.: National Center for Education Statistics, 2001), 10–11. Since parents could respond in more than one way, the total is greater than 100 percent. Data in the paragraphs that follow are also from this survey. A number of other surveys have been published, and results have on occasion differed. I have given here the results of a survey that appears to me to reflect the reality that I know after over two decades of studying home-schoolers and working in this field. Voluntary surveys of this population performed by various interest groups are fraught with difficulty. Home-schoolers are, by their nature, independent. Many do not consider their choices for education of their children to be the business of others, including state and federal governments. They feel little need to participate in surveys. The purpose of this essay is not to give an exhaustive review of the literature, but a reasonable picture of home schooling.

9. Patricia Lines, "Home Schooling," *ERIC Digest*, no. 95 (Eugene, Ore.: ERIC Clearinghouse on Educational Management, 1995), 4.

15

Schools for Students with Special Learning Needs

Marcie C. Roberts

$\mathcal{O}$ver the past ten to fifteen years, a wealth of information generated about learning development and delays has raised the public and parental awareness of the issues that are often at the root of why a child may struggle to learn. As a result, parents are more attentive to the "red flags" that may trigger a delay in language development and lead to problems in reading and writing skill development. Improvements in early identification have led to an increase in the diagnosis of disorders such as learning disabilities, autism, Asperger's syndrome, attention deficit/hyperactivity disorder (AD/HD), and other disabilities that can significantly affect the development and learning of students.

More than 3 million school-age children struggle to learn with a learning disability or related disorders that affect the acquisition of knowledge in various ways.[1] While many of these youngsters are of average or above intelligence, they may struggle significantly with learning in various areas. These disabilities affect the development of spoken and written language, the ability to listen, think, speak, read, write, spell, or do mathematical calculations. In addition, some disorders create issues in the area of social skill development, behavior, attention, self-monitoring, and self-management, all of which can significantly impact the learning process for the child affected by the disorder and in some cases affect the learning of their classmates as well. However, given the right educational program staffed with teachers who are knowledgeable about effective teaching practice for specialized student populations, children with these learning issues can manage academic demands, reach their full academic potential, and go on to be successful college students and productive, contributing adults.

Parents of children who struggle to learn often find that a traditional school setting does not adequately meet their child's needs. The search to identify an appropriate and effective educational program can be daunting, especially given the broad range of options and programs that exist to meet the various special learning needs of children. Finding the right fit can make all the difference in the world in fostering a student's academic potential and success.

A variety of schools across the United States provide programs for students with special learning needs. Many offer programs designed and staffed to meet very specific needs and, through a comprehensive admissions process, they determine the fit of the child to the program. The task for parents is to gain a full understanding of their child's learning needs and, to the best of their ability, to match the child's needs with an appropriate program.

The first step in determining an appropriate school for a child who struggles to learn or who has been diagnosed with a specific learning disability is to create a profile of the child's learning strengths and challenges. A thorough learning profile not only captures the child's academic strengths and areas of need but also includes information regarding the child's interests, activities, personality, and social style. Observations from the child's current teachers are useful, and comments from family members, friends, and other individuals may contribute meaningful information. In a learning profile, all this information is compiled so it can be analyzed to inform parents about what the child needs most in terms of a supportive educational program.

Other criteria for school selection may also be important. These include (among many others) whether the school is accredited, college preparatory, day or boarding, large or small in enrollment, or single gendered.[2] Information about the school can be obtained by visiting websites, reading brochures, and talking with the admissions officer and, if possible, also with parents of children who have attended various schools. With this information and the child's learning profile, parents can effectively explore and prescreen possible school choices.

Often parents find it useful to establish a set of questions that probe more deeply into the practice and philosophy of a school. Some of these questions may include:

- How does the school describe its educational philosophy?
- What is the school's philosophy and practice in the use of homework? How much time are children expected to spend on homework?
- What is the school's approach to behavior management?
- What kind of additional support or resources are available for the student? For the parents?

For those schools that specialize in serving youngsters with special learning needs, the questions can be expanded to include the following:

- What is the student to teacher ratio? (average size of classes?)
- What type of reading support is available? What type of support for writing is offered?
- Are there programs or activities to support social-emotional skill development?
- Are there programs or activities to support the development of self-monitoring and/or self-management skills?
- Are resources available to support the child's occupational therapy, physical therapy, or medical needs?

These kinds of questions will help parents discern the level of learning support provided by the school and whether it is likely to meet the individualized needs of their child.

The number of schools serving students with different learning needs has grown exponentially with the surge of knowledge and data in the last thirty years pertaining to identifying, diagnosing, and addressing these needs. Although some schools have been in existence for a long time, a great many were founded in the late 1970s and early 1980s to deliver the kind of instruction, particularly in reading, identified by researchers as having significant impact on improving reading and academic skills. Most schools serving the needs of students with learning disabilities design their programs specifically around the acquisition of language and reading skills and deliver reading instruction using a multisensory approach such as Orton Gillingham, Wilson Language System, or Lindamood-Bell Learning Processes. If a child has specific reading needs, parents may want to ask questions such as the following about the nature of the reading program:

- What is the ratio of students to reading teacher? (one to one? small groups?)
- How frequently is reading instruction offered? (two to three times per week? daily?)
- What are the credentials of teachers? Have they received special training in supporting students with special learning needs?

These and other questions can help parents gain a solid understanding of the school's philosophy and approach to educating special needs students.

Students with autism disorders have very specific needs, and parents may require professional assistance in determining the level of program appropriate for their child. This assistance can be provided by specialists in the field of autism and/or spectrum disorders, including pediatricians, psychologists, neuropsychologists, and other medical and/or health professionals. Understanding the level of support and program intensity is a priority issue for parents as they explore educational options. Students with autism spectrum disorders often function best in highly ordered and structured environments, especially those with well-defined social skill development and student behavior management programs that set out explicit academic and behavior expectations. With an accurate profile of the student and a program with the right supportive elements in place, some children with autism or Asperger's syndrome are very adept at handling general classroom settings with minimal specialized instruction. Some of these students may even be quite capable of meeting the demands of a rigorous academic program.

For many reasons, finding the right educational program for children with AD/HD may be the most difficult for parents. Children with AD/HD often have difficulty sustaining attention, listening to instruction, and organizing themselves or their materials. They may struggle with taking turns and controlling their temper or with managing verbal or physical impulsivity. AD/HD often occurs in combination with learning disabilities, and children with both disorders may experience both academic difficulties and social-emotional and behavioral problems. Similar to youngsters with disorders on the autism spectrum, these children benefit from schools offering highly structured settings, with clearly delineated rules and expectations that are consistently applied.

A new type of program supporting the special needs of students places emphasis on developing the child's executive functioning skills. Executive functioning is described as a set of mental processes that help connect past experience with present action.[3] People use executive functioning when performing activities such as planning, organizing, strategizing, and paying attention to and remembering details. Students who have problems with executive functioning have difficulty planning, organizing, and managing time, materials, and space. Executive functioning problems may also affect a student's ability to keep track of multiple tasks, evaluate ideas, reflect on work, finish work on time, ask for help, or sequence a task for completion.

Educational programs that stress executive functioning skill development focus first on assisting students to understand themselves as learners. Academic tasks are coupled with explicit instruction about the process required to complete the task as well as the strategies on which the student can draw for task completion. The environment of these schools is highly structured and supportive, providing students with the skills that will equip them to become self-reliant and resilient.

Finally, some schools provide intensive therapeutic and academic programs for youngsters with significant emotional and/or behavioral difficulties. Many of these children may also have learning disabilities, but the behavioral aspect of their disorder presents the major impact on learning. The behavioral and emotional issues require attention before effective remediation can be undertaken in the classroom.

These programs can be found in fairly standard private schools as well as in day treatment and residential schools. Some include outdoor education opportunities that wrap the physical demands and challenges around academic topics. Parents considering placement at a program designed to provide emotional and behavioral support are urged to screen the program for its possible fit to the child's needs. It is extremely important that they fully understand the nature of the academic and emotional support program, the way that students learning needs are met, and the level of supervision and adult support students will receive.

Most schools with programs designed to meet the special needs of children who struggle to learn have a fairly rigorous process for admissions. Selection is based on a child's fit to a program that is targeted to a specific learning need. The first step for parents is to schedule a visit to the school and a meeting with the admissions officer, or to attend an admissions information seminar for prospective families. The school visit or admissions seminar gives parents a chance to gain an in-depth view of the school's program and information beyond that presented in promotional materials or on the website. These opportunities also provide parents with a better understanding of the kinds of students that benefit from the program and the specialized methods of instruction and support, as well as a sense of the culture and philosophy embraced by the school.

Once parents have determined to pursue admission, the next step is to prepare the application, which often requires submission of student information and/or documentation. In addition to standard school information such as past report cards, schools may request the results of psychological or cognitive testing that has been conducted privately or by a school, pertinent medical information, teacher assessments or observations, parent assessments or observations, and if applicable, a copy of the child's 504 Plan or Individual Education Plan. In addition, many schools have a parent questionnaire or assessment that assists in the review of the child. This information is compiled and reviewed thoroughly through the admission officer's perspective of wanting to determine if the school can meet a particular child's needs.

Many schools require a day (and, in some cases, a several-day) visit for students whose profile appears to be a good fit. The visit generally includes an interview with the parents and the student. In many cases, the student is also asked to spend the day in a classroom. School administrators and teachers use the visit to observe the child and to assess his or her academic and interpersonal skill level. General comfort and interest in the program and school environment are also evaluated, though school personnel take into account that many children are uncomfortable in a new and different setting. During the school visit, the student may also be asked to take additional standardized or customized school-based assessments so that the admissions officer can further understand the child's academic strengths and areas of need.

With documentation about a child's learning, personal strengths, areas of need, and observations and assessments from the visit, the admissions officer is ready to make a decision regarding acceptance. If a child is not accepted into the program, it is perfectly appropriate for parents to seek clarification as to why the child was not accepted and, perhaps more important, use that information to understand from the school's point of view what type of program might provide the right level of support for their child.

For example, parents may view a specific school as attractive for their child with special needs because of the school's small class sizes, structured student management program, and staff who are well trained in supporting youngsters who struggle to learn. The school's website indicates that the program features individualized instruction and a strengths-based holistic approach and serves youngsters with language-based learning difficulties. The child, who is diagnosed with AD/HD and has some weaknesses in the area of auditory processing, is above average in intelligence, a good reader, and strong in math and science. The child struggles with maintaining attention, has problems staying on task, has had some difficulty with behavior issues, and often does not turn in homework. Given the description of the school, there is a distinct possibility that this program may not provide the level of support for the child's primary issues, which are related to AD/HD. Perhaps more important, this program may also not provide the level of academic rigor necessary to keep the child engaged and learning. Many students with AD/HD are capable of meeting the demands of an academically rigorous program and so may not be a good fit in schools designed to serve youngsters with language delays, especially since the pace of instruction has often been modified to ensure student understanding and acquisition of knowledge.

The process of identifying a school likely to deliver an appropriate and effective program that meets the needs of a child who struggles to learn can require a great degree of parents' time, attention, and tenacity. There are many resources available through the Internet, independent school associations, and various community-based organizations that support youngsters with learning disabilities and related disorders. Still, finding the right fit can be a long and frustrating task. It is important for parents to take the time to explore various programs and to seek to identify a school that has the capacity to meet the majority of the child's needs. And it is equally important for parents to maintain a sense of perspective throughout the process of the search, reminding themselves of the most important factors for their child at that particular time in his or her educational life. Children have often experienced a great deal of frustration and failure by the time parents reach the point of pursuing alternative educational options. Through the process of exploration and proper placement, the failure factor can be turned around to success, opening up potential for academic, social, and emotional growth and providing the child with a chance to thrive.

NOTES

1. National Center for Learning Disabilities, LD InfoZone, Learning Disabilities at a Glance, http://www.ncld.org/content/view/448/.

2. National Association of Independent Schools, Admissions and Financial Aid, Admissions Facts for Families, http://www.nais.org/admission/index.cfm?itemnumber=145880&sn.ItemNumber=142477.

3. National Center for Learning Disabilities, LD InfoZone, Specific LD Fact Sheets, Executive Function, http://www.ncld.org/content/view/447/391/.

· 16 ·

Specialty Arts High Schools

Mitzi Yates Lizárraga

$\mathcal{A}$ budding mezzo-soprano sings her voicemail recording, "Please, please, please send me audition information about your school." Audition day arrives. A dancer, with hair in a tight bun, stretches her limber muscles. A young writer stands quietly; his observations of the moment are for his next short story. A young actor confidently and loudly states, "Ever since I was born I wanted to attend this school." Chuckles confirm the thoughts of other prospective students with similar dreams. The atmosphere crackles with anticipation and anxiety. The audition area is jammed with anxious young aspiring artists and their families. Like peacocks strutting their feathers, a handful of current students, who only a year ago endured a similar entrance requirement, offer supportive glances and encouraging words to the prospective students. Parents, students, and staff begin the journey yet to unfold, in the lives of these young artists, scholars, and leaders.

The admission process for arts specialty high schools varies but typically includes an audition that requires significant preparation and so gives prospective students and their families an indication of the demands of arts-focused schools. Students present their audition materials before a panel of arts teachers from their field of interest. The number of years an applicant has studied his or her art form carries some weight but is not the determining factor, as the process is designed to prevent social and economic factors from limiting access. Audition panels seek students who are talented, passionate, and open to grasping new concepts of learning and receiving constructive feedback. Students should have a strong desire to work diligently and should possess an aching, burning desire to explore a life in the arts.

At the audition, prospective dance students may take a traditional ballet and a modern dance class, join an improvisation workshop, and present a self-choreographed dance. Writing students may be asked to submit a short personal essay along with additional writing samples (perhaps a narrative, short story, or poem), participate in a dialogue about literary works, and respond to a writing assignment. Music students may perform a selection that they have prepared, take a theory placement test, and sight-read. Theater students may perform a monologue from a play they have read and are expected to be knowledgeable about in response to questions from the audition panel. Visual arts students may present a portfolio of their works (a self-portrait, a still life, or a subject of their choosing using color) and be asked to draw and to write a short essay on a work of art on the day of the audition.

The audition carries the most weight in the admission process into arts specialty high schools. Following the audition, the admission team reviews a student's academic and arts portfolios, attendance records, letters of recommendation, and personal essay. Some arts high schools include an interview as part of the admission process to allow students and parents another opportunity to assess the capability and capacity for the school to meet the needs of the whole child as a student, aspiring artist, scholar, and leader.

New York's LaGuardia School of the Arts is credited as the first publicly funded arts high school in the United States to combine a rigorous arts training and an academic education for gifted and talented students. It began in 1936, when New York City Mayor Fiorello H. LaGuardia founded the High School of Music and Art, followed by the School of Performing Arts in 1948—a public school with an arts focus in dance, music, and theater. In 1961, the two schools merged in preparation for their move to a new facility at Lincoln Center, which was accomplished in 1984.[1]

Since the 1970s, the number of arts-focused high schools has significantly increased. These schools embrace a combined academic and conservatory curriculum with a focus on preprofessional arts training. They take many different forms. Magnet K–12 public schools include Duxberry Park Arts I.M.P.A.C.T. Elementary School in Columbus, Ohio, and La Villa Middle School of the Performing Arts in Jacksonville, Florida, as well as the Cook Elementary School of the Arts in Pensacola, Florida, which was created to meet federal desegregation requirements. Independent boarding schools include Walnut Hill School for the Arts in Natick, Massachusetts, Interlochen Arts Academy in Interlochen, Michigan, and Idyllwild Arts Academy in Idyllwild, California. The South Carolina Governor's School for the Arts and Humanities in Greenville, South Carolina, is a statewide residential boarding school. Arts-focused schools are sometimes housed within a school, such as the Coronado School of the Arts in Coronado, California. Other arts-focused schools are half-day schools: students attend their neighborhood school in the morning for their academic courses and receive their arts classes in the afternoon at places such as the New Orleans Center for the Creative Arts in

Louisiana, the Greater Hartford Academy of the Arts in Connecticut, or the Fine Arts Center Greenville County in South Carolina. Summer residential programs, created to appeal to highly talented students, include the Center for Creative Youth at Wesleyan University in Middletown, Connecticut, as well as statewide governor's schools such as the Kentucky Center Governor's School for the Arts in Lexington, Kentucky, or the Tennessee Governor's School for the Arts in Murfreesboro, Tennessee.

Regardless of geographic location, level, form, or structure, arts specialty schools share many similarities in mission, admissions processes, curricula, faculty and student body composition, and expectations. One of the schools I headed, the Duke Ellington School of the Arts in Washington, D.C., is a helpful case study.

The Ellington School began in 1968 with Workshops for Careers in the Arts, a summer and after-school program created by Peggy Cooper Cafritz and Mike Malone, who recognized that African American youths in Washington, D.C., in the late 1960s lacked opportunities for arts training. The workshop classes in theater, dance, music, and visual arts quickly became very popular. By 1974, Workshops for Careers in the Arts expanded into the Duke Ellington School of the Arts under the auspices of the District of Columbia Public Schools (DCPS). In September 2000, Duke Ellington School of the Arts formed a partnership with DCPS, the John F. Kennedy Center for the Performing Arts, the George Washington University, and the Ellington Fund for the purpose of managing and operating as an independent public school with some autonomy from DCPS. The goal was to implement innovative and challenging programs and arts residencies; to recruit, hire, and retain outstanding faculty; to build a financial base; and to improve the curriculum, teaching, and learning of highly talented students in the arts, regardless of their academic standing or prior arts training.[2]

Naming the District's only arts high school after one of America's most celebrated musicians was wise. Edward Kennedy Ellington, a native Washingtonian, was an extraordinary artist, composer, orchestral bandleader, and arranger. He also cared deeply about the plight of African Americans, and many of his compositions illuminated their social history. For example, his 1934 musical masterpiece entitled *Black, Brown and Beige* traces the plight of blacks from Africa to the Harlem of the first half of the twentieth century. Ellington was a leader who negotiated seventy-five years of dramatic social change for all Americans from his birth in 1899 to his death in 1974. Today, his story continues to inspire students and faculty in the Ellington School. Commitment, responsibility, empowerment, excellence, and dignity are qualities that are inculcated in the school environment, and Ellington's success as an artist, a lifelong learner, and a leader is held up before the school community.[3]

Since its inception, the Ellington School's vision has been to meet the needs of talented students who are considering careers in the arts by providing intensive arts instruction of the highest quality and a strong academic curriculum; to prepare students for postsecondary education and/or professional careers; and to serve as a vital community resource that contributes to the vitality of the arts community at the local, national, and international levels. The school's mission is to encourage each student to reach his or her intellectual and creative potential; to develop a personal sense of discipline, cooperation, and the hard work necessary to succeed in professional occupations; and to learn skills that will contribute to personal fulfillment and proficiency in art and academics.[4]

Teaching strategies are reinforced through professional development, constructive teacher evaluations, and an atmosphere that encourages cross-disciplinary openness in the classroom. Care and attention to students' well-being are essential. Faculty and students share passions for learning and exploring, leading to meaningful instruction and assignments and high levels of engagement. Faculty members encourage students to probe deeply, to develop an analytical approach, to reflect, and to consider the application of course work in other subjects. Students might, for example, investigate how romanticism is reflected in literature, architecture, paintings, choreography, music, and their own lives.

Successful arts schools value the artist as teacher and the teacher as artist; they cultivate communities of educators and artists who possess a breadth and depth in subject areas. Faculty remain active participants in the art world, which enhances, by example, the opportunity for students to become lifelong learners, readers, writers, and communicators. Arts schools benefit when faculty achieve recognition and awards such as National Board certification, Fulbright scholarships, National Endowment for Humanities Teacher grants, and summer fellowships or when they publish works, stage concerts, and present gallery exhibitions.

Ten-hour school days are not unusual in arts specialty high schools, for classroom studies, rehearsals, studio time, and performances. Many students travel from distant neighborhoods to attend arts specialty schools, adding to an already long day. Once home in the evening, additional classroom assignments must be completed.

Arts specialty high schools often attract students who feel out of place in traditional schools where sports and athletics are valued. Students often find their place and the support they need at arts schools with like-minded peers. Some behaviors that are discouraged at traditional schools may be viewed less harshly at arts specialty schools. For example, at arts schools doodling may be seen not as a distraction but rather as a starting point for learning about drawing, two-dimensional concepts, painting, sculpture, photography, computer graphics, art history, and the self-discipline required to be an artist.

Duke Ellington School of the Arts is particularly sensitive to the educational and cultural realities of the District of Columbia's demographics. Ellington students possess widely varying academic abilities, with reading and math skills ranging from fourth grade through post–high school. Household incomes range from below the poverty level to affluent. The racial and heritage background of Ellington students reflects its urban school district, with a majority of black and a growing number of Latino students. Caucasian students constitute a small percentage of Ellington's enrollment. All students benefit greatly and develop lifelong friendships. In the classroom or on stage, they experience an intimate exposure to a diverse world, a world that challenges basic assumptions and generalities about other people.

Regardless of the challenges, Ellington expects students to excel in all their academic and arts classes. Ellington's supportive and well-designed mentoring program provides the scaffolding for students to succeed. This program matches students with teachers, counselors, administrators, and staff and contributes to student achievement by providing a personalized and consistent educational framework. A successful program that positively affects the lives of students, it also offers career-oriented counseling and guidance, facilitates parent-school interaction, promotes and accelerates serious studies, supports and nurtures marginal students, identifies and assists students at-risk, and provides tutoring for students who need academic assistance. In general, arts specialty schools are demanding, and students benefit from supportive student programs. Self-affirmation, a sense of accomplishment, and shared values propel students to excel. Arts schools are personally empowering for students.

The intense curriculum, institutional expectations, and a more personal approach to learning force arts-focused students to demonstrate what they have mastered. Studio and course work guide students to develop technical skills, aesthetic appreciation, and an imaginative approach to interpreting the world. They encourage students to problem-solve, to think creatively and critically as independent learners, and to create and to express themselves—attributes valued throughout the world of work, regardless of profession. Mutual respect and goodwill are pervasive dynamics in teaching and learning in arts specialty schools. A close-knit community of students, parents, and collegial and caring faculty and administrators add to the success of students at arts high schools.

Student achievement extends beyond test scores and grade point averages. The notion of doing your best every day prevails. Students learn the importance of carrying their weight and making individual contributions, and they demonstrate what they have mastered and conduct self-assessments through ensemble projects and collaborations, particularly in their performing and visual arts classes, concerts, exhibitions, and publications—all effective assessment tools.

Students are recognized locally and nationally through the National Foundation for the Advancement in the Arts' National Recognition and Talent Search, Presidential Scholars in the Arts, National Scholastic Art Awards, All-State festivals, and other venues. They often receive numerous scholarships and acceptances into prestigious schools such as Juilliard, Harvard, the University of California, Cooper Union, New York University, Carnegie Mellon, Eastman School of Music, and Rhode Island School of Design.

Schools, too, win awards—Excellence Awards, Blue Ribbon School Awards, the Kennedy Center School of Distinction, Downbeat Magazine Awards, Grammy Awards, and President's Council on Arts and Humanities Recognition. International and national invitational performances may include performances at the White House, the presidential inauguration, the Edinburgh International Theater Festival, and Lincoln Center. These programs may facilitate student placement in Advanced Placement courses and can lead to internships with cultural institutions and networking opportunities with symphonies, ballet companies, and museums. Artist residencies in the schools and internships with professional artists and arts organizations enhance the learning experiences of the students and the teaching strategies of the faculty. Partnerships and collaborations with major cultural institutions such as the John F. Kennedy Center for the Performing Arts and the New England Conservatory supplement the curriculum. Arts schools are designed so that, upon graduation, students will continue their studies at the best universities, colleges, or conservatories or aspire to sing at the Metropolitan Opera, act on Broadway or in regional theater, be in a film or direct one, write a Pulitzer Prize–winning book, or exhibit at the Museum of Modern Art.

Heads of arts schools, in addition to providing educational leadership, are often charged with the responsibility to raise funds and to establish or grow an endowment in collaboration with volunteer boards or committees. But the primary purpose of arts school heads must be articulating and incorporating the vision, mission, and goals of the school as a starting point for all decisions, including hiring and evaluating faculty, developing and assessing the curriculum, and setting expectations for students and the school community, including parents and other constituents. The school head must ensure that the entire school environment is committed to caring for the intellect, the heart, and the physical well-being of students. Arts schools must adopt practices that recognize that students learn in a variety of ways—visually, kinesthetically, linearly, mathematically, and audibly. Cooperative learning, stimulating professional development workshops for staff, well-prepared teachers, authentic student assessment, and parental involvement contribute to the success of arts school students. Students, parents, teachers, and administrators must forge partnerships of open communication, mutual respect, honesty, clear expectations, and a common vision to pursue what is best for the child's success. The school environment must reflect a philosophy of action that affirms the diverse, global world that surrounds us and that taps into the passions and convictions of students.

Volunteer boards are critical to the success of arts specialty schools. They advocate and raise funds for, and raise the profile of, the school; they provide governance and policy guidance; and they serve as liaisons to elected or appointed community officials. Adequate financial resources are also essential. Longer school days, a dual curriculum, and dual faculty result in higher costs than in traditional schools. Tuition or the per pupil allocations do not fund expenses associated with student services, theater productions, recitals, publications, orchestras, art supplies, exhibitions, computer laboratories, and equipment for theater and film programs. The need for additional resources has prompted many arts schools to establish a development department or a private foundation to raise funds and market their programs.

Arts specialty schools prepare their students to pursue further studies and careers in the arts and to consider other professional options. With an entrance process that emphasizes self-learning, initiative, and preparedness, arts schools set high expectations. And they achieve impressive results, with overall high graduation rates; a high percentage of students attending colleges, universities, and conservatories; high daily student attendance rates; and low drop-out and suspension rates.[5] Arts schools have tapped into the essence of what keeps students in school—a nurturing, supportive environment that helps them fulfill their dreams.

Training in the arts connects learning to real work as evidenced by orchestral or ensemble performances, poetry readings, gallery exhibitions, and theater or dance productions. Arts schools create bridges between technology and the creative arts. They blur boundaries between the creative and technological skills required in filmmaking, publishing, software design, the visual and performing arts, architecture, advertising, and marketing. In so doing, they reveal career opportunities. The arts work force is expansive and will continue to grow throughout the twenty-first century. More, today's arts schools prepare a well-rounded work force for tomorrow. They cultivate attractive and transferable skills such as creative thinking, problem-solving, communication, emotional development, social development, global appreciation, and the ability to understand other cultural perspectives and ideas.

Arts specialty schools are an investment in young people and the future of society. They provide a supportive environment for aspiring artists to discover who they are capable of becoming. They empower young people to fully grow into their fullest capabilities as young leaders, to follow their passions, to be open to global ideas, and to uncover and explore questions intellectually and creatively.

NOTES

1. LaGuardia Arts website, www.laguardiahs.org.
2. *Duke Ellington School of the Arts Community Handbook*, 2005, 9.
3. Ibid., 10.
4. Ibid., 9.
5. Warren Hodge and Jackie Cornelius, *A Research Report: Patterns of Success among Network Arts Schools*, ed. Bennett Lentczner and Linda Whitesitt (Washington, D.C.: International Network of Performing and Visual Arts Schools, 2001), 4.

• 17 •

New Age Academy

An Experimental Village School Model

Gloria H. Cooper

> The educator believes in the worth and dignity of man. He recognizes the supreme importance of the pursuit of truth, devotion to excellence, and the nurture of democratic citizenship. He regards as essential to these goals the protection of freedom to learn and to teach and the guarantee of equal educational opportunity for all.
>
> —California Administrative Code,
> Title 5, Education, Sections 5480-5485

My personal commitment to the learning process has been lifelong. I was fortunate to experience the joy of learning early in life. Therefore, in 1976, when reports revealed that increasing numbers of American young people were estranged from this natural and transformative process, I felt compelled to find out why. I was a veteran of three public school systems, and yet I had not been aware of the pervasiveness of our children's struggle. The critical question was why. Why were our youth becoming less and less successful with this essential part of the human experience? Why were so many children having such difficulty developing intellectually? Why were they less willing to focus, pay attention, and do homework assignments? What changes in our schools contributed to their failure? Because I suspected the answers to these questions were beyond conventional educational practices, and because I was ashamed of the possible role I played in our children's struggle, I retired from teaching in the public schools and began independent research. What I discovered alarmed me.

The family, the child's first and primary learning environment, was in trouble. Parents, struggling to provide the basic needs for the family outside the home, had less time for family bonding: daycare facilities replaced their caretaking; fast foods replaced the family meals; television had usurped family values and replaced them with visions of violence and irresponsibility. At the same time, record numbers of our youth were living in poverty and experiencing the chaos of being shuffled between broken homes. It was clear that many school-age children were living harsh lives. No wonder that so many were struggling into adulthood emotionally, intellectually, and socially disabled.

The public school, the child's formal learning environment, was also in trouble. Falling test scores, rising truancy, and increased violence were some of the obvious indicators of failing schools. Teachers, society's key agents for change, were overworked and underpaid and often unsupported as they struggled with reluctant learners. Ours was a nation of children at risk.

Especially troubling to me was the plight of the middle school student. Apparently uninspired and bored, these young people seemed far from experiencing the intellectual joys of learning. Their tendency to engage in high-risk behaviors gave outward expression to their angst. Again the question was why. What drove adolescents to bouts of depression and self-destructive behavior? To understand, I had to become an active learner in the adolescent world. I had to learn about their issues directly from them in order to profile their needs. Thus I rented a garage space in Berkeley and, by 1981, had founded the New Age Academy. I was determined to construct a supportive, nongraded environment that facilitated a positive relationship to the learning process.

Recognizing nature's impact on the ability to perceive truth and beauty in the world, I used elements of the natural environment to design the school's physical space. The garage had two large skylights. I added lots of color, indoor trees, flowers, and a water fountain. I wanted my students to hear the sounds of running water, to experience the size and structure of trees and plants, and to see and appreciate the colors, shapes, and smells of flowers in the natural world. I added colorful art and geometric models, hoping to inspire wonder and to lead students toward new ways of knowing and being creative about the world around them. Having trained as a classical pianist, and understanding the power of nonverbal communicating and learning, I added classical music and created music compilations. I displayed art and artifacts from around the world. I collected wisdom stories from many cultures. I added personal computers (at the time new to education) and brain puzzles and games designed to stimulate thinking and problem-solving skills. The school's motto, "Let Each Day Be Your Masterpiece," was visible above the classrooms.

Those first efforts seemed to work immediately. After their initial queries—Is this a real school? Why do we have long tables and director's chairs instead of desks? Do we have to learn about computers? Are we going to have lockers?—students started to interact and explore the school. I noticed that they were coming earlier and staying longer. It was also clear that, although rewarding, middle school youth were extremely challenging. More than once, after a difficult day, I had to fortify my original determination.

As it turned out, I had to move beyond the indoor staging of trees, fountains, and experimental curricula and into the raw attitudes and emotions of adolescents in order to understand my students. They tested me—Did I harbor any personal perceptions that compromised their learning potential? What did I have to offer beyond the curriculum? Did I see them as empty vessels waiting to be filled? Was I trying to save them? Did I have emotional buttons they could push? I was asking students to focus, be responsible, and have respect. Was I doing the same? Was I really paying attention to them? Could I really be responsible with their truths? Did I believe that they were all lovable, smart, and worthy of my respect? To answer honestly, I had to be willing to explore new teaching strategies that would honor everyone's learning style.

"If learning were food," said one 13-year-old, "then I'm starving." Some of the students were literally starving, physically starving, for real food. Some were emotionally starving for positive, adult attention. Still others were starving for authentic social and spiritual experiences. First, because research showed a direct correlation between sugar and aggressive behavior, candy—their favorite food—was banned during school hours. Instead, students were encouraged to eat more fruit. Then, assisted by private donors and parents, we started a daily vitamin program. Twice a day, students chewed nutritional gummy bears. The results were so immediate that we added a breakfast program, a lunch program, and later cooking and nutrition classes to the curriculum.

Yet unresolved emotions continued to lurk beneath the surface and to interfere with the students' ability to learn. Conflicts happened almost daily, and they were impossible to ignore—"That's my seat!" "He called me a name." "She was talkin' about my momma." A simple word or comment could trigger a whole series of negative reactions. At such times, I stopped class and called a circle to process the incident with all the students. After establishing basic agreements for active listening—unconditional respect, no put-downs, what is said in the circle stays in the circle—we processed the conflict together. Although there were times when that process took up an entire day, I realized that the students' discussions were a rich source of insightful information. I also realized that my success as a teacher depended on their resolving their interpersonal problems.

One of the student's parents introduced me to a lawyer's mediation program, which I adapted to structure the school's conflict management classes.

Before each school year, students learned how to reframe and resolve their conflicts. Again, the results were dramatic. Giving students as well as teachers a structure within which to communicate their emotions has, I believe, been one of the keys to our school's early successes. Students who came to school in some degree of pain, anger, or fear began to learn how to take responsibility and discharge their emotions without hurting themselves or others. A successful learning environment, I concluded, is able to ground negative emotions. I was grateful for the lessons I was learning from my teachers—who were my students.

With each year, seemingly as demanding as the last, I recorded what I suspected were the attributes and qualities of our successes and noted those questions that still needed to be researched. My records, a hodgepodge of observations, geometries, and personal revelations, became a creative blend of the architect's blueprint and my interpretation of Euclid's mathematical method of proof. Working with a yearly theme, I was able to develop a flexible, integrated curriculum with the intent to honor and support all students' innate genius and innate ability to mature.

The students started to excel exponentially, both academically and socially. They were becoming increasingly focused, creative, and committed to the learning process. They were more active in cultural activities, such as plays, music and dance programs, and community service. They were being noticed in the educational community as more mature and advanced than other middle school students. Alums received local, national, and international awards for photography, animation, film, photo-journalism, linguistics, poetry, essay writing, scripts, musical compositions, dancing, singing, and achievements in technology. They were also recognized in the traditional fields of architecture, science, law, education, and business.

As the school grew, I grew. But still, even though the annual end-of-year student performance and portfolio demonstrated the school's success, each new year began with returning students having to refresh their connections along with new students who had fewer skills, shorter attention spans, and a lowered commitment to the learning process.

Why? Where do my students get their attitudes? The truth is that children are always learning: at home, watching television, on the playground, on the bus, in the supermarkets. The classroom is only part of a much larger environment that includes the community of businesses, government, industry, and media. Sadly, our society has been thoughtless and irresponsible. For too long we have dumped raw and unfiltered emotions into this larger environment. The media creates images that stimulate violence, sex, and fear and that block higher-order brain functions. Easily swayed to engage in high-risk behaviors, some adolescents lose their courage and become infected with the ills of society. Some never recover. The abusive attitudes and violent behavior of youth are evidence of our society's emotional, social, and intellectual immaturity.

I now recognize the power and importance of this larger, informal learning environment. Teachers and the school cannot turn the tide of at-risk students until we—a collective of families, communities, media, industry, and government—take responsibility for the ongoing learning experiences in that larger learning environment in which we are all teachers. Children cannot swallow enough pills to compensate for the lack of values in the total collective environment, nor can schools discipline sufficiently or develop curricula to make up for what is lacking. Respect, honor, responsibility, and compassion cannot be learned by rote. Children become what they behold. Every moment of every day, our youth are in an environment that shapes their thoughts, animates their words, and influences their actions.

Yes, it takes a village to protect, nourish, support, and educate a child. Our common ancestors, ever conscious of how beliefs, attitudes, and behaviors influenced the whole, knew that the village was more than sharing the land and common resources. The village, as a collective, took responsibility for maintaining a safe and supportive learning environment while nourishing each child with positive emotional, intellectual, and social-spiritual experiences. Village children became adults when their right relationship to themselves, the earth, their thoughts, and their actions were appropriately wedded. Villagers understood that by endowing each child with active qualities of love, the village—the collective—was enriched.

Yes, families must create safe home environments where children are loved unconditionally. Nurturing children with love and compassion fosters trust and self-worth, their keys to learning success. Yes, teachers and schools can respect all students, unconditionally, and schools can teach students to perceive without judgment and to think without boundaries, their keys to interpersonal peace and happiness. Society, however, must do its part. The media, industry, and government must also be held responsible for honoring our children for who they are and who they are becoming. In order to learn, children must be free of poverty, hunger, and war. They must be able to transform their intuitive expressions of beauty and truth in a tranquil environment. In a truly free society, unadulterated food, clean water, safe and affordable housing, access to health care, and a meaningful education are basic to life.

Today's educators also have a special responsibility. In this information age, freedom comes with an informed mind. Not only must we create high-quality learning environments in our schools; we must also instill new wisdom in the learning environments outside the classroom. We must help society liberate itself from belief systems that discriminate against social and intellectual potential. We must eliminate embarrassing educational labels that imprison children. We must also confront our old habits of exclusion and educate our-selves about all forms of social, class, and ethnic bias.

With truth in our stories and honesty in our reporting, we may end the nightmare reality in which children are trapped. Children need to develop in a context in which their intelligence can discover unity and wholeness in beauty and truth. For children to maintain their natural curiosity and wonder, they need to learn the language of love that emerges from the collective. Thus our relationship to each other is everything.

I propose that when society realigns with our historical, village principles and endows all young people with a learning environment in which they can only succeed, then we become truly educated, self-actualized, self-governing adults. Only then will we have peace in our homes, our schools, and our com-munities. Until then, we must continue to experiment in our schools and emancipate our thinking.

Ours is a union abundant with talent and ingenuity. We can afford to give each generation the means to share freely in the sweet fruits of liberty. To that end, may we, the educators of the twenty-first century, have the courage to do what we must do. From the timeless wisdom of Ralph Waldo Emerson: "Do not follow where the path may lead. Go, instead, where there is no path and leave a trail."

· 18 ·

International and Internationally Minded Schools

Anne-Marie Pierce

$\mathscr{F}$or several decades now, the word "international" has been fashionable. The white pages of the San Francisco telephone directory contain three full columns of listings beginning with "international"—from appliances to waterproofing! Similarly, many schools now use the word "international" as part of their name. But the word itself does not automatically make a school "international." In fact, some "international" schools signify British or American schools outside the home country that are often more "British" or "American" than their respective home counterpart.

WHAT IS AN INTERNATIONAL SCHOOL?

To be international, a school does not need to have the word "international" in its name. Nor does it require a multinational student body or faculty. Authentic international schools espouse an internationally minded philosophy that respects differences. International schools are deeply committed to diversity of all types. They can be defined as schools that deliver an international education in an atmosphere of respect for differences, preparing students for an interdependent world with the aim of promoting world peace. Idealism is at the heart of international education.

Not all international schools have a diverse student body, but those located in areas with a relatively homogeneous population make extra efforts to implement exchange programs, develop long-term partnerships with other schools abroad, establish e-connections with other internationally minded schools, organize study trips to other countries, and participate in programs such as Model U.N., Model O.A.S., Habitat for Humanity, Amigos de las

Americas, or others that promote understanding of international issues or offer opportunities for international service.

Many international schools have adopted an international curriculum, often the programs offered by the International Baccalaureate Organization (IBO), but such a curriculum is not a requirement. They link with schools in other countries, teach second languages seriously, or teach in several languages, thereby offering bilingual programs. International schools prepare students to be citizens of the world. They promote "intercultural literacy."[1]

THE FIRST INTERNATIONAL SCHOOL

Historically there has been an extensive network of American, British, French, or German schools abroad, but they tended to serve the needs of their expatriated citizens and delivered the curriculum of their home country. In the 1960s, several French-American and German-American schools began to be established in the United States. Students of other nationalities as well as American students attended these schools, and they continue to do so, but these are not necessarily international schools. They are rather national schools outside their own country.

Although a thorough history of international schools will usually mention the founding of several institutions beginning at the end of the nineteenth century, the International School of Geneva (ISG), created in 1924, is traditionally recognized as the first bona fide international school. It was founded by a group of parents working for the League of Nations and other international agencies to meet the needs of their children and those of other diplomatic families. The school's early handbooks contain the basis of international schools' mission everywhere, describing it as "an institution inculcating qualities of sympathy and understanding and a devotion to human service, to the end that those whom it may serve will realize the essential unity of all mankind."[2] At the time, no international curriculum existed; therefore ISG prepared its students for the various national exams of its participating students (A-levels, French Baccalaureate, Habitur, SATs, etc.). It was created as a multilingual school with an English track and a French track.

As ISG's population grew over the years, the need for an international diploma that would be recognized in universities in Europe and the United States became clear. Teachers from ISG joined educators from England and France and developed the basic framework for the International Baccalaureate Diploma to be implemented in the last two years of high school, under the impetus of Desmond Cole-Baker, then English section director at ISG, and Alec Peterson, director of Oxford's Department of Educational Studies.

The International Baccalaureate (IB) Diploma Program was launched in 1968 and has grown exponentially. It is now complemented by two curricular frameworks to cover all other grades from prekindergarten to tenth grade: the Primary Years Program for grades Pre-K–5 and the Middle Years Program for grades 6–10. To date, IBO programs are used in nearly two thousand schools in 125 countries, of which more than half are in the United States. These numbers are growing daily as more and more schools become authorized as "IB World Schools." It should be noted that in the United States 92 percent of these schools are public, while worldwide only 55 percent are state schools.[3] Although there are other international curricula, none are as widely used as the IBO programs. In 1999, Washington International School became the first school in the Western Hemisphere to be authorized for all three IBO programs.

The IBO was founded on the vision that a shared academic experience among students around the world would lead to greater tolerance and intercultural understanding. United World Colleges were the first schools to implement IB as the sole curriculum. There are currently twelve United World Colleges around the world. These college preparatory schools recruit students from all continents for grades 11–12, irrespective of their race, religion, politics, and ability to pay. Selected entirely on personal merit, students live in residential communities for two years. The first, Atlantic College, opened in Wales in 1962.[4]

The number of IBO-authorized schools has been growing at an annual rate of 10 to 20 percent worldwide, and particularly rapidly in the United States.[5] The first international school in the United States was the United Nations International School in New York founded in 1947. Since then, many international schools have been created throughout the country, including independent schools, religious schools, charter schools, and public magnet schools. It is important to understand that being an international school does not preclude any of the above classifications. Any school in agreement with the philosophy of international education may internationalize its program and become internationally minded in its practices. There is no obligation to implement the IBO programs to be considered an internationally minded school. These programs simply provide a proven, well-developed, convenient vehicle through which to implement a high-quality international education.

THE ADVANTAGES OF INTERNATIONAL EDUCATION AND IBO PROGRAMS

International education in general and the IBO programs in particular serve the needs of an increasingly large mobile population in the United States and abroad. Their attributes are particularly well-suited to the needs of the twenty-first century, as they:

- choose to emphasize process over content
- emphasize strong communication skills
- develop solid learning and higher-order thinking skills
- encourage students to become familiar with the world
- foster creativity, action, and service
- integrate various disciplines
- develop principled, caring, and compassionate thinkers
- strive to develop mastery in more than one language
- offer a balance between individual and team work

The IB Diploma has become widely recognized and respected in colleges and universities around the world as a demanding and rigorous study program. The most prestigious universities commonly grant a year or more of university credits to diploma recipients because the IBO guarantees consistent quality thanks to an externally moderated system of examinations and a rigorous authorization process for schools, above and beyond usual accreditations.

THE UNDERPINNING OF IBO PROGRAMS

The IBO mission statement affirms key concepts important to international schools around the world:

> The International Baccalaureate Organization aims to develop inquiring, knowledgeable and caring young people who help to create a better and more peaceful world through intercultural understanding and respect.
>
> ... [IBO] programs encourage students across the world to become active, compassionate and lifelong learners who understand that other people, with their differences, can also be right.[6]

The three IBO programs share a common philosophy and similar pedagogical principles. They are perfectly suited to the developmental level of the age groups they aim to serve. All offer a holistic underpinning within an inquiry-based approach. Their challenging curricula serve average as well as gifted students. To differing extents, all are multidisciplinary in their approach. All offer values-laden education independent of any specific religious denomination. All develop higher-order thinking skills and critical thinking. A service component is integral to all.

IB programs encourage exchanges and partnerships with schools in other countries as well as teachers' collaboration within each school. The primary and middle schools are student-centered, promote cross-disciplinary learning, and emphasize the acquisition of solid study skills. The Diploma Program distinguishes itself by its depth and breadth, requiring students to select six courses from various disciplines: math and computer science, experimental sciences, social sciences, the arts, and two languages, one at the native level.

In addition, a course in epistemology (theory of knowledge) helps students understand *how* we learn. The program also requires participation in extracurricular activity and a demonstrated substantial commitment to service. Finally, each student must complete a four thousand–word original research paper in a subject of his or her choice. To obtain the diploma, students must undergo a demanding series of externally moderated essay examinations with rigorous standards.[7]

THE FUTURE OF INTERNATIONAL EDUCATION

The ever-increasing pace of globalization fosters the growth of international schools. Since there are currently no comprehensive educational programs comparable to those offered by the IBO, it is therefore reasonable to assume that they will continue to grow in national and international schools all over the world.

However, IBO programs are expensive to implement. Consequently, the IBO has made a deep commitment to addressing the accessibility issue. Major initiatives are under way to offer these programs in third world and developing countries as well as inner-city and nonaffluent districts in the United States. The need to "internationalize" schools is widely recognized. To this end, the U.S. Department of Education instituted an International Education Week several years ago.

STUDENTS IN INTERNATIONAL SCHOOLS

Not surprisingly, international schools have continued to serve the families for whom they were first conceived: internationally mobile families in the diplomatic corps, multinational businesses, international agencies, and the press. They also often have been the choice of multicultural families. However, the majority of families currently choosing an international education are simply internationally minded families who want their children to be prepared for an interdependent world, capable of adapting to the rapid pace of change, comfortable in a variety of cultures, proficient in more than one language, and prepared to enter work environments that are increasingly multinational.

International school students are dedicated to an ethos of service and sustainability. They are highly aware of the interdependence of people everywhere. They are sensitive to and respectful of cultural differences. They have developed critical thinking, higher-order thinking skills, and solid study habits. They are comfortable with research and are eminently ready for college. IBO programs aim to develop internationally minded people who are striving to become inquirers, critical thinkers, communicators, and risk-takers and who also are expected to be principled, caring, knowledgeable, open-minded, well-balanced, and reflective.[8]

As many international schools are dual language schools or emphasize the acquisition of a second language at a high level of proficiency, they may not be suited to students with serious learning disabilities, particularly those with central auditory processing problems. By definition, international schools welcome a wide diversity of beliefs, religions, and cultures. Hence, families with a rigid belief system or religious fundamentalists would rarely choose an international school.

CONCLUSION

Speaking to the International Baccalaureate North America conference in 1999, Dr. George Walker, then director general–elect of the IBO, offered five objectives to an international education:

1. to celebrate diversity as desirable for improving the human condition
2. to promote understanding and respect for one's own and other's cultures
3. to encourage a knowledge of issues of global concern
4. to recognize the limitation of a humanist education
5. to share with others an understanding of the human condition."[9]

International schools everywhere strive to fulfill these objectives. Most schools could incorporate many of the elements that define an internationally minded education without undermining their own philosophical approach. In fact, many international school characteristics are shared with other types of schools; what distinguishes any school is the level of emphasis placed on any particular set of those characteristics. In the case of international schools, it is the ubiquity of a world lens toward peace that underpins its ethos.

NOTES

1. See Mark Heyward, "From International to Intercultural," *Journal of Research in International Education* 1, no. 1 (2002): 9–29. This article argues that "engagement with host culture," with the objective of achieving knowledge, understanding, and comfort in intercultural experiences, is necessary for becoming "interculturally literate" for a "globalized future."

2. International School of Geneva brochure, cited in Robert Sylvester, "Mapping International Education," *Journal of Research in International Education* 1, no. 1 (2002): 103.

3. International Baccalaureate Organization website, www.ibo.org.

4. Consult www.uwc.org for further information about United World Colleges.

5. For further information on the history of the IB Diploma, consult A. D. C. Peterson, *Schools across Frontiers: The Story of the International Baccalaureate and the United World Colleges* (Chicago, Ill.: Carus Publishing Company, 1987), the first history of the IB. The latest is Jay Mathews and Ian Hill, *SUPERtest: How the International Baccalaureate Can Strengthen Our Schools* (Chicago, Ill.: Carus Publishing Company, 2005). Mathews is the *Washington Post* education reporter, and Hill is deputy director general of the IBO.

6. See the IBO mission statement on the IBO website, http://www.ibo.org/mission/index.cfm.

7. Visit the IBO website, www.ibo.org.

8. See IBO Learner Profile at the IBO website, http://www.ibo.org/programmes/slideh.cfm.

9. George Walker, "To Educate the Nations," in *Reflections on an International Education* (Great Glemham, UK: John Catt Educational Publishers, 2002), 52. This compendium of speeches delivered by the IBO director general offers an excellent understanding of the most important considerations afforded by an international education.

19

Virtual Schools Are the Future

Lisa Snell

$\mathcal{A}$ recent *Christian Science Monitor* feature on virtual schools provides a good example of just how far virtual schooling has come. The article describes how the use of Skype, an Internet-based phone service, has enhanced the teaching of foreign languages online. Yu-Hsiu Lee, a doctoral student in the Language Education Department of Indiana University, Bloomington, explains that "anyone who wants to learn Chinese" can have "one-on-one instruction with a native speaker. Skype allows students to both see and hear the instructor on their computer screens." Unlike using a CD to learn a language, Lee says, Skype allows students to get instant feedback and to ask instructors specific questions.[1]

With such technological advances, more and more students are taking online classes. The 2007 Sloan Survey of Online Learning found that one-fifth of higher education students are now taking at least one class online.[2] While online learning and virtual schools are widely accepted in higher education, they are still in the very early stages of adoption in the K–12 public school sector. Yet these schools are growing at an annual rate of 25 percent.[3] The North American Council for Online Learning reports that there are forty-two statewide programs and more than 180 virtual charter schools across the nation.[4] Current estimates of elementary and secondary students taking virtual classes range from 500,000 to 1 million nationally, compared to a total public school enrollment of about 50 million.[5] Similarly, in a recent survey by the Sloan consortium, 63 percent of school districts reported one or more students enrolled in online courses.[6] A study released by Project Tomorrow reveals that 47 percent of high school students and 32 percent of middle and high school students are interested in taking courses online that are not offered at their schools.[7] All told, in the fall of 2006 (the last year for which statistics are available), 3.5 million students were taking classes online.[8] Virtual schools are used by both full-time students in online schools and in a supplementary blended role with traditional schools where virtual classes offer students a wider range of curriculum choices.

It may be something of a cliché to say that virtual schools offer the promise of a classroom without bells or walls. More significantly, virtual schooling represents an educational shift toward truly individualized learning. In my role as a board member of the California Virtual Academies (CAVA) in Los Angeles and San Diego and as a parent who has enrolled my own child in a virtual school, I have been fortunate to experience firsthand how these schools can offer students a high-quality individualized learning experience. In full disclosure, the CAVA are a group of nonprofit charter schools that contract with K12 Inc. for school management, online school, curriculum, and materials. It enrolls more than 5,200 California students.[9] In this essay I will discuss my personal observations of the virtual school experience as well as the national trends and controversies surrounding virtual schools.

THE ATTRIBUTES OF VIRTUAL SCHOOLS

Three unique aspects of the CAVA virtual schools have convinced me of the vast potential for virtual schooling. First, every child has an individualized learning plan. Each child in CAVA works on his or her individual skill level and moves through the curriculum based on assessment and mastery. Our virtual schools take a mastery approach to learning. Each child has mastered the content before moving to the next concept. Assessment is a regular part of each lesson and gives parents and teachers instant and continuous access to each child's strengths and deficits so that curriculum and instruction can be custom-tailored to fit each child's needs.

Second, I have seen how this individualized approach has helped special needs children. By truly focusing on the individual child and adapting the curriculum to the child's need, CAVA charter schools have actually moved children out of special education categories. In other words, we have seen a shrinking special education population as children master content and become proficient at grade level.

Finally, I have been impressed with the research and development that goes into the course development of CAVA's curriculum. Each course has a team of curriculum experts who carefully craft every aspect of the course design, and their care is evident. My child has been through a curriculum based on California's state standards in reading, math, science, and history in both a traditional public school and the CAVA virtual classroom. While my child's traditional public school experience has been positive and acceptable, there is no comparison to the depth and subject matter discussion available through the virtual course.

Every aspect of the CAVA course is designed to appeal to the child. My son loved the weekly science experiments in the first grade CAVA science curriculum. At his public school, there was rarely a hands-on experiment in science in the first grade. Similarly, he loved the immersion of history and the actual books on mummies and Greek mythology provided through the K12 Inc. materials.

This curriculum is designed by content specialists and based on the K–12 standards in California and Indiana, the highest in the nation. The courses are field-tested on K12 Inc. students to fine-tune them so that they are even more effective. Parents and students have a feedback loop with curriculum developers. When material is confusing, unclear, or contains an error, the curriculum can be instantly adapted to make it better based on the experience of real CAVA students. In addition, when significant historical changes affect course content, changes can be made without having to wait for the next textbook adoption cycle. For example, when Pluto was demoted from planet status, our science curriculum reflected that change immediately.

K12 Inc. is one of the fastest growing for-profit virtual operators, growing from serving 11,000 students in fiscal year 2005 to serving 27,000 in fiscal year 2007, for a growth rate of 35 percent.[10] It is a well-researched curriculum that uses both technology and traditional materials to teach students the core subjects of reading, math, history, science, music, and art. Its materials, according to the *Cleveland Plain Dealer*, allow students to "review books like *A Walk in the Deciduous Forest*, listen to the works of Beethoven, and look at paintings by Matisse. They work with phonics tiles, listen to expert storytellers read great literature, and see 3-D replicas of the geography they study in history."[11]

My positive experience is not unique. The demand for virtual schools continues to grow. For many parents, virtual schools offer middle ground between home schooling and a traditional public school. With virtual schooling, parents have more control over their child's education than they would if the child were in the public schools, but they do not have to design lesson plans, as they would for a home-schooled child. The child also benefits from the high-quality prepackaged curriculum.

High-quality virtual schools offer students a flexible, well-researched online curriculum that is accessible at all times and is not constrained by a physical building. Since virtual schools do not have high capital costs in terms of physical infrastructure, they can invest most of their resources in curriculum research and development and into the hiring of talented teachers. These schools have the potential to provide an array of new educational options to students offering almost complete flexibility to children best served by a custom-tailored curriculum. While any child may benefit from individualized learning, virtual classrooms are especially useful for students who are either far above or far below grade level, students with special needs, and students whose lifestyle or extracurricular activities do not fit within the confines of a traditional public school.

VIRTUAL SCHOOLS AND THE CHARTER SCHOOL MOVEMENT

The growth of full-time virtual public schools gained momentum through the charter school movement. Charter school laws offer flexibility and provide opportunities for innovation with school design. A 2002 report by Neal McCluskey, a former Center for Education Reform education policy analyst, explains how, in many ways, "cyber charter schools are the same as more traditional brick and mortar charters. They are independent public schools sponsored by local or state educational organizations. The charter issuing authority monitors their quality and integrity, but they are otherwise free of traditional bureaucratic and regulatory control." McCluskey argues that a "cyber charter school's success—and existence—is dependent on its meeting student achievement goals specified in its charter, and on effectively managing its financial and operational responsibilities."[12]

Virtual charter schools are often nonprofit institutions that contract with for-profit companies, such as K12 Inc. They embody the philosophy that every student should have an individualized education plan—whether at grade level, advanced, or special needs. The key advantage to virtual learning is that it utilizes an assessment-based approach to learning in which children have mastery of content before moving ahead to the next lesson.

THE GROWTH OF STATE-SPONSORED VIRTUAL SCHOOLS

Another important trend for virtual schools has been the growth of state virtual programs and the use of virtual schooling for supplemental education. According to the think tank Education Sector, state virtual schools are among the fastest growing programs in K–12 public education:

Twenty-eight states now have virtual school programs that enroll students statewide, up from five such programs in 1997. Last year, some 139,000 students enrolled in at least one course through a state virtual school. Two of the oldest and largest state online programs, in Utah and Florida, have both expanded by more than 50 percent over the past five years. If trends continue—if states continue to create virtual schools and recently created programs grow at even half the rate of the programs in Florida and Utah— we can expect a half-million students to enroll in state virtual schools in just a few years.[13]

Perhaps indicating that supplemental online courses will continue to become a normal part of the high school experience, Michigan recently began implementing a 2006 law that required every high school student to participate in an "online learning experience" as a requirement for graduation.

VIRTUAL SCHOOL CONTROVERSIES

The growth of virtual schools has led to both innovation and controversy. Critics question everything from virtual school funding to the suitability of parents serving as teachers. In addition, the home-schooling community has mixed feelings about state-sponsored virtual schools, believing they intrude on traditional home schooling.

The largest controversy surrounding virtual schools concerns their funding. Under many state laws set up to encourage competition, a district that loses a student to a school chartered by another district is mandated to make payments for the child's education. Online schools, freed from geographic boundaries, have entered the competition for students and the tax dollars that follow them. In other words, a virtual school could draw funds from multiple school districts within a state, even when those school districts have no oversight of how the online schools operate.

Many policy makers are convinced that virtual schools should operate at a much lower cost than traditional schools. Some states have explicitly mandated what percentage of virtual school funding must go to instruction. For example, in California 80 percent of student funding to a virtual school must be spent on student instruction. California law also mandates that at least 50 percent of resources go to salaries for certified teachers. These mandates do not take into account the research and development costs of a high-quality online curriculum or the cost that an online school may devote to materials. For example, the CAVA schools spend more than $800 on materials per student, compared with an average of $237 in traditional California schools.[14]

In most states, virtual schools are funded at a lower rate than traditional classrooms. In some states critics have objected to virtual schools because they drain resources from traditional schools. In 2007, Indiana lawmakers refused to fund virtual charter schools. The opponents' winning argument was that virtual schools are unproven and would have siphoned millions of dollars from traditional public schools.

Pennsylvania was one of the first states to grapple with the funding controversy. More than 100 of Pennsylvania's 501 school districts joined in lawsuits challenging the legitimacy of virtual charter schools. The suits argued that Pennsylvania's 1997 charter school law did not cover cyber schools. Claims that the legislature never intended to include Internet delivery of public education in this law are now resolved by the amendments to that law, which were included in Pennsylvania's budget legislation for 2002–2003. Previously, the responsibility to evaluate charter applications and monitor an established charter school lay with local school districts. In recognition of the unique structure of cyber charter schools and the challenges they pose to local school-district governance, Pennsylvania's new education law places the evaluation, approval, and oversight responsibilities for cyber schools with the state Department of Education. Under the new law, the Department of Education assesses annually whether each cyber school meets the goals within its charter. The state conducts a comprehensive evaluation before granting a five-year renewal of cyber schools and reviews the school's performance on the Pennsylvania System of School Assessment (PSSA) and other standardized tests every year.

To enhance educational accountability, Pennsylvania cyber charter school applications now must include a description of the school's proposed curriculum, showing how course work aligns with the state's academic standards and assessments; a description of the school's education delivery system, including technologies used and the amount of time students will spend online; a list of the materials and services, such as computers and Internet access, the school will provide to students; a description of the school's attendance policy and how it will be monitored; and a description of the school's special education services. In addition, the state of Pennsylvania will reimburse local school districts 30 percent of the total funding due to the charter school by the district, based on the number of students enrolled.[15] In 2007, the Pennsylvania Department of Education joined state legislators in calling for a single uniform funding rate for online charter schools across the state.[16]

There are also several controversies surrounding the home-schooling aspect of virtual schooling. The first surrounds parental qualifications to teach students at home using an online curriculum. In Wisconsin the Appeals Court recently heard oral arguments in a case in which the state's teachers union attempted to close down the Wisconsin Virtual Academy (WIVA). WIVA opponents argued that parents are "untrained, unqualified, and inexperienced" and thus incapable of teaching their children. Attorney Mike Dean, representing the intervening group of WIVA parents, was quick to point out to the court that his "untrained, unqualified, and inexperienced" group of parents included doctors, lawyers, engineers, and master's degree–holding homemakers.[17]

Many virtual school critics simply object to subsidizing home-schoolers. They argue that virtual schools are in actuality state-subsidized home schools and that charter school laws do not cover home-schoolers. In Colorado, for example, the state charter school law specifically bans online schools from enrolling students who previously were taught at home or went to a private school.

In addition, home-schoolers themselves have been very reluctant to embrace virtual schools and publicly funded home schooling. Home-schoolers fear that institutionalizing home schooling will lead to more government regulation of home-schoolers. For example, in most states charter school students are required to participate in mandatory state testing, while home-schoolers are not. Home-schoolers fear that this mandatory testing might eventually be required of all home-schoolers, even if they are not receiving government subsidies. For example, the Home School Legal Defense Association urges its members not to enroll in the Idaho Virtual Academy, saying that for "'families who become dependent on the 'free' government equipment and funds, their freedom is gradually exchanged for their 'freebies.'" "This is simply an attempt by the government to create small public schools in our home," the association warns.[18]

VIRTUAL SCHOOL PERFORMANCE

Like all types of public schools, there are variations in the quality of virtual school programs. Yet, overall there have been only a few weak schools, as the online learning community works hard to police itself through best practices recommended by the North American Council for Online Learning and accreditation efforts through numerous independent organizations from Advanced Placement to the Commission on International and Trans-Regional Accreditation (CITA).[19] Overall, according to a 2007 report by Education Sector, the small body of research focused on the effectiveness of K–12 virtual schooling found "no significant difference" in student performance in online courses versus traditional face-to-face learning.[20] While there are no systematic data on student performance in virtual schools across the nation, the performance of individual virtual schools indicates that they can be just as effective and sometimes more effective than traditional classrooms.

Florida is the case in point. According to an April 2007 *American Chronicle* report on Florida's Virtual schools, the Florida Virtual Academy (FLVA) exceeded the state average in every subject and every grade on Florida's 2006 Comprehensive Achievement Tests (FCAT).[21] According to the Florida Department of Education, 83 percent of FLVA student scored at or above proficiency on reading tests, compared to 80 percent of Connections Academy (FLCA) (K12 Inc.'s nearest competitor) students, and 66 percent of those in public schools. In math, 68 percent of FLVA students achieved proficiency, compared to 53 percent of FLCA students and 67 percent of students attending public schools.[22]

Similarly, a November 2007 study by Florida Taxwatch of the Florida Virtual School (FLVS), the largest online program in the country, with more than 100,000 course registrations and more than 50,000 students in 2006–2007, found that the FLVS outperformed the statewide counterparts on the FCAT and AP exams. For example, there were 1,900 course enrollments for AP classes at the FLVS in 2005–2006, and FLVS students scored an average of 3.05 on AP exams compared with an average of 2.56 on AP exams statewide.[23]

VIRTUAL SCHOOLS AND THE FUTURE

The legal future of virtual schools is unclear, and public schools may win a few temporary battles against virtual education in the short-term. However, one thing is certain: traditional public schools will have to face competition from virtual education. As a 2001 report by the National Association of State Boards of Education on e-learning concluded, "The most valuable benefit of e-learning is its potential to deliver high-quality instructional services to all learners regardless of location, family or cultural background, or disability."[24] This experience has held true in my role with the CAVA for more than 5,200 students working through an individualized learning plan. Perhaps the successful FLVS's motto says it best: "Any Time, Any Place, Any Path, Any Pace."

Table 19.1. Florida FCAT Results, 2006 (Percentage of Students at or Above Proficiency by Grade Level, Subject, and Type of School)

School	4th Reading	4th Math	5th Science	8th Reading	8th Math	8th Science
Florida Virtual Academy	83	68	59	69	82	39
Connections Academy	80	53	53	52	53	28
Public Schools	66	67	35	46	60	32

Source: Florida Department of Education, FCAT, 2006.

NOTES

1. Tom Regan, "Online Learning Grows More Popular: Improved Technology Has Made Online Classes More Attractive to More and More Students," *Christian Science Monitor*, October 31, 2007, 17.

2. I. Elaine Allen and Jeff Seaman, *Online Nation: Five Years of Growth in Online Learning*, Sloan Consortium, October 2007, http://www.sloan-c.org/publications/survey/pdf/online_nation.pdf.

3. Bill Kaczor, "Although Still in Its Infancy, Virtual Learning Catching On at Elementary, High School Levels,"Associated Press column, September 7, 2007.

4. John Watson, *Keeping Pace with K–12 Online Learning: A Review of State-Level Policy and Practice*, North American Council for Online Learning, November 2007, http://www.nacol.org/docs/KeepingPace07-color.pdf.

5. Kaczor, "Although Still in Its Infancy, Virtual Learning Catching On."

6. Anthony G. Picciano and Jeff Seaman, *K-12 Online Learning: A Survey of U.S. School District Administrators, Sloan Consortium*, 2007, http://www.sloan-c.org/publications/survey/pdf/K-12_Online_Learning.pdf.

7. *Learning in the 21st Century: A National Report on Online Learning*, Project Tomorrow and Blackboard Inc., October 18, 2007, http://www.blackboard.com/K12/OnlineLearningReport.

8. Regan, "Online Learning Grows More Popular," 17.

9. See the website of the California Virtual Academies, www.caliva.org.

10. "Technology-Based Education Provider K12 Inc. Plans Initial Public Offering of 6 Million Shares," Associated Press, November 30, 2007.

11. Scott Stephens, "Online Schools Earn Mixed Grade," *Cleveland Plain Dealer*, August 25, 2002, AA1.

12. Neal McCluskey, *Beyond Brick and Mortar: Cyber Charters Revolutionizing Education*, Center for Education Reform Report (Washington, D.C.: Center for Education Reform, 2006), 1.

13. Ethan Gray and Bill Tucker, *Students Are Streaming to State Virtual Schools*, Education Sector Report, November 7, 2006, 1, http://www.educationsector.org/analysis/analysis_show.htm?doc_id=420347

14. Elizabeth G. Hill, *Reforming California's Instructional Material Adoption Process*, California Legislative Analyst Office, May 2007, http://www.lao.ca.gov/2007/instruct_material/instruct_material_052407.pdf.

15. For more on the Pennsylvania story, see John Watson, *Keeping Pace with K–12 Online Learning: A Review of State-Level Policy and Practice*, Learning Point Associates, 2005, http://www.learningpt.org/pdfs/tech/Keeping _Pace2.pdf.

16. John Watson, *Keeping Pace with K–12 Online Learning: A Review of State-Level Policy and Practice*, North American Council for Online Learning, November 2007, http://www.nacol.org/docs/KeepingPace07-color.pdf.

17. Patrick McIlheran, "Educrats to Parents: Bug Off," November 11, 2007, 3, Center for Education Reform Newswire, November 13, 2007, http://www.edreform

.com/index.cfm?fuseAction=document&documentID=2756&sectionID=72&NEW SYEAR=2007.

18. Taryn Brodwater, "Virtual Schools Offer Alternative," *Spokane Spokesman-Review* (Idaho ed.), August 28, 2002, B1.

19. See the websites of the North American Council for Online Learning, www.nacol.org, and of the Commission on International and Trans-Regional Accreditation, www.citaschools.org.

20. Bill Tucker, *Laboratories of Reform: Virtual High Schools and Innovation in Public Education*, Education Sector Report, June 7, 2007, http://www.educationsector .org/research/research_show.htm?doc_id=502307.

21. Daniel Downs, "Virtual Public Schools: Why Nationwide National Achievement Test Scores Engender Their Support, Part III," *American Chronicle*, April 3, 2007, http://www.americanchronicle.com/articles/viewArticle.asp?articleID=23255.

22. Ibid.

23. *Final Report: A Comprehensive Assessment of Florida Virtual School*, Florida Taxwatch, November 2007, http://www.floridataxwatch.org/resources/pdf/110507 FinalReportFLVS.pdf.

24. *Any Time, Any Place, Any Path, Any Pace: Taking the Lead on E-Learning Policy*, National Association of State Boards of Education, October 2001, 7. http://www.nasbe .org/e_Learning.html.

20

The Rise and Fall and Rise
of Catholic Schools

Robert Mattingly

$\mathcal{I}$t would be difficult to think of any educational system that is as old, global, and internally diverse as Catholic education. Sixteenth-century Peruvian children sitting in a hut listening to missionaries; nineteenth-century immigrant children sitting in a classroom in the United States, listening absolutely silently to one of the sisters; contemporary law students at Georgetown University in Washington, D.C., or at Sophia University in Tokyo, Japan: all are experiencing Catholic education. Further, over the past few decades Catholic education has undergone some of the most radical transformations of its long history. To get a sense of where Catholic education is going, it is important to have a basic sense of its roots.

YESTERDAY

Catholic education can be defined as starting with the Roman Catholic Church itself. A necessary aspect of membership in the Christian community is the acquisition of information about the faith, and so education must be provided for the faithful. Seminaries were established so that priests could learn, preserve, and teach the faith, and Catholic education traces its earliest roots to these seminaries. While over the centuries Catholic education broadened its student body to include the members of the nobility and later people of all classes, the core mission of Catholic education as a way to preserve the faith has been retained. In the United States, Catholic schools expanded rapidly as Catholics feared that the nation's public schools favored Protestantism and were hostile to Catholicism.

Catholic education in the United States reached the greatest number of students during the 1950s and 1960s. These were the children of the post–World War II baby boom. In 1950, 3 million students were in roughly 10,000 elementary or high schools. By 1960, more than 5 million students were in roughly 13,000 elementary or high schools. During these years, too, orders of priests, brothers, and sisters were flooded with record numbers. In 1950, 93 percent of the elementary and 84 percent of the high school faculties were members of a religious order, who from a financial perspective, required little more than room and board in exchange for their work.[1]

The revitalization of the mission of the Catholic Church during Second Vatican Council caused a dramatic exodus of members of religious orders to other walks of life.[2] The religious orders that constituted such a huge proportion of Catholic school faculty in the 1950s have fallen to a current level of roughly 4 percent.[3] This staffing change has presented two major challenges for Catholic schools. The first has been economic: lay teachers need to be paid a salary, and to meet this unexpected budgetary challenge schools that had charged little to no tuition quickly had to start charging tuitions that were difficult for some families to pay. The second impact of this staffing change was a challenge to the identity of Catholic schools. For many people what made a school a "Catholic" school was that students were taught by a member of a religious order. As schools suddenly had very few or no members of religious orders on their faculties, they had to redefine and market a new identity.

In recent years there have also been demographic challenges, as the number of school age children has declined. At the same time many Catholics moved from urban areas, where Catholic schools were located, to the suburbs. Catholics have also migrated from areas of the country such as the Midwest and Northeast, where there were many Catholic schools, to the South and West, where there are few Catholic schools.

TODAY

Given all the challenges of the past few decades, it is a credit to the strength of Catholic education that it has survived. Today, 2,363,220 students attend one of 7,507 Catholic elementary or high schools.[4] This number represents more than half of all students attending nonpublic schools, but despite changes and challenges, Catholic schools are able to charge less than half the tuition charged by other nonpublic schools.[5] While much attention is given to those Catholic schools that have closed, many new Catholic schools have opened to serve new areas where Catholics now live. Others have opened to serve new needs. Those schools that have survived the reconfigurations of the past decades have not only worked through demographic, financial, and marketing challenges; they have also redefined what it means for them to be a Catholic school. Now that it is increasingly rare to have any priests, brothers, or nuns teaching in Catholic schools, various constituencies have reflected and mapped out what makes their school Catholic. Various publications, too, have emerged to help boards to articulate what it is that makes a school Catholic. Most religious orders have framed ideals that they hope all of the schools they founded work toward. All these conditions have come together to make Catholic schools more mindful and explicit about their mission and pedagogy than probably ever before in their history. What follows are some of the common markers that schools have articulated that make them Catholic.

Community

The backbone of a Catholic school is its community. Members of the student body often form deep relationships that last well after graduation. The sense of community often extends beyond students and faculty to include parents and alumni, and the school often plans events and gatherings that make everyone feel at home and a part of the school community. Catholic schools also have a strong sense of community, or relation, with other Catholic schools.

Academic Excellence

Although all schools aspire to academic excellence, Catholic schools answer the question, "Why aspire to academic excellence," a bit differently. The goal of academics is not to ensure that graduation leads to a prestigious next school or job or even simply produces a more learned person. Catholic schools affirm that an important way to come to know the Creator God is through an understanding of creation, just as one gets to know an artist by looking at his or her art. Thus Catholic education looks beyond the surface knowledge to seek to understand how God creates our world and supports the human genius. The wonders of gravity, evolution, or the Pythagorean theorem are wonders not just in themselves but in the One who caused them to be.

Understanding the Person of Jesus Christ

Catholic missionaries believed Catholic education to be an important aspect of proselytization. Receiving the sacraments and practicing the faith were the major goals. Today, while preparation and the practice of faith are of key importance to some schools, all share the goal of presenting an understanding of the person of Jesus Christ. While non-Catholic students might not share Catholic belief in Jesus Christ as Lord and Savior, it is important for all to have a clear and accurate understanding of who Jesus Christ was and what he stood for. The goal here is not to require faith, but literacy, in the message of Jesus Christ.

Loving

A specific teaching of Jesus Christ is to love your neighbor as yourself. This teaching is an import ideal for Catholic schools. As a goal, it demands a value system that guides how one person treats any other person. Catholic education strives to mold hearts that deal with all people with love, understanding, and generosity.

Social Justice

Another teaching of Jesus Christ was, in His time, a special concern for those who were marginalized—lepers, women, the sick. Today, Catholic schools have taken this teaching to heart. Most schools have outreach programs for those who are poor or marginalized today. School administrations typically make great efforts to ensure that those of lower social economic status have the means to afford Catholic education.

Religion

Catholic schools encourage the practice of faith, whatever that faith may be. Obviously, many Catholic schools seek to ensure that Catholic students practice their Catholic faith. But many schools, too, have broadened what worship is and how it is practiced so that students of other faiths can still practice their faiths in the school. Catholic colleges often have chaplains of various faiths performing services on campus. High schools often have retreat programs designed so that people of many faith backgrounds feel a part of the retreat experience.

TOMORROW

The reflection, innovation, and stability of the recent past are good predictors of the future of Catholic education. To understand how Catholic schools are going into the future, it may be helpful to consider them in three unofficial categories—parochial, religious ordered, and social service. Each serves an important but very different aspect of Catholic education.

Parochial Schools

The most numerous and well-known aspect of Catholic education can be categorized as parochial. These schools are managed by a diocesan education office. The grade schools are often physically adjacent to a parish. High schools are situated to serve geographic regions of a diocese. These schools differ from the others in that they are populated by and seek to foster a local Catholic community. A goal of a parish-based grade school is to accommodate as many members of the parish as possible. The school community is intertwined with the parish community. The school prepares students for the reception of sacraments such as First Communion and Confirmation. The school may also be involved with the liturgical life of the parish by training and organizing the parish choir or altar servers. The pastor of the parish may have a leadership role in the school. These schools are growing, especially in areas where Catholics are migrating to the suburbs and in the southern and western parts of the country.

Religious Ordered Schools

While virtually all Catholic schools were founded or staffed by a religious order, some were founded not as links to a parish or a diocese but rather as a work of the religious order. These can be grade schools, high schools, colleges, or graduate schools, intended to serve some special segment of the Catholic population or to educate in a different way. Thus these schools have some type of selection process or requirement for attendance. Examples of the special segments served include students with physical or mental disabilities, students with high intelligence, and orphans. Some orders founded schools using Montessori, bilingual, or other specialized educational techniques. Within this category are also the hundreds of Catholic colleges and universities as well as many Catholic high schools. These schools often have competitive admissions and generous alumni.

Social Service Schools

In recent years, a third type of Catholic school has emerged, especially in inner-city parishes whose schools experienced enrollment declines as parish members left cities for the suburbs. Some of these schools closed, but others were soon filled with students who now live in these neighborhoods but are not Catholic. These new families have been eager to be a part of a school that can provide their children with a high-quality education. In these schools, it is not uncommon for less than 5 percent of the student body to be Catholic. Thus, these schools have changed their focus from serving the parish to serving the greater community. In this regard they are like Catholic hospitals, which provide an important service to the community without regard to the religious affiliation of those served.

The success and importance of community service have led to the recent founding of Catholic schools specifically for the economically disadvantaged. In 1971 the Nativity School in New York City began to provide yearlong and almost all-day education for economically disadvantaged middle school students. This model has grown into a network of 64 schools around the country serving more than 4,300 students.[6] Ten years ago in Chicago, Cristo Rey was founded to provide high school education for economically disadvantaged students. At this high school students receive a high school education part of the day and do an internship at a local business for the rest of the day. A percentage of the student's tuition is paid by the business where the student does his or her internship. Today there are 2,882 students in 12 Cristo Rey schools, and in 2008, 7 more schools on this model are expected to open.[7] The number and kind of these Catholic schools will probably continue to expand in the coming years.

CONCLUSION

In conclusion, Catholic education started as a means to ensure that the message of Jesus Christ was passed to succeeding generations. The visible reality of this educational system has constantly changed through the centuries. Over the past few decades the people on both sides of the teacher's desk have changed, and new teachers and students have prompted the Catholic school mission to become more explicit and inclusive. Catholic education has become more conscious of not simply teaching, but practicing the message of Jesus Christ while providing quality education to an increasingly diverse student body.

NOTES

1. Dale McDonald, PBVM, Ph.D., "Catholic School Data," National Catholic Education Association, http://www.ncea.org/news/AnnualDataReport.asp.
2. Rev. Frank H. Bredeweg, comp., "Catholic School Data," unpublished data on file at the National Catholic Educational Association, Washington, D.C.

3. Ibid.

4. Dale McDonald, PBVM, Ph.D., "Catholic School Data," National Catholic Education Association, http://www.ncea.org/news/AnnualDataReport.asp.

5. Great Schools, http://www.greatschools.net/cgi-bin/showarticle/CA/197/improve/print/.

6. NativityMiguel Network of Schools, "Facts and Figures," http://www.nativitymiguelschools.org/about_schools/facts_figures.shtml.

7. Cristo Rey Network Schools, "Facts and Figures," http://www.cristoreynetwork.org/about/facts_figures.shtml.

· *21* ·

Jewish Day Schools in
the Twenty-First Century

Laurie Piette

*W*hat are "Jewish schools"? The answer is not simple. There are many types, including, but not limited to, supplementary schools, Sunday schools, and day schools. The first and second lie outside the scope of this essay; they often overlap, include extensions of individual temples, and are after-school or weekend programs for students who do not attend Jewish day schools. Yet the day school itself can take many forms, according to the branch of Judaism to which it belongs—Orthodox, Conservative, Reform, even Reconstructionist[1]—and its individual school mission. There are also "community" schools that ascribe to the tenets of no single denomination but may be more or less conservative (or liberal) than any single sect. Thus the thriving local Orthodox school may not meet the needs of a group of neighborhood Hasidim,[2] while a Reform Jew may choose to send his or her child to a Conservative school. In short, there is nothing monolithic about Jewish day schools. While individual communities ascribe to certain doctrinal commonalities and there are supportive Jewish organizations such as the Board of Jewish Education, the Jewish Theological Seminary, and the Hebrew Union, there is no one centralized power or administration that unifies all Jewish schools, who teaches there, and what is taught.

THE HISTORICAL CONTEXT
AND CULTURAL SURROUNDINGS

Add to this complexity the obvious truth that Jewish schools have been deeply affected by their historical contexts and cultural surroundings. Even

185

as I limit my scope to discussing, in broad strokes, the development of Jewish schools in America since the late nineteenth century, I offer only an overview of trends and a few comments from contemporary experts. In many ways, the modern Jewish school could not have come into existence until the work of John Dewey had been popularized. Until Dewey's concept of school as social center took hold in the United States, the family and synagogue necessarily assumed the role of educating Jewish youth. Moreover, Jewish immigration came to the United States in what Nathan Winter describes as three successive waves: "the Spanish-Portuguese, the German-Jewish and the Eastern European Jewish settlements."[3] Though there were some attempts to establish day schools during the first two waves, most Jewish education was organized at the time through the synagogue via supplementary and, later, Sunday schools. By the beginning of the twentieth century, with the arrival of close to a million Jews of Eastern European descent, these educational measures were not enough. In this era day schools were created, and an American version of the *heder*, "a one-teacher, one-room school," was often housed in the parlor of the teacher's home or tenement.[4]

Samson Benderly's communal schools, established first in Baltimore and later in New York, were based on "Ahad Ha'am's cultural Zionist concept of a spiritual center and . . . Dewey's vision of the school as social center."[5] Benderly, a reformer of Jewish schools, tapped into an immigrant's (and the nation's) fascination with American democratic values while privileging Jewish identity. Though he forswore the day school model, he revolutionized Jewish education by placing child-centered methods in modern buildings at the heart of his efforts. His emphasis on progressive education extended to his treatment of subject matter, but he also claimed that "the main question of the Jewish school" is "not so much the amount of knowledge obtained, as the creation of a Jewish atmosphere."[6] Benderly's schools also taught Hebrew as both a scriptural and a modern language, thus alienating many Reform constituents, yet his schools were simultaneously considered too liberal and earned the distrust of Orthodox communities.

While Benderly's followers continued to promote communal schools, supplementary and Sunday schools persisted alongside a growing number of day schools. Initially, Orthodox communities took the lead in the day school movement by establishing various Orthodox Jewish schools, or *yeshivot*. Meanwhile, Jewish organizations such as the Melton Research Center for Jewish Education at the Jewish Theological Seminary undertook a study of curricula and worked to create teaching modules that appealed to a range of Jewish constituencies. In keeping with a deep-seated love for nonsectarian, public education, Reform congregations in general withheld their support for day schools until the mid-1980s.[7]

JEWISH SCHOOLS AND JEWISH IDENTITY TODAY

Since the 1980s, the numbers of Jewish day schools of all denominations have risen sharply. The 2000–2001 National Jewish Population survey found "29 percent of children ages 6 to 17 attending a Jewish day school or yeshiva. Only 23 percent of adults 18 to 34 reported attending such a school; while just 12 percent of adults 35 to 44 say they attended a Jewish day school."[8] Jack Wertheimer, provost and professor of American Jewish history at the Jewish Theological Seminary in New York, has observed:

> Thanks to a quiet revolution over the last several decades, day schools at the elementary, junior-high, and even high-school level are thriving as never before, boasting some 200,000 pupils and 700 schools around the country. Although afternoon and Sunday schools still continue to enroll the majority of children receiving some formal Jewish education (apart from those receiving none at all), the proportion in day schools has risen to around 40 percent (again not counting those outside the formal system altogether). In New York, the figure is closer to two-thirds; in Los Angeles, to half.[9]

Further, the Avi Chai Foundation cites "a 20 percent to 25 percent increase in the number of non-Orthodox students entering day schools."[10] This trend is partially explained by the view, held in many contemporary Jewish circles, that day schools can help to address issues facing the future of Judaism.

One issue is the tremendous success of Jewish integration into American culture, and its tradeoffs. Citing historian Haym Soloveitchik, Wertheimer explains:

> If it had once been possible for Jews to assume that "Jewishness was something almost innate, and no school was needed to inculcate it," the fuller participation of many Jews in modern Western life rendered any such assumption suspect. As segregated living patterns collapsed and families proved increasingly incapable on their own of teaching essential beliefs and practices, Jewish identity ceased to be, in Soloveitchik's words, "a matter of course" and became a matter "of choice: a conscious preference."[11]

One measure of this effect was the 1990 National Jewish Population survey, which found an intermarriage rate of 43 percent and a decline in Jewish observance.[12] A few years ago Fred Fox, chair of the Jewish Federation of Greater Philadelphia's Center for Jewish Life and Learning's Task Force on Day Schools, described the intermarriage rate at closer to 50 percent.[13] But countering these trends, Wertheimer and other commentators cite:

> studies linking the amount of time spent in Jewish education during one's youth to adult participation in Jewish life. In this regard, recent research points unmistakably to the unique benefits of attending Jewish day schools. Their alumni are far more likely than others to observe a range of rituals and holidays, to contribute to Jewish causes and institutions, and to maintain a strong attachment to Israel. Most impressive, perhaps, is the finding that graduates of day schools are considerably more inclined to wed other Jews.[14]

In fact, Yeshiva University published a 1994 study noting the effectiveness of Jewish day schools at keeping "Jews Jewish."[15] The study found that "a Jewish day school education—no matter the ideology—when combined with a positive family environment and other Jewish experiences is the key to Jewish survival. The greater the exposure to Jewish day school education, the more pronounced one's adult Jewish behavior and attitudes."[16]

The implications are tremendous: fewer children are being born to successive generations of Jews, the observance level of those children overall is dropping, and these children are almost as likely as not to marry outside the faith, thus perpetuating (and perhaps intensifying the implications of) the cycle. Accordingly, when day schools were found to stem this tide, they offered not only a chance for Jews to receive a good education but also a way to ensure the continuity of American Judaism. It is difficult to come up with a more compelling argument for an educational system.

THE CHARACTERISTICS OF JEWISH DAY SCHOOLS

Given that the nature of Jewish education is not monolithic and that chief among its goals is inculcating Jewish identity, it is distinguished by two central components: the disciplines of Hebrew and Jewish studies.

Jewish educators have been struggling with and debating the role of Hebrew in the day school curriculum from the very beginning of American Jewish education. An 1804 piece lamented that "few, very few indeed are concerned about it ('a compleat [sic] and full knowledge of the Hebrew language, being that in which all our prayers are read')."[17] In the 1940s, Ben Rosen, an officer of the National Council for Jewish Education, and Hebrew scholar

William Chomsky asked why Jewish schools fell short of their avowed aim to teach Hebrew: "Some say it is because of a wrong emphasis upon teaching children to *speak* Hebrew, rather that to *read* with understanding."[18] In contrast, in 2004 Vardit Ringvald, director of the Hebrew and Arabic Languages Program at Brandeis University, asserted, "When teaching Hebrew in a Jewish setting, teaching for acquisition should be the preferred approach." She also notes:

> In order to execute the Proficiency goals they [Hebrew teachers] are first required to understand most of the aspects related to the language teaching professions, such as second language acquisition theories, teaching methodologies, principles in identifying appropriate teaching materials for their learners and how to develop them, assessment methods as well as some principles that are related to formulating lesson-plans and incorporating the use of technology in the classroom.[19]

An implication seems to be that many Hebrew teachers bear the strain of conflicting demands and may not develop as accomplished teaching practices as their peers in secular studies and/or in other foreign languages.

To flatten the debate into simple terms, there seem to be two main conflicts in the approach to teaching Hebrew. One model is to teach scriptural Hebrew, that is, the Hebrew of the Tanakh, Midrashim, and other commentaries. One could compare this kind of language instruction to teaching Cervantes in Spanish or, more approximately, to teaching non-English speakers literature ranging from Beowulf to Chaucer to Shakespeare. The vocabulary is text-specific and replete with language forms not often encountered today. To make such a comparison, however, borders on blasphemy since, much as I hold authors like Shakespeare dear, they are not writing or interpreting the word of God. The second approach is to teach Hebrew as a modern language that, given the establishment of the State of Israel, offers students a living language to use in a modern country. Here one must consider the effects of teaching students how to order French fries in Hebrew, the language of the politically and religiously charged homeland of the Jews. An ideal solution might be to use both approaches, but how can schools realistically do that when they also need to teach all of the general studies curricula that students receive in public and other private schools? Even with their longer school days, Jewish day schools simply may not have enough time. The breakdown in the teaching of Hebrew involves, then, not only matters of teacher preparation and training but extends all the way to the organizational level.

The second central component of Jewish day schools is Jewish studies programs, which face a number of additional issues. First is the question of what, exactly, constitutes Jewish studies. The discipline seems to include *t'fillot* (ritual prayer observance), scriptural text study, the holidays, life cycle events, Jewish history, a knowledge of Jewish customs practiced around the world, and the application of *mitzvot* (moral obligations) to daily life. Just as other disciplines need a scope and sequence that delineates which skills are to be taught at which grade levels (hopefully in keeping with students' developmental abilities and based on educational research), Jewish studies curricula need this kind of articulation. This level of detail is lacking, at times, when schools try to do it all in spite of difficult choices that should be made; these choices may be made clear or further complicated by the denominational affiliation of the school, the opinions of the congregation's rabbi, or the views of the school's parent body and the level of involvement of each of these constituencies. In addition, teachers need to be well-versed in the intricacies of Jewish theology, history, and ritual observance and also in sound pedagogical practices so they can communicate a love of Judaism to, say, preschool, second-, fifth-, eighth-, and eleventh-grade students. This problem is twofold: "the serious shortage of qualified teachers for Jewish schools and the lack of a systematic program for education of non-Orthodox Jewish teachers."[20] And sitting in the classroom are students who may or may not hear messages about the nature of God that are dissonant from the ones they hear in their homes, in their synagogues, and in their peer groups.

Other issues facing Jewish day schools are those familiar to day schools in general, such as competition with other private schools, the question of voucher programs, the financial burdens of running private institutions, and the managing of financial aid.

THE BENEFITS OF JEWISH DAY SCHOOLS

What do Jewish day schools have to offer? The benefits are many: a multiplicity of vision that runs the gamut from Hasidism to interdenominational, Jewish faith-inspired schools; small classrooms with devoted, if underpaid, teachers; an environment in which the rhythm of Jewish life is lived and the school calendar reflects the Jewish calendar, with its holidays and rituals; an atmosphere where character education is intrinsic and stems from religious obligations to do the right thing (*mitzvot*) instead of being tacked on as community service projects that embellish college applications.

Aware of the limitations of after-school religious training, officials in the various Jewish communities have championed day schools. In 1961, Rabbi Louis I. Newman of Temple Rodeph Sholom, New York City, asserted that the Jewish day school would "aid us in overcoming the abysmal ignorance among Jewish children regarding Jewish history, archaeology, literature, and life which we seek to overcome by the inadequate Sunday or Mid-week School."[21]

Today Jewish leaders continue to address the various shortcomings of day schools while simultaneously trumpeting their incredible possibilities. Not least among these is the felt sense that Jewish schools preserve an ethnic and cultural sense of identity in a people who have successfully become part of the fabric of American society. Rabbi Simeon J. Maslin boasts, "When I look at kids who have Jewish day-school education—and I'm not talking now about yeshiva education, which I myself went through, I'm talking about [Solomon] Schechter schools and these Reform day schools—when I look at the kids who come out of those schools, they have Jewish educations. They know what the holidays are. They're familiar with a name like Maimonides. They have a grounding in Judaism." He continues, saying that students attend the kind of schools that are "totally American and totally Jewish . . . living in two civilizations."[22] In keeping with this dialectic, Jenna Weissman Joselit, professor of American studies and modern Judaic studies at Princeton University, writes that Jewish day schools have become "a true-blue American phenomenon, a testament to the promise of pluralism."[23]

NOTES

1. These movements can be difficult to define. In essence, the Orthodox, Conservative, and Reform movements range from most conservative to most liberal levels of observance. Major ideological differences involve the authenticity and transmission of the Torah. Orthodox believers hold that God gave Moses the entire Torah (written and oral) on Mount Sinai. Reform believers espouse that the Bible was written by several different human beings. Conservative members believe that the Torah comes from God but was recorded and influenced by humans. Reconstructionists view Judaism as an evolving community. While they do not believe that God chose the Jewish people, they are often very observant of Jewish laws.

2. Hasidim are the followers of Hasidism, a subcomponent of Orthodoxy that is very observant of Jewish laws and in which members often choose to live together in Hasidic communities.

3. Nathan Winter, *Jewish Education in a Pluralist Society: Samson Benderly and Jewish Education in the United States* (New York: New York University Press, 1966), 2, 4, 8.

4. Ibid., 9.

5. Miriam Heller Stern, "A Dream Not Quite Come True," *Journal of Jewish Education* 70, no. 3 (Fall 2004): 19.

6. Samson Benderly, "Samson Benderly on the Problem of Jewish Education," speech to the Achavah Club, November 26, 1910, in "Israel Friedlaender's Minute Book of the Achavah Club," *Mordecai M. Kaplan's Jubilee Volume*, ed. Moshe Davis (New York, 1953), 188–91, reprinted in *Jewish Education in the United States: A Documentary History*, ed. Lloyd Gartner (New York: Teachers College Press, 1969), 128.

7. "Reform Jews' Debate on Day Schools," *New York Times*, April 6, 1986, available online at *New York Times Online*, nytimes.com.

8. Faygie Levy, "More Jews Find an Outlet in Day-School Education," *Jewish Exponent* 18 (September 2003), available online at ProQuest, www.highbeam.com.

9. Jack Wertheimer, "Who's Afraid of Jewish Day Schools?" *Commentary*, December 1, 1999, available online at Gale Group, www.highbeam.com.

10. Levy, "More Jews Find an Outlet."

11. Wertheimer, "Who's Afraid of Jewish Day Schools?"

12. Stewart Ain, "Stay in School: Yeshiva U. Survey Concludes That Day School Education Is Key to Jewish Survival," *Jewish Week*, November 3, 1994, available online at ProQuest, www.highbeam.com.

13. Jan L. Apple, "Advocating the Need for a Day-School Education," *Jewish Exponent*, August 25, 2005, available online at ProQuest, www.highbeam.com.

14. Wertheimer, "Who's Afraid of Jewish Day Schools?"

15. Ain, "Stay in School."

16. Ibid.

17. Quoted in *Jewish Education in the United States*, ed. Gartner, 48.

18. Ben Rosen and William Chomsky, "Improving the Teaching of Hebrew in Our Schools," 1940, reprinted in the *Journal of Jewish Education* 69, no. 1 (Spring–Summer 2003): 57.

19. Vardit Ringvald, "Proficiency-Based Instruction," *Journal of Jewish Education* 69, no. 3 (Winter 2004): 5, 8.

20. Irving Barkan and Sarah Elkin Braun, "About the BJE: BJE History," Board of Jewish Education of Metropolitan Chicago, April 2004, www.bjechicago.org.

21. Louis I. Newman, "The Jewish Day School: Why I Favor It," January 14, 1961, reprinted in *The Jewish Day School in America*, ed. Alvin Irwin Schiff (New York: Jewish Education Committee Press, 1966), 78.

22. Quoted in Bertram Korn Jr., ed., "Reform Day Schools: An Idea Whose Time Has Come?" *Jewish Exponent*, August 26, 1994, available online at ProQuest, www.highbeam.com.

23. Jenna Weissman Joselit, "The Wonders of America; School Daze; How American Jewish Parents Learned to Make Their Peace with the Jewish Day School," *Forward*, September 2, 2005, available online at ProQuest, www.highbeam.com.

Islamic Schools

The Struggle for Successful Integration

Farhat Siddiqui

*E*ducation of young people has long been the means whereby civilizations ensure the continuation of their values and beliefs even as they cultivate independent thought, from one generation to the next. In the United States, the influx of people of many different ethnicities and religions has long inspired community efforts to educate young people in the culture of their ancestors. The purpose and mission of Islamic schools are similar. Private Islamic schools in the United States are committed to providing a high-quality education in an environment that nurtures spiritual, intellectual, and moral development in order to create community leaders dedicated to the service of society as a whole. In the nineteenth century, Irish Catholics and eastern European Jews established places of learning for their communities. In the twentieth and twenty-first centuries Muslims from the Middle East and the subcontinent of Asia are following in this practice.

Currently there are about three hundred private Islamic schools in North America; together they serve less than 2 percent of the Muslim student population.[1] Typically, Islamic schools are community-based and supported. They are created to meet the needs of the community they serve. Some schools have evolved out of home-schooling efforts; some have been initiated by a community center or a mosque; and some were founded by groups of parents who shared similar educational and social goals for their children. These schools range in size from just a handful of students in one or two grade levels to schools with more than six hundred students, from preschool through grade 12. Many schools begin with just one or two grade levels, often preschool or first grade, and expand one grade level each year. The majority of Islamic schools serve students in the elementary and middle school grades. Following their eighth-grade graduation, these students attend local area private or public schools, in some cases Catholic schools. Their parents are reassured that their children have received a strong moral and academic foundation.

In some Muslim communities, students start their education in Islamic schools in preschool and continue through high school. These "crayons to college" schools are much like private schools in that they charge tuition and much like Catholic schools in that they provide moral and spiritual guidance in addition to a liberal arts education. These schools hold themselves to high standards. Like private and Catholic schools, they plan their curricula, programs, and extracurricular offerings to provide opportunities for student advancement and to ensure student success. These schools generate resources through fund-raising efforts on a community level, and they are supported by the local community in providing opportunities for students. Their resources include involvement by parents and community members in career development programs, such as career days and job-shadowing opportunities. Parents and community members give presentations on social welfare topics and involve students in community service projects such as providing food to the homeless. Islamic schools also obtain state accreditation and accreditation from private agencies such as the North Central Association Commission on Accreditation and School Improvement. Students are evaluated with national assessments such as the Iowa test for elementary and middle school students and the ACT and SAT tests for high school students. But the real measure of success—for school administrators and educators, for parents and families, and for the larger community—comes when the students are recognized as positive contributors to the global society. Their success in the larger social context affirms the mission of Islamic educational institutions. Although Islamic schools are relatively young and have yet to establish and statistically analyze long-term results, they are proud of what their students have achieved.

Islamic schools impart Islamic values. Students come to understand that school is not just a series of classes, seminars, and retreats, and that learning is not just mastering a set of beliefs. At Islamic schools, they learn a way of life. The values they learn—honesty, integrity, and the importance of good citizenship and service—guide the choices they will make throughout their lives. The practical application of values is included in the teaching of secular subjects. In addition, in Islamic studies classes students learn Islamic beliefs as well as the history of the faith. They also learn Arabic, the language of the Quran, and they learn the Quran itself, memorizing passages and understanding their meaning. Islamic schools also seek to combine the values of Islam with existing "character education" programs. Teachers and staff members shape school policy to reflect Islamic values, and these values permeate the school environment. The task of imparting Islamic values is not easy, given the dominance of a teen culture in American society. But when schools are supported by parents who apply Islamic values in their personal lives and in their homes, success is achieved.

Students in Islamic schools thus acquire a strong academic foundation, a strong set of social values, and a reliable moral compass that will help them to integrate into American society in a positive and meaningful way without losing their heritage and culture. In the United States, the image of the salad bowl conveys the kind of integration Islamic schools aim for their students to achieve—a mixing that involves maintaining one's identity even while contributing and flourishing as an individual who is a unique part of a whole. An objective of Islam is to maintain the concept of *ummah* (Arabic for "community" or "nation"), which supports the moral development of a healthy society; thus integrating into American society means contributing to it. Ultimately the concept of *ummah* can be achieved only when individuals are committed to maintaining a sound democracy and a good government.

Students in Islamic schools are individuals who come to understand their roles in society and their responsibilities to the community. They use their educational experience to contribute needed intellectual and economic resources. Their values are in harmony with the values of their parents and with the values of the American nation, and they are the beneficiaries of the resources the schools make possible for them. Recently a student of Middle Eastern descent joined our Islamic school in middle school. He was, like so many young people, uncertain of his faith in the context of the larger environment. But the school allowed him to search for understanding, to explore, and to reach maturity. He used his interests and talents to create a documentary examining the reasons that Muslim women in Western society choose to wear the *hijab*—the head covering that observant Muslim women use in practicing modesty. Through work on this documentary he gained a clearer understanding of Islamic values and their direct application to individual choice as well as their impact on society and morality. Through this understanding, he came to a strong sense of faith, a belief system that is rooted in the democratic way. The strength and the confidence he gained allowed him to compete with America's best students. He submitted his documentary to Harvard University, where he began classes as a first-year student in the fall of 2007.

In the United States a wide variety of public and private schools are available. Islamic schools are a sound alternative for Muslim families who are seeking high-quality education in a morally guided atmosphere that supports the values taught in Muslim homes. Islamic schools offer commendable curricular challenges and enjoyable extracurricular programs. Although these programs may not be abundant, they certainly flourish with student participation, since they are specific to the student population. As tuition at Islamic schools is considerably lower than that at most private and Catholic schools, the popularity of Islamic schools will continue to grow. They have increased rapidly in their short thirty years in North America. In the 1980s there were only about ten Islamic schools. Today there are thirty times that number.[2] One reason for this growth is the strong commitment of the older generation, who have taken responsibility for preserving their identity through education. The immigrant Muslim population arrived in this land of opportunity as a well-educated and economically stable group, and Muslims know they derive benefits in proportion to their contribution to society. Another reason for the growth of Islamic schools is that they offer what all American parents seek for their children—the opportunity to gather with other young people to learn a common heritage for the purpose of academic, social, and moral understanding and for the achievement of compatibility and success.

NOTES

1. Muslim Students Association, www.msanational.org.
2. Ibid.

• 23 •

Christian Schools

Redeeming Lives and Culture

Erik P. Ellefsen

*C*hristian schools in the United States were the primary choice of parents for their children's education from the colonial period until the modern public school movement of the early 1900s. These early Christian schools were generally connected with the mainline Protestant denominations, including the Episcopalian, Presbyterian, and Lutheran denominations; many were also Quaker. The Catholic Church, too, started and administered schools, especially to counteract what was viewed as the Protestant influence over public schools. The modern Christian school movement, however, began in the 1900s in Dutch immigrant communities and, later, as part of the Evangelical Christian movement.

BACKGROUND ON REFORMED AND EVANGELICAL CHRISTIAN SCHOOLS

Dutch immigrants from the Reformed Christian denominations were greatly influenced by Dutch Prime Minister Abraham Kuyper (1901–1905). Kuyper encouraged the establishment of Christian schools that would use Calvinist theology to develop in students a worldview bringing about personal and cultural redemption. In his famous Princeton lectures, Kuyper highlighted the impact of Calvinist worldview and education:

> Calvinism [Reformed Christianity] did not stop at a church-order, but expanded in a *life-system*, and did not exhaust its energy in a dogmatical construction, but created a *life-* and *world-view*, and such a one as was, and still is, able to fit itself to the needs of every stage of human development,

197

in every department of life. It raised our Christian religion to its highest spiritual splendor: it created a church order . . . ; it proved to be the guardian angel of science; it emancipated art; it propagated a political scheme . . . ; it fostered agriculture and industry, commerce and navigation; it put a thorough Christian stamp upon home-life and family-ties; it promoted through its high moral standard purity in our social circles.[1]

The Christian schools founded out of the Reformed perspective are organized today under an umbrella organization known as Christian Schools International (CSI). CSI, established in 1920, was the first organization to serve Christian schools. It has grown from eight founding schools to more than three hundred, serving 77,000 students today. Due to this growth, CSI began to offer services to help support constituent schools in the areas of curriculum, consulting services, and certification programs.[2]

Reformed Christian schools are not the only type of Christian schools available to parents and students. In the 1960s the Evangelical Christian school movement arose in response to the secularization of public schools. In 1973, the Association of Christian Schools International (ACSI) was formed by a conglomeration of regional Evangelical school associations that represented 150,000 students in 1,200 schools. Thirty-five years later this organization has grown to more than 4,000 schools with well over 700,000 students.[3]

The differences between the two types of Christian schools can best be seen in their history and organization. Reformed schools tend to have parent-run boards that are voted upon by a society of supporting churches; have a closer identity with a Reformed denomination such as the Christian Reformed Church, Reformed Church of America, or Presbyterian Church of America; and have Dutch immigrant heritages. Evangelical schools tend to be organizationally diverse, with a mix of parent-run boards, church-run schools, or schools that are modeled after independent schools. Evangelical schools also tend to be more flexible in regards to admissions requirements for students and church affiliations of faculty members, which allow them to attract a broader constituency. Even though the Reformed and Evangelical Christian schools have different foundations, their goals are so similar that CSI and ACSI have had numerous discussions over the past ten years about merging into one international organization that supports the development of Christian schools.

YESTERDAY: AIMS OF CHRISTIAN SCHOOLS

The unique nature of Christian schools allows for some variation in the purpose of the individual school, but among the larger Christian school associations and movements, there are some agreed upon foundational points. These include the general purpose of the schools, the redemptive work in the individual student, and the redemptive work in society through these students.

First, the purpose of the Christian school is usually to act as an arm of the Christian church and family to train students in the way they should go.[4] Yale philosopher Nicholas Wolterstorff says, "From the beginning of the Christian church, Christian parents have considered it desirable and even obligatory to educate their children so as to induct them into the vision and life of the Christian community."[5] Therefore, Christian schools promote and teach the integration of faith and learning for the development of a coherent Christian worldview because "it is virtually impossible for a teacher to avoid seeking to shape students' tendencies . . . and it is certainly impossible for a teacher to act in such a way that he or she will *in fact* not alter the student's tendencies."[6] This worldview shapes the individual and the action of the individual in the local, national, and global community.

Second, the redemptive work in the individual student is a key to the education process. Students do not live their faith in a bubble, nor is their faith impotent to impact their lives and the surrounding culture. Therefore, the work of the Christian school is to produce change in each individual student by increasing cognitive abilities and skills. But more important, the Christian school acts to bring about greater internal change in the student by altering inclinations or dispositions. This redemptive education is called *decisional learning*, which is "growth in right choosing, in accepting or rejecting what is in light of what things *ought to be*. It includes moral and aesthetic, legal and logical choosing, based on relevant Christian standards. Included in this dimension is growth in appreciation, attitude, judgment, and commitment."[7]

The Christian school becomes an agent of Christian discipleship. It is effective when the academic, spiritual, social, and physical spheres are combined as part of the overall educative process. Christian school education, therefore, becomes much more than academic content or even character development; rather, it is centered on individual transformation in the development of a unique Christian worldview that fosters unique Christian action. Wolterstorff reiterates this emphasis: "Christian education points to a certain way of living and acting—one in which a person lives and acts responsibly, in obedience to God's will, as an agent of God's cause in the world."[8]

Last, Christian schools seek to bring about the redemption of God's world. Ultimately, the outcome of the Christian school is to partner with churches and families to develop and train Christian disciples who will produce beauty, goodness, peace, justice, and joy in all aspects of life. Simply put, Christian schools desire to prepare students who will serve God by serving others to overcome alienation from God and allow for human liberation from oppression, deprivation, and suffering.

TODAY: CHRISTIAN SCHOOL
SUCCESSES AND IMPROVEMENTS

Often in Christian schools anything but perfection is a disappointment because the purposes, aims, and goals are so grandiose. However, while Christian schools have shown that they are successful at being inclusive and fostering a commitment to a religious identity, they have also become more academically rigorous and distinctive. Christian schools will have to build upon their strengths and continue to improve as they are challenged by charter schools, home schools, and the reemergence of public school accountability.

Success One

The community of the Christian school promotes and fosters an inclusive nature. Students at Christian schools report more positive opinions of the education experience, the diversity within the school and society, and their acceptance within the community.[9] Christian schools are often wrongly accused of being bigoted, punitive, or uniform in their actions in developing students, when in reality they have been shown to have a welcoming and caring school climate and culture.

Success Two

Christian schools cultivate and encourage in students their religious identity. Students from Christian schools tend to develop and maintain their families' religious identity as their own and are more likely to stay committed to their religious beliefs. This area of success displays the ability of Christian schools to develop and support a more coherent worldview in their students.

Improvement One

Christian schools are often maligned for not being academically rigorous. The critics claim that religious schools provide a substandard education delivered by substandard teachers. However, a current study which adjusted for demographics shows that Christian school students achieve parity with public schools in math and have an advantage in reading. But this same study shows that Catholic and Lutheran school students achieve at a higher level than their Christian school counterparts.[10] Even though Christian schools do have better outcomes than their public school competitors, there is a clear need to produce better achievement gains.

Improvement Two

Christian schools are working to become more distinctive. At the conclusion of his famous study of Christian schools, Alan Peshkin seemingly compliments them by saying:

> The Christian students I know are spontaneous, fun-loving, friendly, accepting, and warm human beings, who—like the rest of American students—romance, cheer on their teams, and cheat on exams. Which is to say that . . . Christian schools are recognizably like most public schools in . . . subjects taught, topics covered, games played, examinations taken, rules broken, and punishments awarded.[11]

However, many critics within the Christian school community do not take this statement as a compliment. Instead they "denounce the lack of distinctiveness in Christian education and its failure to produce radical, Christian disciples."[12]

There are two primary criticisms of Christian schools in this regard. The first is that Christian schools were often founded as reactionary institutions to combat the deep-seated concerns about public education.[13] For example, in ACSI schools the education can often be criticized as containing substandard curricula because of a fear of engaging in modern academic disputes. In reality, many Christian schools become labeled as intellectually inferior because of the inability to use the religious truths of Christianity to challenge modern dilemmas such as human origins, moral law, and economic injustice. On the other hand, CSI schools struggle today with the Dutch roots that for many decades created cohesion and purpose. One critic states, "Historically, Reformed Christian schools have tended to isolate and protect. . . . To maintain doctrinal and ethnic purity, they segregated Dutch immigrant children from the rest of society."[14] Today, however, the loss of cultural hegemony has created a sense of crisis within CSI schools.

The second criticism is that Christian schools are too similar to public schools. Because most Christian schools are modeled after the comprehensive public school, many of the same problems exist, such as a lack of academic focus, a lack of a clear school ethos, and organizational inflexibility. Christian school leaders, say the critics, are mimicking an institutional model that needs fixing and ultimately does not fit the demands for Christian school competitiveness.

In response to these criticisms Christian schools have made radical changes. They have chosen to build upon their inclusive nature to take part in the diversification of American culture; they have developed academic programs that promote growth in students both intellectually and spiritually; they have been more specific about creating a distinct Christian school ethos; they have continued to promote student commitments to religious beliefs and values; and they have created comprehensive plans to positively impact their communities, the nation, and the world.[15]

TOMORROW: OPPORTUNITIES FOR CHRISTIAN SCHOOLS

Due to this response, Christian schools are growing, impacting student lives, and changing communities. Likewise, Christian schools continue to make adjustments to compete and grow in the future. In order to enhance growth, leaders have focused on making Christian schools more rigorous, distinct, and affordable for all students.

First, Christian schools are becoming more academically rigorous. Many Christian schools have shed the public school model of comprehensive education and have embraced the independent school model of a strong liberal arts core coupled with electives that allow students to prepare for collegiate academics. This college prep focus within Christian schools prepares students to compete academically with the best Catholic, independent, Episcopal, and public school students throughout the United States.

Second, Christian schools are focusing more attention on being distinctive based upon clear religious beliefs and values. According to researcher and policy maker Charles Glenn, "Research evidence . . . suggest[s] that schools with a religiously-based ethos have an advantage over schools committed to value-neutrality."[16] Christian schools are now better defining how religious beliefs impact student learning, development, achievement, and success. This religious foundation allows Christian schools to develop a countercultural learning environment that embraces not only the truths of the past but also the dilemmas of the present.

Third, resources and capital are being developed for more students to attend Christian schools. Traditionally, Christian schools have had academically open admissions requirements, but parents have sacrificed to pay the tuition. Affordability is especially burdensome in urban areas where parental choice in education is most necessary because of the poor state of urban public schools. Therefore, instead of waiting for the government to provide vouchers to parents, Christian schools have begun to take action to become more affordable in both the poorer urban and more affluent suburban areas. Many small schools have consolidated or joined together in associations that have embarked on professional fund-raising efforts to offset the cost of tuition. In addition, schools have formed financial support groups to support the development of Christian schools.

CONCLUSION: CHOOSING A CHRISTIAN SCHOOL

Christian schools were founded as a way to encourage the development of a Christian worldview in students who would not only be changed internally but would also act to bring about change in the world. Even though Christian schools have struggled at times to achieve this outcome perfectly, they have been shown to be very effective in developing people who think differently and have a distinct commitment to their beliefs and values. As Christian schools adjust to the future, they are building opportunities to increase the influence of their alumni. Ultimately, Christian schools exist to bring God glory by partnering with churches and families in the great task of educating young people who will serve others.

NOTES

1. Abraham Kuyper, *Lectures on Calvinism* (Grand Rapids, Mich.: Eerdmans Publishing Co., 1931), n.p.

2. See Christian Schools International's website, www.csionline.org.

3. See the Association of Christian Schools International's website, www.acsi.org.

4. Proverbs 22:6, *The Spirit of the Reformation Study Bible (NIV)* (Grand Rapids, Mich.: Zondervan, 2003).

5. Nicholas Wolterstorff, *Educating for Responsible Action* (Grand Rapids, Mich.: Eerdmans Publishing Co., 1980), vi.

6. Ibid., 6.

7. H. J. Triezenberg, *Principles to Practice* (Grand Rapids, Mich.: CSI, 1979), 2.

8. Wolterstorff, *Educating for Responsible Action*, 14.

9. Alan Peshkin, *God's Choice: The Total World of a Fundamentalist Christian School* (Chicago, Ill.: University of Chicago Press, 1986), 329–36. .

10. P. E. Peterson and Elena Llaudet, "The NCES Private-Public School Study: Findings Are Other Than They Seem," *Education Next* 7, no. 1 (Winter 2007): 75–79.

11. Peshkin, *God's Choice*, 47.

12. John Bolt, *The Christian Story and the Christian School* (Grand Rapids, Mich.: CSI, 1993), 15.

13. Ibid.

14. Steve Vryhof, "Christian Schools: Ripe for Change," pt. 1, *The Banner*, September 9, 1991, 6–7.

15. The following schools are, in the author's opinion, exemplary: Oaks Christian School, Westlake, California; Valley Christian School, San Jose, California; Wheaton Academy, Wheaton, Illinois; Lexington Christian Academy, Lexington, Massachusetts; Boston Trinity Academy, Boston, Massachusetts; Unity Christian High School, Grand Rapids, Michigan; and Westminster Academy, Fort Lauderdale, Florida.

16. C. L. Glenn, "School Distinctiveness," August 1995, unpublished.

· 24 ·

Episcopal Schools

An Anglican Legacy

Ann Gordon

*P*arents look for schools that will help shape their children's lives. They want a school that provides a moral vision for their children through which life decisions can be made. They want their children to have an intellectual foundation that will serve them all their lives. They want their children to live responsibly in the twenty-first century with a worldview that appreciates different points of view and different cultures. Those who want their children exposed to a religious tradition want one that preserves and honors their own family's religious heritage and values. Finally, they want all of this to take place in a caring and nurturing atmosphere. For three hundred years, Episcopal schools have served these needs with excellence and integrity.

YESTERDAY: THE ANGLICAN LEGACY

From their inception, Episcopal Schools have been known for their rigorous educational program that is informed and influenced by the Judeo-Christian heritage and tradition. As church schools, their values-oriented mission goes beyond what most secular schools consider their calling. But what exactly does it mean to be a "church" school, and why should Episcopal schools have several hundred years of success?

To understand the nature of an Episcopal school, it is first necessary to understand the unique nature of the Episcopal Church in regard to education. The glue that binds our individual and collective community of schools is found in our historic ties with Anglicanism and, as Americans, the Episcopal expression of that heritage. The school and the culture of which it is a part are inescapably and historically linked. Fostering a sense of awareness about Anglican tradition

205

and our Anglican legacy is crucial to the success of an Episcopal school's mission, since each school defines its Episcopal identity, mission, and goals according to its own history and culture (that in itself is a very Anglican approach!).

The distinctive ethos of the Anglican way provides our schools with a spiritual framework on which we build a caring and accepting community with a strong academic purpose. Since faith and culture are partners in this endeavor, these values are integrated into all aspects of school life, from the choice of curriculum, to the quality of the relationships within the community, and to the form and style of leadership and governance. A legacy of Anglicanism is that intangible values and beliefs are matched with tangible manifestations, creating a singularly effective ethos.

A high regard for *intellectual discipline* is probably the first tenet most people would identify as typically Anglican. The Church of England instilled a strong commitment to the life both of the mind and the spirit in the earliest forms of American education that still enrich the present. Therefore, we see scholarship as hard work expressed by open discourse, intellectual inquiry, and a melding of reason and faith. We challenge our students and ourselves to that effort. The exemplary reputation for academic excellence that Episcopal schools hold in the independent school community demonstrates that principle of strengthening the intellect.

Second, *tolerance and inclusivity* are foundational principles of Anglicanism. To be faithful to its gospel mission, the Church of England and its counterparts around the world obligated themselves to accepting differing points of view, divergent opinions, and varied practices. This respect for differences is embodied in every Episcopal school's admissions and hiring policies, financial aid programs, and curriculum. The common threads of Anglicanism that draw us together also encourage us to anoint our differences.

Whether we identify it as social responsibility, social justice, or the acting out of the Episcopal baptismal covenant to "seek and serve Christ is all persons," *service to others* is a third hallmark of the Anglican legacy that Episcopal schools inherited. The fact that some of the most outstanding models of community service programs in American independent schools are found in Episcopal schools is no accident. From nursery school to boarding school the importance of giving the gift of self to someone else is a vital part of the Episcopal school culture and an essential component of each student's education.

As part of the Episcopal baptism rite, we pray that the person being baptized have an "inquiring and discerning heart." Therefore, *faith and reason are partners* in an ethos that places learning solidly in the context of each person's lifelong exploration for truth. Episcopal schools teach students to challenge as they learn and to seek out and form arguments that support their convictions. Questioning must be an accepted part of the curriculum. An Episcopal education teaches students to struggle with questions as they move beyond "right" answers to many viewpoints and even more questions.

Finally, it is in *worship* that an Episcopal school is more emphatically Anglican than at any other time. Anglican doctrine supports many diverse points of view, but it is through worship that we are unified, through common form and structure and through shared ritual and tradition. By observing similar patterns of worship, we are then able to differ from one another in other circumstances. The rich heritage of Anglicanism provides Episcopal schools with the dignity of our liturgical traditions. Each school creates meaningful celebrations that express the unique needs of that community and, at the same time, draw it into the unifying liturgical tradition of the Anglican Church.

These qualities—intellectual discipline, tolerance and inclusivity, service to others, learning through faith and reason, and worship—attract families outside the Episcopal Church to enroll their children in Episcopal schools. The appeal of these distinctly Anglican features is evidenced by the fact that about 75 percent of the families in Episcopal schools are not Episcopalians.[1] Who and what we are as church schools are why they enroll their children. It is only by remaining clear about our mission that we will serve them well.

TODAY: CHALLENGING THE LEGACY

Ironically, the unity of the worldwide Anglican Church today is being threatened because of issues of diversity and inclusiveness. At the center of the controversy is the Episcopal Church in the United States, whose decisions on ordaining gay clergy has heightened tension between theological traditionalists and their more liberal counterparts. The nature of Anglicanism is comprehensive, celebrating diversity through *via media*—the middle way—as a bridge between widely divergent theological opinions. These core values of tolerance and respect for all are being challenged, with repercussions for Anglicanism worldwide.

What overall effect this international turmoil might have on Episcopal schools is unknown at this time. Church polity and practices are at issue, not the educational mission of the schools. That is not to say there will be no fallout. If a parish with a day school decides to disassociate itself with the Episcopal Church, the school and parish leadership will need to reexamine its Anglican heritage and identity.

One of the most important things any church school can do is to continue to explore the central unifying Anglican concepts on which its Episcopal identity and strength are built. Hopefully, in light—or in spite—of the decisions that are made by Episcopal or Anglican church leadership, Episcopal schools will adhere to a most basic Anglican tenet and hold together even with different or opposing positions.

TOMORROW: EXTENDING THE LEGACY

Periodic evaluation and assessment provide the occasion to extend and enhance the performance and the mission of a school. Through the institution's strategic planning or the accreditation process, the school's vision is honed, and issues are identified where growth is both possible and desirable. As Episcopal schools reassess and reflect on fulfilling their vocation as church schools, they will be addressing three specific challenges for the twenty-first century: the greater inclusion of early childhood programs, the opportunity to move out of the mainstream, and the role of worship and religion in church schools in a diverse society.

Early Childhood Programs

There are approximately 1,040 Episcopal schools in the United States, and about 900 Episcopal early childhood programs. Some 300 of these are programs within a larger school, and about 600 are self-standing.[2] The majority of the early childhood programs are small nursery schools or childcare centers under the jurisdiction of a local Episcopal parish or diocese.

Many early childhood programs in Episcopal schools model the highest standards and practices in the field of early education. These exemplary programs are often part of a larger K–8 or K–12 institution. There are many self-standing early childhood programs that are excellent as well. But many church early childhood programs lack connections to the larger concept of Episcopal schools, affiliated with neither the National Association of Episcopal Schools nor the National Association for the Education of Young Children (NAEYC), the professional organization for the early childhood field. These schools may consider themselves a parish outreach program, and some faculty and staff may consider themselves a ministry of the church. Lines of accountability (e.g., does the director receive direction from the parish?) may be unclear. As a consequence, these schools do not benefit from the validation that comes from full membership in the community of Episcopal schools and from exemplary programs created by NAEYC and from its experience in high standards, policies, and practices. There is work to be done in making these schools aware of the importance of relationships with the larger church and early childhood community.

Schools Out of the Mainstream

In the mid-1990s, there were a number of attempts to extend the mission of Episcopal schools in areas not normally served by independent or Episcopal schools, primarily in the inner city, serving at-risk youth. These attempts failed because they lacked sufficient funding sources. Fortunately, exciting changes have been taking place in the first decade of the twenty-first century. Close to a dozen Episcopal schools are newly open or planning to open in urban and rural areas with the expressed purpose of educating students not normally served by Episcopal and/or private schools. An industrious collaboration among religious, business, community, and independent school leaders is making this high-quality education available to economically disadvantaged and culturally diverse students. These new Episcopal schools are designed to address their needs. Some schools are tuition-free; others have a sliding scale appropriate to the income level of the community they serve.

Location plays a role in the mission of each school. One school chose to locate in its city center in order to reach a greater diversity in the student body. Another chose to locate near the crossroads of several urban communities where it could serve the greatest number of eligible students. One middle school that serves economically disadvantaged girls is located in the neighborhood where the annual median household income is $16,000. Another school collaborates with community services in the area to meet student needs that go beyond academic requirements.

Those great Anglican hallmarks of inclusivity and a respect for differences are manifested in the way these new Episcopal schools live out their mission. Christians from all denominations, Buddhists, Muslims, and Jews create a religious diversity within the schools. One school has a student population that is 96 percent racially and ethnically mixed; another school represents its neighborhood with a 44 percent enrollment of African American students.

The face of Episcopal schools is changing with these schools' fuller commitment to our baptismal covenant's charge to "strive for justice and peace among all people and respect the dignity of every human being." These schools serve others by educating children who need education the most. Their support by the entire Episcopal school community will help this ministry flourish in the twenty-first century.

Religious Diversity

Reflecting their Anglican heritage, Episcopal schools are not proselytizing institutions. On the contrary, Episcopal schools have long held the position that their role in spiritual formation is to further a student's understanding and commitment to the values and faith found within their own families. One longtime school head, the Reverend John Verdery, explained the concern with spiritual formation by saying that he hoped a student who was a Jew or a Muslim or a Baptist or a Catholic would, through Episcopal education, become a better practitioner or his or her own faith. Veredy went on to say that the purpose of an Episcopal school was to "confront the young with the importance of deciding what they believe in by letting them know by our actions more than our words, what we believe in."[3] Therefore, worship and religious education in an Episcopal school are not just denominational exercises—or as Bishop Stephen Bayne would say, "a tribal rite of the initiated"[4]—but vehicles for all students to question, explore, and find their faith and then strengthen the bonds with their own faith community.

Religious inclusivity is a given in most Episcopal schools. As the century progresses, however, the issue of religious plurality may become increasingly important. Chaplains in Episcopal schools struggle with the question of how the church should convey its message in a pluralistic school community. More recently, the intensity of the question has been heightened by the plurality within the Anglican Church itself.

At the first national gathering of Episcopal school leadership in 1960, the Reverend E. Allison Grant suggested a solution. Although Grant was not referring to the issue of religious plurality in the schools, his remarks are timely. "It appears to me," said Grant, "that both the Church and the Schools must develop what may be called 'a doctrine of the Church school.'" He asks, "What are the presuppositions that must of necessity underlie all that we attempt to do?"[5] The answers to that question are critical at this time when the fabric of Anglican unity is being tested. A guide to the nature and nurture of Episcopal schools in a pluralistic society, from preprimary through high school, can benefit those who serve the Church in this extensive ministry.

HOLDING THE LEGACY IN TRUST

As academic institutions, Episcopal schools will continue to thrive during the twenty-first century. As educational institutions whose calling includes a spiritual and moral dimension, Episcopal schools will continue to fulfill a vital role in independent education.

Preserving and protecting the legacy on which Episcopal schools are founded are demanding tasks for church school leadership today. There is a delicate balance between making legitimate room for differences in the school's life and its fulfillment of its vocation as a church school. For hundreds of years, Episcopal schools have been models of this *via media*, and, God willing, they should be able to hold the schools in trust for many generations to come. The twenty-first century world needs students who are educated in matters of the heart and soul as well as the mind.

NOTES

Some material used in this essay was first published in my article, "Looking Back to the Future," *NAES Network*, May–June 1997, and is used with permission.

1. National Association of Episcopal Schools, www.spiscopalschools.org.
2. Ibid.
3. John D. Verdery, *Why Church Schools? In Episcopal Church Schools: Their Reasons for Being*, ed. Peter W. Sipple (New York: National Association of Episcopal Schools, 1981), 9.
4. Stephen F. Bayne Jr., "The Christian Witness of the Church's Schools," in *The Church's Schools in a Changing World*, ed. Clarence W. Brickman (Greenwich, Conn.: Seabury Press, 1961), 28.
5. E. Allison Grant, "The Address of the President of the Episcopal School Association," in ibid., 69.

Boarding Schools

The Boarding Advantage

Elisabeth Griffith

$\mathcal{A}$ttitudes about boarding schools are rooted, for many people, in geography and fiction. New Englanders accept them as part of the landscape, where the campuses of schools such as Choate, Groton, Taft, and Deerfield are the centerpieces of picturesque villages. An image of ivy-covered, red-brick academic buildings surrounded by playing fields is part of our visual vocabulary. Southern prep schools evoke images of horse paddocks and golf courses, while western boarding schools conjure up corrals and sun-drenched, flower-filled plazas. In the Midwest, people tend to think of boarding schools as detention centers for the spoiled or delinquent, or as military schools with parade grounds.

Movies, from *Goodbye, Mr. Chips* to *Dead Poets Society*, reinforce those visual stereotypes. There is also an entire genre of "prep lit," beginning with Charles Dickens, almost entirely set in boarding schools. The reading list would include *All Loves Excelling* by Josiah Bunting, *The Headmaster's Papers* by Richard Hawley, *Academy X* by Andrew Trees, *Saving Miss Oliver's* by Stephen Davenport, *The Headmistress* by Angela Mackail Thirkell, *Special Topics in Calamity Physics* by Marisha Pessl, and *The Fall of Rome* by Martha Southgate.

Because of their compelling myths, accomplished alumnae, and expensive tuitions, and because they are not only independent schools but separate communities, boarding schools evoke a sense of not just white but WASP male privilege, despite their contemporary diversity. The overused descriptive adjective "elite" applied to boarding schools repels as well as attracts applicants and families. Old stereotypes linger, so the challenge for boarding schools today is to catch the attention of families who cling to the old stereotypes that only privileged, problem, or neglected kids go to boarding school. A larger challenge is to persuade parents who cling—period—to give their children an opportunity to grow up away from them.

A BRIEF HISTORY OF BOARDING SCHOOLS

Boarding schools in America began as religious institutions. Like medieval guilds, these schools trained acolytes and apprentices. They "prepped" their students for elite colleges, some even becoming the feeder schools for specific colleges. Except for the occasional Moravian or Quaker seminaries, these institutions were single-gender and predominantly male. Initially, boarding schools proposed to instill specific values—values of religious orthodoxy or reform, values of traditional academic inquiry or of scientific investigation, values of Americanism or the dominant culture. When Americans forced indigenous peoples onto reservations, the children were sent to boarding schools where their hair was cut and they were punished for practicing tribal customs or speaking native languages. All boarding schools inculcated a sense of uniformity. Whether or not there was a required uniform, school ties were binding.

The female model was a seminary like that founded by Emma Willard. In 1819 the newly married Mrs. Willard moved to Troy, New York, with the intention of founding a school for bright young women. To that end, she had copied the lessons and texts used by her brother at Middlebury College. She planned to offer science and language courses. When she appealed to the town fathers to underwrite her enterprise, they were appalled at the idea of young women studying physics or physical education. She tried again for funding, this time promising a curriculum that would educate the "Republican mothers" of the future, young women who would happily reside in their assigned "separate sphere." With her finances secure, Mrs. Willard offered her original course of study. In 1833, Mary Lyon established a similar seminary at Mount Holyoke, which eventually evolved into a college.

Until colleges admitted women, following the Civil War, there was no demand for college preparatory work for girls. The best and the brightest white girls "finished" their education at seminaries. However, after public school boards discovered that women would accept lower wages than male teachers, "normal" schools—a hybrid of seminary and teachers' colleges—flourished. Freed black women also attended normal schools, pursuing an education in order to teach. African American families, in fact, gave priority to the education of daughters over sons to protect girls from the sexual coercion of the Reconstruction South.

Once the eastern Seven Sisters colleges and western coeducational state universities opened, preparing girls for college prompted single-gender girls' schools to open. For example, Bryn Mawr School for Girls in Baltimore became Bryn Mawr College's feeder school; graduation from the former depended on matriculation at the latter.

Whereas in the late eighteenth century education had been linked to literacy because democracy depended on educated citizens, in the late nineteenth century education seemed increasingly essential for economic success, especially as curriculum became more scientific and practical. The influx of immigrants from regions other than Western Europe added "Americanization" to the agenda of public schools. At the same time, required school attendance, through the eighth grade or age 16, was a controversial reform promoted to keep children out of factories and sweat shops. In this era, boarding schools took on dual purposes: sanctuaries of privilege for the elite and reformatories for the poor.

THE BENEFITS OF BOARDING SCHOOLS TODAY

Today, boarding schools provide a model of superior and diverse education that might revolutionize public education—if school boards were gutsy enough to try the experiment. Public school boards have less flexibility than private school boards, but Boston and Detroit have launched pilot programs. The SEED Foundation in Washington, D.C., has established charter boarding schools.

Like all independent schools, boarding schools are characterized by small classes, knowledgeable teachers, customized curriculum, and shared values. In addition, boarding schools engender in students greater independence and responsibility. Because they constitute a community of adults and young people who are not related by family ties, they inculcate their own values, goals, and expectations. At boarding schools young people have opportunities to lead, to be responsible for the consequences of their behavior, to live with all kinds of people, to develop habits of self-discipline, to become more self-reliant—in short, to grow up.

For the overscheduled, overmanaged, overindulged, and overprotected adolescents of contemporary American society, boarding schools are antidotes. They espouse and achieve the goal of producing independent and ethical adults. In boarding schools, young people frequently spend more time interacting with adults than they do at home. They see those adults at work—teaching, coaching, monitoring, mentoring, running dorms, and at leisure, with their families. Every level of engagement is possible. Reflecting on the experience, boarding school students repeatedly report how much the attention of the soccer coach or the math teacher mattered. And, in fact, boarding school teachers are often experts in adolescence because their judgments are based on a database much larger than the nuclear family—one hundred ninth graders as compared to one's only child. Adults who are not their parents can be objective and realistic about students' actions because they have less ego invested.

The boarding school model is also an antidote to the struggles of some public schools whose teachers have successful interaction with their students during the school day but cannot influence what happens after school. At the public boarding schools in Boston and Detroit, supper is served and study hall is monitored. In some cases students are bused home at 11:00 P.M. and picked up again at 7:00 A.M.

In boarding schools, students are also held to standards of behavior regarding community norms such as sportsmanship, study hours, or room inspection that some parents find a challenge to enforce. Similarly, being part of a community of people with more ethnic, racial, religious, and economic diversity than most zip codes gives students a preview of the real world of global interaction and communication. For majority Christians to learn about Ramadan or the Days of Awe, for Americans to room with mates from other countries who speak three or four languages, for affluent young people to be in the same classes or on the same teams as young people who take much less for granted, can be enlightening.

Boarding schools are not only college prep in the traditional sense; they also teach students to live independently: how to budget time and sometimes money, do laundry, make new friends, and deal with roommates and dormitory life. Almost every boarding school alum believes that experience made the transition to college much easier, and they testify that the friendships developed away from home are lifelong.

BOARDING SCHOOL PARENTS, BOARDING SCHOOL STUDENTS

All of these benefits of boarding school life would accrue more easily if parents would trust schools more and micromanage their children less. The four-decade decline in boarding school enrollment documented by the National Association of Independent Schools and the Association of Boarding Schools can be attributed to many factors—the growth of local day school alternatives, the high cost of boarding tuition, lingering antiboarding biases—but the most powerful factor is the recent role of parents.

An unintended consequence of the success of the twentieth-century women's movement and of women having greater opportunities in the paid work force has been that women postpone marriage, delay childbirth, and have fewer children, frequently only one child, and may have more discretionary income.

(Interestingly, later marriage and children were also characteristics of the first generations of college-educated women, ca. 1880–1930.) When well-educated, affluent couples have children, they are often in a position to focus all of their energy, ambition, and financial resources on their offspring. Whether the mom leaves her job or juggles paid employment with motherhood, or the dad can afford to stay home, these parents tend to overprotect and overparent their offspring, interrupting and delaying the standard developmental steps toward maturity. These are the parents who have been derided as "helicopter parents"—hovering, employing cell phones as harnesses, using GPS to locate their child at any and every moment. They are motivated equally by affection and anxiety.

Helicopter parents like the caché of boarding school but are reluctant to share supervision of their offspring with any other adult authority. Some of these parents are buying second homes in the towns where their children go to college. Such parental behavior stunts the ability of kids to grow up. One head refers to this behavior as overwatering house plants, drowning rather than nurturing their growth. In the best cases, of course, schools are partnerships between teachers and parents, both nurturing greater maturity, responsibility, and independence of the students.

While this assertion is evidence of author bias—an author educated in excellent Midwestern public schools in the 1950s—I believe boarding schools benefit every kind of student. Besides the pampered and privileged, boarding schools advantage students whose local schools cannot afford extensive arts or athletic programs; students with special needs who are served in "niche" schools; students with learning differences or therapeutic issues or a passion for horses or outdoor education or the cello; American students whose parents work for the Foreign Service or the military or for multinational corporations; international girls who hope to attend an American university; students seeking single-gender classrooms or religiously rooted curriculum or other opportunities not widely available.

Boarding school communities offer students a sanctuary, a place to be or become their genuine selves, guided by adults who expect them to study hard, behave ethically, take responsibility, and accept consequences, who nurture success but are not emotionally daunted by setbacks. Learning to navigate the "real world" within the safe confines of a boarding school is like taking the training wheels off. It allows students to practice independence, wobbling along until balance has been achieved and they soar ahead. Perhaps another way to think about boarding schools, in this era of disconnection and anxiety, is to see the communities they create not as exclusive but inclusive, as welcoming students and their families in joining with school faculty to create a lifelong transformative connection.

· 26 ·

Cultivating Manliness

The Case for Boys' Schools

Damon Bradley

*E*xperience has shown that most prospective parents seeking their child's admission to an independent school are interested primarily in the quality of the education, often determined by a school's standardized test scores, college placement record, and reputation in the community. For these benefits, parents are willing to make a significant monetary outlay for a long period of time. Only secondarily do they acknowledge that the particular school they are considering may have distinctive qualities of its own. To the point, a school may not only provide excellent educational preparation but may be single-gender in structure, a fact that parents may at first consider inconsequential. It is not unusual for some parents to arrive at the admissions office, not only unaware of a school's single-gender character, but despite it. Imagine their astonishment at learning that single-gender schools often consider gender-specific education to be a focal point of their program, a core value fundamental to their very mission.

Coeducational schools are relative newcomers on the American educational scene, only supplanting single-gender schools as the norm in the late nineteenth and early twentieth centuries as arguments for gender homogeneity and equality of the sexes grew in favor. Proponents of the movement maintained that students in a coeducational setting were more likely to develop mutual understanding and respect for members of the opposite sex. Coeducational schools, they argued, better prepared students for a world in which men and women would one day work side by side as equals. The argument ultimately won the day; as a result most Americans living today have been educated in coeducational schools and know only that option. As one educator put it in 1870 with the advent of coeducation, single-gender education had once and for all been "retired to the museum of pedagogical paleontology."[1]

219

Yet the report of the extinction of single-gender education in America was premature. Over the past three decades, the case for girls' schools and boys' schools has gained in prominence, reaffirming for our day the pedagogical rationale for educating boys and girls separately. Indeed, a number of school systems across America, historically coeducational, are now expanding the idea of "school choice" to include schooling in a single-gender environment. What revelation has caused this about-face? The case for all-girls single-gender schools is made elsewhere in this volume. The focus of this essay is on boys in a single-gender setting.

THE REASONS FOR BOYS' SCHOOLS

Ironically, the raison d'être for the boys' school may be more sound today than at any other time in its long history and provides persuasive justification not only for the continuation of the model but also for its expansion. To a reasonably perceptive individual, it may appear tautological to suggest that boys' schools know boys, but it is a notion that is often overlooked. It seems hardly imprudent to assert that because boys' schools are dedicated to the education of boys, they are in a better position to understand boys more fully and to meet their developmental needs more successfully. Because boys' schools specialize in boys, the range of developmental levels in the classroom is narrower than the developmental spectrum reflected in a coeducational setting, where the girls typically mature cognitively at an earlier age than boys. A classroom of boys exhibits a more compressed pattern of maturity; and the boys demonstrate a developmentally predictable receptivity to instruction. Boys' schools provide a setting in which learning can occur in keeping with the tempo and sequence of boys' development. They offer many advantages.

Boys' schools model maleness. Boys are more likely than not to be taught by male teachers in an all-boys' school. Boys' schools tend to recruit and hire a vastly larger percentage of male teachers than a typical coeducational school hires, including staffing at the elementary level. Indeed, some boys' schools intentionally maintain a male-to-female faculty ratio of four- or five-to-one. The reason is self-explanatory: every man was once a boy and presumably retains some primal recollection of what it was like to be a youngster, with all the same foibles and inadequacies now exhibited by the students in his classroom. Likewise, the coterie of men who have chosen to teach in boys' schools instinctively appreciate the challenges of teaching boys and innately apprehend how to engage them in productive schoolwork. Men such as these can be powerful role models for the boys they encounter precisely because they retain the germ of their own boyishness and regard boys nonjudgmentally, without disapproving assumptions. The male teachers not only know how to connect with the boys in the classroom; they also serve as coaches on the athletic field and personal advisers during free periods. These teachers engage the boys in the hallways, sit with them at the lunch table, share tales of adventure, critique the current action movie, and recount the most recent jokes found on the Internet. And while I do not wish to disparage the women who elect to teach boys, many of whom after all have vicariously mastered the tricks of this special trade, there remains a unique bond between a man and a boy.

Boys' schools favor a core curriculum. I lightheartedly call boys' schools "meat and potatoes" schools (as opposed to schools inclined more toward trendy "quiche and sprouts"). That is, of course, a metaphorical way of describing the programs and curricula offered in boys' schools, where there is a preference for focusing more on substance and less on whatever subject matter is currently in vogue. I do not think it is an overstatement to suggest that boys' schools tend to be traditional in their culture, typically emphasizing the verities of human knowledge, the enduring questions, the eternal moral issues, the ageless great books. A preponderance of boys' schools still value breadth and depth typically conveyed through a core curriculum shaped by a healthy skepticism of specialization, especially when it surfaces too soon and too zealously. Frill is viewed as extraneous, even inappropriate. To continue the metaphor, the educational program at most boys' schools is quite unlike the aisles of a supermarket where one can take a little of this and a little of that, satisfying one's personal tastes and partialities, often with little regard for the nutritional value of the selection. Boys' schools want to know what a student has acquired as he exits the checkout line, with some assurance that his shopping basket is filled with provisions that will help sustain him in life.

Boys' schools encourage engagement in the fullness of school life. In a typical coeducational setting, such pursuits as the arts (music, studio art, and drama), journalistic clubs (newspaper, yearbook, and literary magazine) and community service programs are routinely populated by a high proportion of girls, leaving the more physical activities—and too often the monkey business—to the boys. In a boys' school, predictably, if students want a band, a chorus, a literary magazine, or a SADD chapter, then it is up to the boys to make it happen; there are no girls to turn to. And happen it does. The very activities boys would be inclined to leave to the girls, if they could, flourish in boys' schools. Unlike in a coeducational school, there are no girls to make boys self-conscious and insecure, and boys do not feel like sissies in front of the other boys. Boys *sans* girls have been unfettered to seize appealing opportunities they once would have nothing to do with. Although the term "well-rounded" has no doubt become stale through overuse, it still intimates with some accuracy what boys' schools accomplish—namely exposure to the full range of a school's program, including rigorous academics; vigorous athletics; arts, both fine and lively; extracurricular activities; and community service. Boys' schools remain determined to protect those pursuits.

Boys' schools "stand for the hard right." Canon Charles Martin, headmaster of the all-boys St. Albans School from 1949 until 1977, was fond of quoting a line he included in his "Prayer for Boys": "Help me to stand for the hard right against the easy wrong."[2] Canon Martin knew that boys tended to see morality in absolutes, in black and white, and seldom with any gray tones. Boys' schools have recognized that this (some may say) rigid and naive outlook actually presented an educational opportunity by setting expectations of behavior that are at once demanding and lofty. Over the years, boys' schools have built on this uncomplicated moral code by inculcating clear-cut core values and establishing high ethical standards. For example, many boys' schools have adopted formal honor codes as a standard for student conduct. The expectation that the school community will not tolerate lying, cheating, stealing, or plagiarism of any kind is an ethical precept most boys can comprehend and embrace. Honor codes signify the "hard right" and set the criteria of trust and personal integrity by which each member of the community is judged. Boys' schools promote principles that mean something to their students, such as civility, personal accountability, social responsibility, respect toward those who may be different—all virtues to which each boy might aspire in his own life. (I have often pointed out in my own school that the very word "virtue" incorporated the Latin word for man (*vir*), suggesting that "virtue" and "manliness" are closely linked, or certainly were in the eyes of the Romans.) In this male setting, boys are encouraged to do the right thing, exhorted to set their sights on noble endeavors, and persuaded to value right over might. Boys' schools seek to mold boisterous boys into gentle-men who discover more charitable, more compassionate manliness.

THE BENEFITS OF BOYS' SCHOOLS

Not surprisingly, there are those who assume that lack of exposure to the opposite gender is a clear inadequacy of single-gender education. This conclusion is evidently based on the supposition that the only place boys and girls cross paths is in school. Remarkably, they do seem to find one another in other settings, whether casual or structured. In the past, I have described the exit interviews I have conducted with senior boys as they prepare to leave school and head off to college: "Virtually to a last one, each young man attests to the value of being in an all-boys' school. No longer saddled merely with the *anticipation* of the absence of girls, he has by the twelfth grade had the *experience* not only of the presence of girls in many walks of life, but of the unique benefits of an education among boys."[3] Skeptics might also argue that single-gender schools provide an inhospitable environment for exploring sensitive topics such as sex, date rape, sexually transmitted diseases, and other modern gender issues. They will no doubt find it counterintuitive to discover that these schools provide an atmosphere conducive to discussions on delicate subjects of this nature, without the awkwardness and discomfiture that commonly attend such candid exchange. My own familiarity with boys' schools persuades me that students talk about touchy matters more openly and with less hesitation because of the healthy rapport they have with their teachers, the vast majority of whom are also males. Male teachers have the advantage of being able to talk candidly with boys about the gender issues that have preoccupied our society over the past couple of decades without appearing to have an ax to grind or too great a stake in the outcome of the discussion. I maintain that a man can more effectively teach boys of such things—precisely because he is a man.

The friendships that arise in a boys' school are uncommonly deep and often lifelong. There is more sturdiness to male relationships in this setting, if only because these interactions are not diluted by the lure of the opposite sex or eroded as attention is increasingly directed toward the girls. There is a distinct difference between the experience boys have in a single-gender school and their experience in a coed school, a difference that becomes more and more apparent as they move into their high school years. A boy certainly cannot be expected to like every boy in his class or in his school; but absent the distaff side, at least one key stumbling block to male bonding is eliminated.

The camaraderie and closeness that prevail in boys' schools have generated a cadre of loyal alumni, willing to devote considerable time to advancing their school's reputation in the community and sizable resources to assure their school's financial well-being. Fully aware that the mere mention of monetary support may to some border on the indelicate, I would be remiss if I did not mention in this context the historically generous pattern of charitable giving among alumni.

The cynic may assert that these numbers may be easily explained as a result of the higher levels of compensation men still receive in our society. Clearly that is a factor. However, while possessing wealth is a necessary condition of eleemosynary zeal, it is hardly a sufficient cause. People ultimately give to institutions they are proud of and believe in. Financial largesse by itself will not beget philanthropy. There must be lasting good feeling about the school and continuing loyalty to its mission, both of which have their roots in the special relationship boys in a single-gender setting have to one another and the singular affection they have for the school that helped shape their lives.

The playing field, too, is a vital part of life in a boys' school. Boys need daily activity, not only to burn off excess energy but to allow them to focus more successfully on the less physical requirements of the classroom. Activity of this kind also helps keep them fit. Sport in a boys' school is best understood as an extension of the classroom, emphasizing important lessons having more to do with sportsmanship, perseverance, fair play, and teamwork than it does with winning. Learning to lose gracefully, indeed learning to win humbly, are important life lessons that can only be effectively taught on the field. It may be true that an emphasis on athletics can easily slip into overemphasis, into an extreme, at times fanatical obsession that can assume far too large a profile. At its best, however, sports offers a kind of institutional glue that helps to bond disparate constituencies and provides a sense of solidarity like no other aspect of school life. The playing field is the breeding ground for many a life-long friendship. It is also the place where boys learn quickly that differences of race, religion, and ethnicity are irrelevant. Of far more importance for a boy is whether or not a fellow student can run interference or block for him as he struggles for the first down. Competitive team sports build a rather unique *esprit*, even for the fellow who assists a teammate in scoring a goal or even for the third-string player who cheers on the starting team from the bench. Team play naturally breaks down the predictable barriers among boys. While some schools may seek to produce "rugged individualists," boys' schools tend to turn out lifelong "teammates," who stay in touch with one another as they go their separate ways and who will always stand ready to lend aid to a classmate in need.[4]

Boys' schools may not be right for every boy. Indeed, many boys will flourish in a coeducational setting and fully realize the potential they possess. But boys' schools are good places for many boys. They are not the strange places that many people, out of ignorance, may assume. They are healthy settings for boys to grow in wisdom and stature, where it is all right to be a boy, and where boys can develop into well-educated, thoughtful, kind, and high-minded men. Still, to those who have never encountered or observed this type of education, the concept may seem alien, even a little bizarre. Those who have actually experienced a boys' school education, however, are utterly assured of its worth; and the vast preponderance of alumni recognize that they have been part of something very special. They entered a school as ungainly little boys— some of them seemingly slow academically, raucous in their behavior, or just plain naughty—and departed as accomplished young men, who had been extended academically, challenged physically, stimulated artistically, and sensitized to the needs of others. Herein lies the true worth of a boys' school education: it provides an environment where maleness is not scorned but instead admired, even celebrated; and it affords a setting where boys can fulfill the promise, the God-given gifts, that are at times difficult to discern but in the right hands are almost always accessible and just awaiting release. Boys thrive in these surroundings because, after all, boys' schools do know boys.

NOTES

1. William Warren, president of Boston University, quoted in Rosalind Rosenberg, "The Limits of Access: The History of Coeducation in America," in *Women and Higher Education in American History: Essays from the Mount Holyoke College Sesquicentennial Symposia,* ed. John Mack Faragher and Florence Howe (New York: Norton, 1988), 110.

2. The "Prayer for Boys," written by Canon Charles Martin, is still used at St. Albans School and can be found on the school's website, http://www.stalbansschool.org/home/content.asp?id=1522.

3. Damon Bradley, "Boys' Schools Know Boys," *VincentCurtis Educational Register,* 59th ed. (Falmouth, Mass.: VincentCurtis, 1999–2000), 112.

4. Ibid., 109.

Where Girls Come First

Twenty-First-Century Girls' Schools

Ilana DeBare

$\mathcal{N}$early anyone looking at the American education landscape in the late 1960s and 1970s would have concluded that girls' schools were a dying breed. The top men's colleges like Harvard and Yale were going coed, as were the country's leading boys' high schools. Scores of girls' schools went out of business or were swallowed up by their better-funded, more prestigious male counterparts. The number of all-girl private secondary schools in the United States fell from 1,132 to 551—a drop of more than half—between 1965 and 1978.[1]

But that seemingly inevitable mass extinction of girls' schools never came to pass. And in fact, since around 1990, there has been a remarkable resurgence of single-gender education for girls in the United States. More than thirty new private girls' schools have opened nationally, including the school that I helped start, the Julia Morgan School for Girls in Oakland, California. Hundreds of public schools quietly began experimenting with single-gender classes in subjects like math and science. And for the first time in a century, some communities launched all-girl public secondary schools such as the Young Women's Leadership School in Harlem.[2]

This new wave of interest in all-girl education was spurred in part by research on the challenges girls face in coed environments. The American Association of University Women and scholars such as Myra Sadker and David Sadker documented how, even in the very best schools, girls typically receive less teacher attention than boys and are less likely to pursue math and science.[3] At the same time, feminist scholars such as Carol Gilligan started calling attention to differences in the ways that girls and boys learn. Meanwhile, through the 1980s and 1990s, girls' schools retooled themselves to meet the needs of young women in the twenty-first century, spending millions of dollars on new sports facilities and science laboratories and developing curricula to address issues such as financial literacy and media images of women. The creation of the National Coalition of Girls' Schools in 1991 helped girls' schools exchange information, support each other, and promote themselves to the broader world.[4] The result is that today's girls' schools share a clearly defined mission—empowering young women to succeed in a world that offers them both unparalleled opportunities and some lingering hurdles.

What are contemporary girls' schools like on a day-to-day basis? There is no single cookie-cutter mold. Each school is a product of its own community and history, whether it is a century-old boarding school with a stellar equestrian program, a brand-new public school with a goal of preparing inner-city girls for college, or a Catholic school that aims for spiritual as well as intellectual growth. But amid the differences, there are certain commonalities.

At girls' schools, girls play all the roles. Girls are the student council presidents, not just the secretaries. They are the math whizzes, the athletic stars, the computer gurus, the class clowns. Some girls develop a lifelong interest in subjects such as physics or engineering that they might not have discovered in a coed class. And all girls absorb an implicit message that women can do anything, that it is completely normal for women to be leaders.

Girls are valued for their heads and hearts, not their looks. Alice Rivlin, budget director under President Bill Clinton, attended the Madeira School in McLean, Virginia. She recalled, "I loved the way I didn't have to worry about what I wore. I wasn't competing with girls for the best sweater, which had been part of the public school environment. You didn't have to be embarrassed to be brainy, which was the case at public school."[5]

Girls are freed from the constant internal pressure to please boys. The pressure on teens to be popular with the other sex can be overwhelming. For girls, that often means pressure not to look too smart, too capable, or too ambitious. Many girls respond by "dumbing down" or silencing themselves. Without boys around, many girls say they feel more free to speak up, take intellectual risks, and make mistakes—all of which are key steps on the path of learning. "At my old school I didn't want to stick myself out in classes," said an eighth grader at the new Atlanta Girls' School. "I was kind of passive. Here I talk more."[6]

Girls' schools allow young women to stay girls a little longer. It is not unusual at a girls 'school to see eighth graders doing cartwheels on the lawn at lunch or tenth graders playing Red Rover. The absence of boys allows girls to retain the playful, silly parts of childhood a little longer. In today's world, where 6-year-olds listen to Britney Spears and 12-year-olds feel pressure to have oral sex, this playfulness can be a particularly precious gift.

Girls develop strong female friendships. Many alumnae say that the strongest friendships of their lives are those from their girls' schools. "I value female friendships very highly, maybe because I had more time to forge those friendships," said an alumna of a Catholic girls' school in Seattle. "I saw I could have very close female friendships, which was not an experience familiar to me from junior high."[7]

Girls learn from female role models. Today all schools should include women's lives and experiences in their curricula. But faculty at girls' schools are more likely to go the extra mile to dig up readings on the role of women in the abolitionist movement or to hang a poster of Marie Curie alongside the one of Albert Einstein. Many schools have career days, mentor programs, or internships aimed at exposing girls to the wide range of options available to them in life.

Girls' schools provide strong math and science teaching. Girls' schools are acutely aware of the historical gender gap in math and science and have devoted significant resources to figuring out how best to teach these subjects. They have often been ahead of the pack when it comes to using hands-on approaches or group projects to teach math and science. Some girls' schools have financial literacy curricula that teach everything from how to balance a checkbook to how to invest in the stock market and how to write a business plan.

Girls' schools give attention to the tough social issues facing young women. Walking the halls of a girls' school, you are likely to pass a bulletin board plastered with photographs from fashion magazines—assembled as part of a critical study of how the media portrays women's bodies. Body image, healthy friendships, sexuality, eating disorders: many girls' schools have developed curricula or programs to address these hot-button issues directly, in an atmosphere of trust and candor.

In the past, some parents chose a girls' school in an effort to shelter their daughter from boys, sex, or drugs—a Rapunzel's-tower approach toward schooling. That is the wrong reason for choosing a girls' school today. In our ultrawired world of instant messaging, cell phones, YouTube, and MySpace, no school can truly shelter students from anything. But what girls' schools can do is give young women the information and confidence they need to make healthy choices. They can create a peer culture that encourages girls to maintain those healthy choices when they are on their own, out of sight of teachers and parents.

Along with the many benefits of girls' schools, there are of course some potential pitfalls. Primary among them is stereotyping. Schools and teachers that are new to the idea of single-gender education can sometimes slip into a reliance on gender stereotypes in the classroom—for instance, teaching math to boys through problems about sports and to girls through problems about shopping. While perhaps a quick way to come up with a lesson plan, stereotypes like these undermine the broader goal of preparing girls to be leaders and play a variety of roles in today's world.

And although there is an increasing body of scientific research on girls' and boys' learning differences, teachers need to remember that there is also a range of learning styles within each gender. Many girls learn well by working in small groups, for instance, but there are also girls who are the quintessential lone scholars.

So one question parents should ask when considering a girls' school is what kind of continuing education is provided to the faculty on single-sex classroom dynamics and working with girls. Do teachers attend conferences on gender and education? Do they have group discussions or guest speakers about girls' social and emotional development? Are there mentoring systems in place to help novice teachers who may not have worked with an all-girl population before?

One lingering assumption about girls' schools it that they are the right choice for one particular type of girl—the shy, quiet child who might wilt in a coed environment. That is not true. While the quiet girl may thrive in a girls' school, so do the outspoken leaders and top achievers.

Another lingering myth is that girls will emerge from a single-gender experience socially unprepared for the coed "real world." This assumption was sometimes true fifty years ago, when schools were a more hermetically sealed environment. But girls today have plenty of opportunities to be friends with boys outside of school. Parents who are concerned about these opportunities should seek out healthy coed extracurricular activities for their daughters— whether it is a church youth group, summer camp, or theater club, or simply time spent hanging out with brothers and male cousins. A few girls' schools even have a nearby "brother school" that co-sponsors joint activities such as coed theater productions and service projects.

Over the next few years, it is likely that the public school sector will see the biggest increase in all-girl schools and classes. The 1972 federal Title IX law banning gender discrimination in education had long been interpreted as prohibiting public single-gender schools. But in 2001, as part of the No Child Left Behind reform package, Congress passed legislation allowing public single-gender schools or classes if enrollment is voluntary and if comparable academic opportunities are available to both sexes. That legislation contributed to an increase of single-gender public schools around the country that is likely to continue.

Even with their resurgence over the past two decades, however, girls' schools remain a tiny sliver of the American educational system. And they are likely to remain a small sliver. Attending a girls' school continues to be a "countercultural" choice—for parents, but particularly for their teen or preteen daughters. The media barrage young women with such ubiquitous messages about the importance of boys—of having fun with boys, looking good for boys, being popular with boys—that many girls cannot conceive of spend-ing six hours a day away from boys. It takes considerable guts for an eighth grader to tell her friends that she has decided to enroll in an all-girl high school.

But that gutsy decision may pay off for the rest of her life. Parents some-times ask about the best time to attend a girls' school—elementary, middle, or high school, or college. We started the Julia Morgan School as a grade 6–8 middle school because we felt early adolescence was a particularly critical time for girls. But in the long run, the exact timing of a girl's single-gender expe-rience is less important than the fact that she has had that experience.

"Being in a single-sex setting showed me thousands of examples of smart, funny, unique women and gave me the impression that I could be that too," said an alumna of all-women Mills College in Oakland, California.

> And secondly, it created a terrific sexism barometer for late in life. Now, when I hear a comment that I think is offensive, I know it's offensive be-cause I know that at Mills such a comment never would have been uttered. I have something to bounce the "real world" off of. Because I've been in a place where women are respected I can immediately spot when they are being slighted. I'm not sure I would be as able to do that if I had stayed in coed settings all my life.[8]

At their best, girls' schools turn out young women with self-esteem, in-telligence and character—and also an inner, guiding vision of what a society would look like that truly respected women. The girls' schools of today are not cloisters aimed at keeping girls away from the world. They are training grounds for future leaders—places where girls have room to grow, to take their own talents and ideas seriously, and then emerge to shape a better world.

NOTES

1. Ilana DeBare, *Where Girls Come First: The Rise, Fall and Surprising Revival of Girls' Schools* (New York: Tarcher/Penguin, 2004), 335.

2. For statistics and other information on single-gender public schools, see the Na-tional Association for Single-Sex Public Education website, www.nasspe.org.

3. American Association of University Women, *How Schools Shortchange Girls: The AAUW Report* (New York: Marlowe & Co., 1995). See also Myra Sadker and David Sadker, *Failing at Fairness: How Our Schools Cheat Girls* (New York: Simon & Schus-ter, 1994).

4. For a directory of U.S. girls' schools, see the National Coalition of Girls' Schools website, www.ncgs.org.

5. Quoted in DeBare, *Where Girls Come First*, 315.
6. Quoted in ibid.
7. Sara Klein, interview with author.
8. Quoted in DeBare, *Where Girls Come First*, 326.

FURTHER READING

Datnow, Amanda, and Lea Hubbard, eds. *Gender in Policy and Practice: Perspectives on Single Sex and Coeducational Schooling*. New York: Routledge Falmer, 2002.

Meehan, Diana. *Learning Like a Girl: Educating Our Daughters in Schools of Their Own*. New York: Public Affairs, 2007.

Stabiner, Karen. *All Girls: Single-Sex Education and Why It Matters*. New York: Riverhead, 2002.

Salomone, Rosemary C. *Same, Different, Equal: Rethinking Single-Sex Schooling*. New Haven, Conn.: Yale University Press, 2003.

IV

THE FUTURE COURSE

· 28 ·

Transmogrifying Education for the Twenty-First Century

Patrick F. Bassett

The crusty headmaster of one of America's most prestigious schools said a generation ago, "It doesn't matter what we teach, so long as most of it is boring and all of it irrelevant." The intellectual presumption behind this sardonic comment—that students were supposed to emerge from the American "academy" as critical thinkers with a broad base of erudite (if effete) knowledge—persists at many schools and colleges. Our European counterparts were more likely to specialize in a field (taking fewer courses to prepare for A-level exams in Great Britain, for example), but the expectations were similar: to produce a graduate with a scholarly penchant and at least some level of deep knowledge in one or more academic disciplines.

The three-hundred-year liberal arts tradition in American independent schools and universities was at first partly pragmatic, as indicated in the famous observation by one of America's true intellectuals, John Adams:

> I must study politics and war that my sons may have liberty to study mathematics and philosophy. My sons ought to study mathematics and philosophy, geography, natural history, naval architecture, navigation, commerce, and agriculture in order to give their children a right to study painting, poetry, music, architecture, statuary, tapestry, and porcelain.[1]

Our more contemporary fantasy has been that the academy's broad, liberal arts and discipline-specific orientation is still perfectly suited for "knowledge workers" in the Information Age. What has always been understood but not acknowledged, however, is that only a small percentage of students are inspired to become both broadly educated scholars and experts in at least one field. Yet now that we see how the world has changed in recent years, we are rightfully worried that we are not even doing so well in preparing students for the previous century, much less for the current one.

For one thing, nationally, we've never been very successful in engaging students fully or graduating all of them from high school, much less college. According to research compiled by the National Center for Higher Education Management Systems in 2003, of 100 ninth graders entering high school, 67 earn a high school diploma in four years, 38 enter college, 26 are still enrolled for sophomore year, but only 18 graduate from college within six years.[2] These numbers do not indicate a very good return on the massive investment of time, energy, and resources for the U.S. educational system.

And getting children through the educational pipeline is not the only problem. A recent *Washington Post* article cited research from the American Institutes for Research showing that only 38 percent of graduating college seniors can successfully perform tasks such as comparing viewpoints in two newspaper editorials. The same article also cited findings from the National Survey of Student Engagement, which found that "about 30 percent of college students reported being assigned to read four or fewer books in their entire senior year, while nearly half (48 percent) of seniors were assigned to write no papers of twenty pages or more."[3]

Apparently, the disengagement begins early. An article in *Newsweek* cites the "fourth-grade slump," where declining interest in reading begins, accompanied by a gradual disengagement from school. Fourth grade is also where American test scores, competitive internationally to that point, begin to drop.[4]

So, it turns out, we pay a very high price for teaching what seems to kids, increasingly in the digital age, that which is "boring" and "irrelevant." Ironically, there is already emerging wide consensus among educators, scholars, and the business community about what's necessary to teach and how to teach it for what author Daniel Pink, in *A Whole New Mind*, calls the "Conceptual Age" of the twenty-first century.[5]

In my work with schools in the United States and around the world, I frequently address groups of leaders, not only educators but their boards of trustees, primarily comprised of CEOs, social sector leaders, professionals, and, internationally, the diplomatic corps. When I ask the kind of "generative" question these school leaders should be asking themselves—"What are the skills and values that will be rewarded in the twenty-first century?"—I always, *every time, everywhere, and anywhere in the world*, get the same list:

- integrity and character
- teaming and leadership
- communication skills

- empathy, social and global consciousness
- expertise/competence in some field
- innovativeness and creativity

What's interesting is that this "wisdom of the crowd" is actually confirmed by a whole host of researchers, observers, and commissions that have weighed in on the topic within the last few years. In my opinion, some of the most important recent books and reports for educators and education policy makers include:

- *Tough Choices or Tough Times.* This New Commission on the Future of the American Workforce report emphasizes the importance of: (1) creativity and innovation; (2) facility with the use of ideas and abstractions; (3) self-discipline and organization to manage one's own work and drive it through to successful conclusion; (4) leadership; (5) ability to function well as a member of a team.[6]
- *Five Minds for the Future.* Howard Gardner argues for the: (1) disciplined mind (expertise in a field); (2) synthesizing mind (scanning and weaving into coherence); (3) creating mind (discovery and innovation); (4) respectful mind (open mindedness and inclusiveness); (5) ethical mind (moral courage).[7]
- *College Learning for the New Global Century.* This Association of American Colleges and Universities report cites the following as vital skills: (1) cross-disciplinary knowledge; (2) communication skills; (3) teamwork; (4) analytical reasoning; (5) real world problem-solving skills.[8]
- *A Whole New Mind.* Author Daniel Pink argues that the future will reward those who are masters of: (1) design (beyond function to beauty); (2) story (beyond argument to storytelling); (3) symphony (beyond individual insight or virtuosity to synthesis and orchestration); (4) empathy (beyond logic to empathy and social and global consciousness); (5) play (beyond seriousness to play and flow—and discovering the intoxication of what one loves and is really good at); (6) meaning (beyond accumulation of "things" to "meaning in life," past "making a difference" to "leaving a legacy" and to experiencing the transcendent).[9]

Thus, an act of "symphony" and "synthesis" coupled with an act of "meaning" and "discipline"—to use Pink's and Gardner's terms, respectively—is to see from these disparate sources the same message and meaning: the need to re-engineer the curriculum of twenty-first-century schools to align with these agreed-upon skills, values, and aptitudes if our students are to be well-served (and our economy and culture to prosper) in a much more competitive, global, high-tech, volatile, and uncertain future.

But where to begin? How about starting with a modest redirection, since whole-scale reform never has or never will work in the education industry? *Wikinomics,* by Dan Tapscott and Anthony D. Williams, points us to a much more bottom-up, "peer-negotiated" future that the next generation of teachers, already in our schools, could, for the first time in the history of our industry, lead.[10] So let's ask (in Marc Prensky's term), the "digital natives"[11] of any age in our school (including not just the 20-something "net-generation" new teachers but also their younger brothers and sisters actually in school as students and their older innovation-minded colleague mentors) to co-design the school of the future. All of the following possibilities exist for "experimenting" and co-creating the new design:

- schools within a school open to any or all for part of their program—with the opportunity to concentrate in an area of interest and strength: robotics; the arts; entrepreneurship; inventors' workshop; design workshop; next generation Web 2.0 development; video-casting; or any of the traditional disciplines (foreign language, math, science, English, history) going far beyond what's possible in typical survey courses
- semester school option within one's own school or among a collaborative supported by many schools, like the Mountain School, where kids live on an organic farm in Vermont for a semester; or CITYterm, where New York City becomes the classroom; or SEGL— the School for Ethics and Global Leadership, where students focus on ethics and international affairs with Washington, D.C., as the backdrop[12]
- a one-day per week alternative curriculum, like the service and career internships on Wednesdays at Madeira School, McLean, Virginia, or the internships at the Cristo Rey Schools[13]
- virtual collaboratives that match schools from all over the world to develop project-based curricula addressing real-world projects and problems, such as the online "Virtual Science Fair" produced by the Near-East South Asia Association of Overseas Schools or the National Association of Independent Schools' Challenge 20/20 Program[14] based upon Jean-François Rischard's *High Noon: 20 Global Problems and 20 Years to Solve Them*[15]
- whatever else inspires the R&D design team made up of the volunteer team within the school community (students, faculty, venture capitalists, board members, and parents).

What is likely but sad is that it will be the well-resourced and successful schools in the public and private domains that will be equipped to move forward with the twenty-first-century agenda. But poor kids in marginal schools need this level of experimentation as well: isn't four days of "drill and kill" to meet the government standards and testing agenda punishment enough for all involved? Wouldn't one day per week of truly engaging and exciting schooling be worth coming to school for the other four days of the week for all students in all schools?

No top-down, government-mandated, administrator-required approach need apply. Just take the folks in any school who already possess the twenty-first-century skills identified above and give them resources and a blessing to experiment and permission to fail. If we do so, in the new networked and collaborative digital model of the Conceptual Age, we will quickly find out what works and emulate it worldwide a million times over. Now there's a proposition that will attract just the right next generation of teachers to your school. Here's the cool thing: thinking and acting this way has the potential to attract and keep all-stars at your school. And, it could even pay for them.

NOTES

1. John Adams to Abigail Adams, May 12, 1780, Adams Papers, Massachussetts Historical Society, http://www.masshist.org/adams/quotes.cfm.

2. National Center for Higher Education Management Systems, "Conceptualizing and Researching the Educational Pipeline," *NCHEMS News* 20 (2003): 2–7, http://www.nchems.org/news/NCHEMS%20News%20May2003.pdf.

3. Thomas Toch and Kevin Carey, "Where Colleges Don't Excel," *Washington Post*, April 6, 2007, A21.

4. Peg Tyre and Karen Springen, "Fourth-Grade Slump," *Newsweek*, February 19, 2007, http://www.msnbc.msn.com/id/17083398/site/newsweek/.

5. Daniel Pink. *A Whole New Mind: Why Right-Brainers Will Rule the Future* (New York: Penguin Group, 2006).

6. National Center on Education and the Economy, *Tough Choices or Tough Times: The Report of New Commission on the Future of the American Workforce* (San Francisco, Calif.: Jossey-Bass, 2006).

7. Howard Gardner, *Five Minds for the Future* (Boston, Mass.: Harvard Business School Publishing, 2006).

8. National Leadership Council for Liberal Education and America's Promise, *College Learning for the New Global Century* (Washington, D.C.: Association of American Colleges and Universities, 2006), http://www.aacu.org/advocacy/leap/documents/GlobalCentury_final.pdf.

9. Pink, *A Whole New Mind*.

10. Don Tapscott and Anthony D. Williams, *Wikinomics: How Mass Collaboration Changes Everything* (New York: Portfolio, 2006).

11. Marc Prensky, "Digital Natives, Digital Immigrants," *On the Horizon* (NCB University Press) 9, no. 5 (October 2001), http://www.marcprensky.com/writing/Prensky%20-%20Digital%20Natives,%20Digital%20Immigrants%20-%20Part1.pdf.

12. Mountain School, http://www.mountainschool.org/; CITYterm, http://www.themastersschool.com/CityTerm/index.htm; School for Ethics and Global Leadership, http://www.schoolforethics.org/.

13. Madeira School, http://www.madeira.org/on_campus/cocurriculum.aspx; Cristo Rey schools, http://www.cristoreynetwork.org.

14. NESA Virtual Science Fair, http://www.nais.org/resources/index.cfm?ItemNumber=149603; NAIS Challenge 20/20, http://www.nais.org/go/challenge2020.

15. Jean-François Rischard, *High Noon: 20 Global Problems, 20 Years to Solve Them* (New York: Basic Books, 2002).

• 29 •

Future Stock vs. Future Shock

Richard K. Jung

*J*ohn Dewey, America's most influential twentieth-century educational philosopher, believed in the connection between theory and practice. Dewey both wrote about education and actively participated in it for a time through the creation of a "laboratory school" for children connected to the University of Chicago. As a philosopher, Dewey was a pragmatist who stated in the opening of his treatise *Experience and Education* that "the main purpose or objective [of education] is to prepare the young for future responsibilities and for success in life."[1]

In the spirit of John Dewey, this collection—with essays written by twenty-first-century educators, leaders, and policy analysts—plots for parents and educational practitioners the sometimes familiar and other times less familiar or largely uncharted terrain of American education a century after Dewey's first landmark treatise, *How We Think* in 1910.[2] This present collection, however, does so very much with Dewey's futurist orientation in mind.

Each essayist was asked to describe a particular model or design, including its history, philosophy, and the types of students and families that have most used or found it successful. As a collection, the book provides educators and parents an insider's assessment of the defining characteristics as well the commonalities in the rapidly expanding range of school choices.

As a collection, these essays indicate that modern-day educational leaders still grapple with the fundamental questions Dewey raised almost a century ago: How do we think? What educational experiences are most effective, and for whom? And how do we best prepare our children for their future and future responsibilities? These essays also indicate that the future facing today's parents and youth is multicultural, quickly changing, complex, technologically driven, and global. The premise of this collection of essays, at least when it comes to educational choices, is that the best antidote to what futurologist

Alvin Toffler called "future shock" is to take "future stock" of what options are available on the rapidly evolving educational landscape.[3]

"FUTURE STOCK" TERRAIN MAPPING OF
THE EVOLVING LANDSCAPE

Why is taking future stock so important in a future shock era? Toffler's most concise definition of future shock is that "too much change in too short a period of time" leads to "information overload."[4] Even Toffler might be shocked by a few of the predictions in futurist Jim Carroll's article, "What Comes Next? (And What Should Educators Do about It?)"[5]

A pair of Carroll's observations about the nature of the world into which today's children are graduating, however, provides a useful framework for summarizing the "higher elevation" educational terrain mapped in these collected essays.

Rapid Knowledge Growth

Carroll considers "ever-growing sapiential circles" as the core trend driving rapid knowledge growth that will have the most significant impact on education.[6] With recent technology advances, we can now connect the minds of people around the world who share an interest in a topic or issue. The impacts of living in such a "flat world" are and will become even more dramatic—from the way Facebook and similar websites are changing the social fabric of schools to the amount of medical knowledge doubling every eight years.

Several essays in this collection reformulate this trend into a question: What will today's children need to know in the twenty-first century, and how will they learn it? Anne-Marie Pierce tackles this question directly in her essay "International and Internationally Minded Schools." Describing the attributes of the International Baccalaureate Organization (IBO) and other international programs that "are particularly well-suited to the needs of the twenty-first century," she claims they:

- choose to emphasize process over content
- emphasize strong communication skills
- develop solid learning and higher-order thinking skills
- encourage students to become familiar with the world
- foster creativity, action, and service
- integrate various disciplines
- develop principled, caring, and compassionate thinkers

- strive to develop mastery in more than one language
- offer a balance between individual and team work

In "Independent Schools," Pearl Rock Kane echoes this assessment. Together they underscore Carroll's claim that: "learning is what most adults will do for a living in the 21st century."[7]

Michael Thompson's introductory essay, "School Choice: A Personal History," frames at the outset of this collection why learning about today's and future educational choices is so critical: "My children and my work led me to two conclusions: first, that school 'fit' is the thing that every child needs, and, second, that the parental impulse to find the best possible school situation for a child is absolutely universal and must be honored by society." The essays that follow this introductory essay can guide that universal parental impulse and quest for "fit." In "Virtual Schools Are the Future," for example, Lisa Snell demonstrates the advantages of virtual learning in finding that fit, as students in these schools benefit from "truly individualized learning" and the leaders of these schools are able immediately to incorporate new information into a curriculum that is already heavily research-based.

Rapid Career Changes

Carroll notes that Australian educators estimate that "65% of children in preschool will be employed in roles and jobs that don't exist today."[8] The same will likely be true for American preschoolers today. So, as Patrick F. Bassett emphasizes in his essay, "Transmogrifying Education for the Twenty-First Century," the "generative" skill sets and enduring values that "will be rewarded in the twenty-first century" include:

- integrity and character
- teaming and leadership
- communication skills
- empathy, social and global consciousness
- expertise/competence in some field
- innovativeness and creativity

ALTERNATIVE PUBLIC SCHOOL MODELS' TERRAIN MAPPING

What Americans Think about Their Schools, a recent national survey conducted by Harvard University's Program and Education Policy and Governance and

Education Next, underscores two important values reshaping today's educational landscape: accountability and choice. This report begins by noting "Americans both care about their schools and want them to improve."[9] American adults give the nation's public schools only mediocre grades yet are willing to invest more money in public education, especially if this investment is tied to holding schools more accountable or giving parents more choice. In her essay, "American Public Education," Paula J. Carreiro expands on the various tensions in public schooling based on unequal funding, standards, and accountability measures.

Two essays in this collection map the recent rapid growth of alternative forms of public education that are likely to become more salient forces as the twenty-first century progresses. Merrill Hall describes home schools in "Home Schooling," and Bruno V. Manno describes charter schools in "Chartering Choices: A Strategy for Creating New Schools." Home schooling in America is more than 250 years old, while the charter school movement began less than two decades ago, in 1991. And although together, formal home schools and charter schools educate less than 5 percent of the American school-age population, their enrollment and impacts have grown substantially in a relatively short period of time. Harvard's survey indicates that the public is increasingly supportive of charter schools. In "Financing Education: The Worm in the Apple," Peter M. Branch elaborates on the funding issues for these and other types of public schools historically and currently.

SPECIALTY SCHOOL TERRAIN MAPPING

This collection of essays also maps educational terrain of several types of specialty schools, often but not always outside the perimeter of public schools. Authors address single-gender schools ("Cultivating Manliness: The Case for Boys' Schools" by Damon Bradley, and "Where Girls Come First: Twenty-First-Century Girls' Schools" by Ilana DeBare); religious schools ("The Rise and Fall and Rise of Catholic Schools" by Robert Mattingly, "Jewish Day Schools in the Twenty-First Century" by Laurie Piette, "Christian Schools: Redeeming Lives and Culture" by Erik P. Ellefsen, "Episcopal Schools: An Anglican Legacy" by Ann Gordon, and "Islamic Schools: The Struggle for Successful Integration" by Farhat Siddiqui); developmentally focused schools ("The Right Place: Nursery School in the Twenty-First Century" by Gay Cioffi, "The Preprimary Schools of Reggio Emilia" by Pam Oken-Wright, "The New (Old) Vision: Montessori Education in the Twenty-First Century" by Maura C. Joyce, and "Specialty Arts High Schools" by Mitzi Yates

Lizárraga); schools with students with different learning needs ("Schools for Gifted and Talented Students" by Virginia H. Burney, "Multiple Intelligences: Capitalizing on Strengths" by Thomas R. Hoerr, and "Schools for Students with Different Learning Needs" by Marcie C. Roberts); and year-round schools ("The Too-Long Summer Vacation: School Calendar Reform," by Charles Ballinger).

Learning about the history, critical elements, and students served by each of the models can help parents know about and identify educational options that are best suited for their children and might best prepare today's youth for a world quite different from today.

"Below-the-Surface" Educational Terrain Mapping: Governance and Community

A less immediately obvious, but perhaps more important theme in these essays is that one way parents can separate effective models from ineffective ones is to look not only at but beyond the defining characteristics of these designs. Several of these essays point to the importance of assessing the extent to which the leaders and governance structures at a school can keep it on track and true to its mission. All point to the importance of community as a fundamental, below-the-surface predicate for success. In fact, a sense of community is at the heart of a school's success, whether measured in a school's growth, its fund-raising ability, or its student achievement.

Kane places "self-governance" at the front of her list for what separates independent schools from public schools. Keith Weller Frome, in "Model and Mission: What a School Wants, What a School Needs," uses case studies to point to both the difficulty and importance of mission being supported by viable leadership and governance structures. And Gloria H. Cooper in "New Age Academy: An Experimental Village School Model" calls on the larger community to enhance that leadership.

Eileen Shields-West's essay, "Governance: Trying to Perfect," comparing the governance models of independent schools, public charter schools, and traditional public schools, turns to BoardSource's conclusions about what distinguishes an "exceptional" board. Traits to look for include a board that has a constructive partnership with the school's head or principal, is mission driven, is results oriented, is strategic in its emphasis, values an ethos of transparency, and is committed to continuous learning and revitalization.

What do successful schools as diverse as Montessori, single-gender, boarding, and charter schools have in common? Joyce points to the centrality of "a community with heritage" at the heart of the mixed-aged Montessori model. Bradley emphasizes the "camaraderie and closeness" being at the core of the successful all-boys' school, as does Elisabeth Griffith as she describes the ideal boarding school in "Boarding Schools: The Boarding Advantage." And Manno characterizes the key element of successful charter schools in this way: "Charter schools are created by choices—teacher, parent, and student choices—that produce voluntary associations—in this case, school communities. The choice metaphor is complemented by the community metaphor."

As a collection then, these essays point to the often less visible, but more potent elements of effective governance and strong community when considering choices among a proliferation of choices in America's twenty-first-century schools.

Interestingly, as Richard P. Fitzgerald argues in "The Ends of the Spectrum: A Comparison of Traditional and Progressive Schools," the concluding words of Dewey's *Experience and Education* encourage us, as well, to look beyond educational labels such as "progressive," or "traditional," and a host of other "brand names." Dewey gives the following observation and advice: "We shall make surer and faster progress when we devote ourselves to finding out just what education is and what conditions have to be satisfied in order that education may be reality and not a name or a slogan."[10] Accordingly, this collection not only offers insiders' perspectives on many of the proliferating educational models on today's educational landscape but also provides insights for determining whether the necessary "conditions" are present for that model's success.

NOTES

1. John Dewey, *Experience and Education* (New York: Collier Books, 1938), 18.
2. John Dewey, *How We Think* (Boston, Mass.: D.C. Heath, 1910).
3. Alvin Toffler, *Future Shock* (New York: Random House, 1970).
4. Ibid., 12.
5. Jim Carroll, "What Comes Next? (And What Should Educators Do about It?)," http://www.jimcarroll.com/10s/10education.htm.
6. Ibid.
7. Ibid.
8. Ibid.
9. William G. Howell, Martin R. West, and Paul E. Peterson, *What Americans Think about Their Schools*, www.hoover.org/publications/ednext/8768237.html.
10. Dewey, *Experience and Education*, 90.

About the Contributors

Charles Ballinger is executive director emeritus of the National Association for Year-Round Education, San Diego. He has been a classroom teacher, a central office administrator, a laboratory school instructor at the Ohio State University, a consultant for the Ohio Department of Education, and a professional association chief executive. He is the author of numerous articles for professional journals and the co-author of *School Calendar Reform: Learning in All Seasons* (2006).

Patrick F. Bassett became the president of the National Association of Independent Schools in August 2001, subsequent to a career as an independent school teacher, school head, and regional association director. He was named a Kellogg National Leadership Fellow in 1986 and in March 2000 was honored by the Klingenstein Center for Educational Leadership at Teachers College, Columbia University, with the Educational Leadership Award.

Damon Bradley taught in independent schools, both at home and abroad, for nearly thirty-five years, devoting the greater part of his career to the education of boys. He served as headmaster of two schools, including fourteen years as headmaster of Landon School, a boys' school in Bethesda, Maryland. Following his retirement in 2004, he was appointed lecturer in education at Washington College, Chestertown, Maryland.

Peter M. Branch, the son of public school teachers, attended public schools until college, when he received a BA from Williams College and an MA in history from Indiana University. He has served for more than thirty years as the head of independent schools, including acting head of the Dalton School, New York, and head of Woodmere Academy, Woodmere, New York; Holland

Hall School, Tulsa, Oklahoma; and, since 1996, Georgetown Day School, Washington, D.C. He has served on many independent school association boards, including the National Association of Episcopal Schools, of which he was president.

Virginia H. Burney, PhD, is an educational psychologist and gifted and talented consultant with the Indiana Education Project at Ball State University in Muncie, Indiana, where she works on statewide projects for high-ability students in public schools. She is a current or former member of the boards of the National Association for Gifted Children, the Indiana Association for the Gifted, the College Board's Indiana Advanced Placement Advisory Council, Park Tudor School, and Sycamore School.

Paula J. Carreiro is the head of Beauvoir, the National Cathedral Elementary School, in Washington, D.C. As an educational professional for thirty-five years, she has worked in numerous school settings, both public and private, and traveled to other countries to observe and evaluate a variety of school environments. In addition, she has served on several educational association boards, independent school boards, and university advisory boards, and she chaired the board of the Association of Independent Schools in Washington, D.C.

Gay Cioffi has been a teacher director at the Little Folks School in Washington, D.C., for the past twenty-eight years. She has written extensively about early childhood education and the arts. Her papers on early childhood education have been presented at the Oxford Round Table, Oxford University, and the National Association of Early Childhood Education. She has received two Outstanding Teacher Awards from the Wolf Trap Foundation for the Performing Arts.

Gloria H. Cooper, a veteran of the Philadelphia, Washington, D.C., and Berkeley public schools systems, is the founder of the New Age Academy, a learning institute in Berkeley, California. In June 2007, she was awarded a special proclamation by the mayor for helping guide Berkeley's youth "in these difficult middle school years into growth and understanding of their full value and strengths" and for "facilitating East Bay teachers to achieve their own full potential through the art of teaching."

Ilana DeBare is author of *Where Girls Come First: The Rise, Fall and Surprising Revival of Girls' Schools* (2004). She is a co-founder and board member of the Julia Morgan School for Girls, an independent girls' middle school in Oakland, California, that opened in 1999 and now serves 180 girls in grades 6–8. She works as a business reporter at the *San Francisco Chronicle*, and in

2007 was named journalist of the year by the U.S. Small Business Administration in San Francisco.

Erik P. Ellefsen is principal of Chicago Christian High School, Palos Heights, Illinois. He has worked for ten years in both public and private high schools, has worked for two professional baseball teams, and has held leadership roles with the teachers' union. His research interests include organization philosophy and education history, and he has published articles in the *Journal of the International Community of Christians in Teacher Education* and the *Jazz Age Encyclopedia*. He is currently writing an interpretive biography of AFT President Al Shanker for his dissertation at Boston University.

Richard P. Fitzgerald has been headmaster of Bentley School, Oakland and Lafayette, California, since 2002. Previously, he served as head of Branson School in Ross, California, and of Little Red School House and Elisabeth Irwin School, New York City, and interim director of Live Oak School in San Francisco. He has been an English teacher, a basketball coach, a development director, a house tutor, and has served on the boards of the California Association of Independent Schools, the Multi-Cultural Alliance, the Marin Shakespeare Company, and the Crucible, an Oakland industrial arts center.

Keith Weller Frome, EdD, was headmaster of the Elmwood Franklin School and served as the founding head of Elmwood Franklin's community tutoring center, Achieve, from 1997 to 2007. He is now the chief academic officer and vice president for program of College Summit, a Washington, D.C., nonprofit that helps school districts build their capacity to enroll low-income students in college. In 2006 his book *What Not to Expect: A Meditation on the Spirituality of Parenting* (2005) was named the best book on family life by the Catholic Press Association.

Ann Gordon, MA, was executive director of the National Association of Episcopal Schools for fourteen years, where she focused on church and school relationships, governance issues, and Episcopal identity. Previously, she taught at Stanford University's laboratory school and in several community colleges. She has studied early childhood in Reggio Emilia, Italy, and in Russia. She is co-author of *Beginnings and Beyond: Foundations in Early Childhood Education* (7th ed., 2008), *Beginning Essentials in Early Childhood Education* (2007), and *Guiding Young Children in a Diverse Society* (1996).

Elisabeth Griffith, PhD, has been headmistress of the Madeira School, a girls' boarding high school in McLean, Virginia, since 1988. A product of public schools and a women's college, she is a historian and author of *In Her*

Own Right: The Life of Elizabeth Cady Stanton (1984). Her career includes college teaching and political activism. She serves on the boards of WETA and the White House Project.

Merrill Hall is interim head of Gibson Island Country School in Pasadena, Maryland. For twenty-one years, from 1983 to 2004, he was head of Calvert School in Baltimore, Maryland, and simultaneously CEO of its Home Instruction Department, now Calvert Education Services. Previously he held teaching, coaching, and administrative positions at one public and two independent schools. In 2003 he was the recipient of the Andrew White Medal, given for innovation in education by Loyola College in Baltimore.

Thomas R. Hoerr is head of the New City School in St. Louis, Missouri. Previously he was a public school principal and teacher, and he directed a university nonprofit management program. He has written more than sixty journal and magazine articles and is a regular columnist for the journal *Educational Leadership*. He has also written three books: *Becoming a Multiple Intelligence School* (2000), *The Art of School Leadership*, (2005), and *School Leadership for the Future* (2008).

Maura C. Joyce has been the head of school at Montessori in Redlands, California, since July 2000. She holds both primary and elementary certification from Association Montessori Internationale and had nine years of classroom experience at the elementary and adolescent levels prior to going into administration. She has lectured at the Association Montessori Internationale administrator's workshop, the Montessori Institute of San Diego, and Mt. San Jacinto College, San Jacinto, California.

Richard K. Jung, EdD, founded and serves as a partner for Education Access Strategies, LLC, Bethesda, Maryland, which assists independent schools and other nonprofits with executive searches and provides strategic planning and related consulting services. Previously, he served as head of school for the SEED School in Washington, D.C., the nation's first inner city college preparatory public boarding school, and for the Bullis School in Potomac, Maryland. He has been research director for the presidentially appointed National Advisory Council on the Education of Disadvantaged Children.

Pearl Rock Kane is the Klingenstein Family Chair Professor of Education at Teachers College, Columbia University, New York, and director of the Klingenstein Center for Independent School Education. She has taught and served as an administrator in public and private schools in Michigan, Massachusetts, and New York City. She is the editor of *The First Year of Teaching:*

Real World Stories from America's Teachers (1991), *Independent Schools, Independent Thinkers* (1992), and *The Colors of Excellence: Hiring and Keeping Teachers of Color in Independent Schools* (2003).

Mitzi Yates Lizárraga is head of the San Diego School of the Creative and Performing Arts, a public arts school for grades 6–12. Formerly, she was principal and CEO of the Duke Ellington School of the Arts in Washington, D.C., as well as the general director of the Greater Hartford Academy of the Arts in Hartford, Connecticut, and the Center for Creative Youth, both programs of the Capitol Region Education Council. She is a board member with the San Diego–based AJA Project, a nonprofit organization that provides media arts and educational programs for newly arriving refugee adolescents.

Bruno V. Manno is senior associate for education at the Annie E. Casey Foundation, where he directs the foundation's K–12 education investments. He has also been senior fellow in the Education Policy Study Program at the Hudson Institute in Washington, D.C. From 1986 to 1993 he worked in the U.S. Department of Education, holding several senior positions including assistant secretary for policy and planning. He is the author or co-author of numerous articles and other publications, including *Charter Schools in Action: Renewing Public Education* (2000).

Robert Mattingly, MEd, MA, ThM, MDiv, is currently head of Chesapeake Montessori School, Annapolis, Maryland. He has also taught and been an administrator at St. Joseph's Preparatory School in Philadelphia, St. Mary's Ryken High School in Leonardtown, Maryland, and Gonzaga College High School in Washington, D.C. He has published articles in the National Catholic Education Association journal, *Momentum*, and led numerous diversity workshops for faculties and conferences.

Pam Oken-Wright, MEd, is a teacher-researcher, author, and consultant who has worked with five-year-olds at St. Catherine's School in Richmond, Virginia, since 1979. She is a member of the Lugano Research Collaborative for the Study of Reggio Principles in U.S. Contexts and is on the editorial board of Innovations in Early Childhood Education: The International Reggio Exchange. Among her publications are contributions to *Next Steps Toward Teaching the Reggio Way* (2004) and *Teaching and Learning: Collaborative Explorations of the Reggio Emilia Approach* (2002).

Anne-Marie Pierce, a native of France, completed a thirty-five-year independent school career as head of the Washington International School from 1991 to 2001. She has served on several regional, national, and international association boards, including the IB Council of Foundation, French-American International School, San Francisco, and the Association of Independent Schools of Greater Washington. She is now president of A.M.P. & Associates, LLC, an educational consulting firm offering services in the United States and abroad.

Laurie Piette is the director of studies at the Rodeph Sholom School in Manhattan, where she also serves as chair of humanities. She has taught English, Latin, and history to fifth- through twelfth-grade students in New York independent schools, including Friends Seminary. She presented a reading of her play at the Ensemble Studio Theatre and read at the In Our Own Write series at the New York LBGT Center. She has also been a teacher adviser to the Metropolitan Museum of Art, New York, and has led workshops on integrating math and social studies using Roman coinage.

Marcie C. Roberts, MEd, is the chief executive officer of Education Enterprise of New York in Rochester, New York, and in that capacity serves as executive director of the Norman Howard School, an educational program for students with learning disabilities in grades 5–12; EnCompass: Resources for Learning, an affiliate not-for-profit that provides services for individuals who struggle to learn and the families and professionals who support them; the Sands Academy, a K–6 school for children who have language and learning delays; and Education Enterprise of New York Foundation.

Eileen Shields-West spent more than ten years at *Time* magazine, covering business in the New York Bureau, politics in the Washington bureau, and becoming *Time*'s San Francisco bureau chief in 1981. She then moved to CBS-TV and CNN to broadcast the news. In 1992 she authored *The World Almanac of Presidential Campaigns*. She served as chair of Beauvoir School, the National Cathedral Elementary School, in Washington, D.C., from 1996 to 1999, and is presently vice chair of Refugees International and a director of the SEED Foundation. She continues to freelance as a journalist and writer.

Farhat Siddiqui is principal of Universal School in Bridgeview, Illinois, where she previously served as classroom teacher and assistant principal. She was recognized as the school's Teacher of the Year in 1998 and received its Service Award in 2000. She has gained local and national recognition for her presentations on current topics in Islamic school education, and she plays an active role in organizing annual conferences for educators and academic competitions for students. She is a certified AdvancEd Chair for the North Central Association Commission on Accreditation and School Improvement.

Lisa Snell directs the Education Program at Reason Foundation, Los Angeles, where she oversees research on education issues. She has recently authored policy studies on weighted student funding, universal preschool, school violence, charter schools, and child advocacy centers. Her work has appeared in *Education Week, Wall Street Journal, USA Today, San Francisco Chronicle, Los Angeles Times,* and other publications. She serves on the board of the California Virtual Academy, a K–12 virtual charter school

Michael Thompson, PhD, is a psychologist, school consultant, and co-author of eight books, including the *New York Times* best-seller *Raising Cain: Protecting the Emotional Life of Boys* (1999). He was the host and co-writer of the award-winning PBS documentary, *Raising Cain: Exploring the Inner Lives of America's Boys.* A frequent commentator on the lives of boys, he has been a guest on the *Oprah Winfrey Show,* CBS's *60 Minutes,* and ABC's *20/20.*